Contentious Compliance

Contentious Compliance

Dissent and Repression under International Human Rights Law

Courtenay R. Conrad

Associate Professor of Political Science
University of California, Merced

Emily Hencken Ritter

Associate Professor of Political Science
Vanderbilt University

OXFORD
UNIVERSITY PRESS

OXFORD
UNIVERSITY PRESS

Oxford University Press is a department of the University of Oxford. It furthers
the University's objective of excellence in research, scholarship, and education
by publishing worldwide. Oxford is a registered trade mark of Oxford University
Press in the UK and in certain other countries.

Published in the United States of America by Oxford University Press
198 Madison Avenue, New York, NY 10016, United States of America.

An Online Appendix is available at https://dataverse.harvard.edu/

Library of Congress Cataloging-in-Publication Data
Names: Conrad, Courtenay R., author. | Ritter, Emily Hencken, author.
Title: Contentious compliance : dissent and repression under international
human rights law / Courtenay R. Conrad, Emily Hencken Ritter.
Description: Oxford [UK]; New York, NY : Oxford University Press, [2019]
Identifiers: LCCN 2018045548 | ISBN 9780190910983 (pbk.) |
ISBN 9780190910976 (hardcover)
Subjects: LCSH: International law and human rights. |
Human rights. | Treaties. | Political persecution. |
Dissenters—Legal status, laws, etc. | Government, Resistance to. |
Protest movements.
Classification: LCC KZ1266 .C66 2019 | DDC 341.4/8–dc23
LC record available at https://lccn.loc.gov/2018045548

1 3 5 7 9 8 6 4 2

Paperback printed by WebCom, Inc., Canada
Hardback printed by Bridgeport National Bindery, Inc., United States of America

Dedicated to Will H. Moore

CONTENTS

ACKNOWLEDGMENTS

The progress of science relies on community. We build on the careful work of other scholars. We present our research publicly, opening it to critique, suggestion, and improvement. We depend on organizations and universities for the time, space, and resources to think, process, write, fail, and succeed. We lean on a community of colleagues—from graduate school advisors to senior colleagues, from friends in the discipline to editors who support the research—for advice and encouragement. We contribute to the community, adding our ideas to the body of knowledge in the hopes they will assist others in proving us wrong and thinking differently about social scientific outcomes. We thank our community here.

PROFESSIONAL ACKNOWLEDGMENTS

The two of us first met in 2008 at a small workshop on courts and human rights organized by Will Moore and Jeff Staton and sponsored by Florida State University and Emory University. Although the workshop was filled with prominent senior scholars (many of whom we thank below), this finally forthcoming project developed in pajamas and over the course of car rides, as FSU graduate student Courtenay hosted Emory graduate student Emily on an air mattress for the duration of the conference. Thank you, Will and Jeff, for starting us on a journey that will endure throughout our careers.

Like all good graduate students, we finished our respective dissertations before we really got started on this project, which began with a puzzle and a model and grew from there. The formal theory and its implications for government repression were published in the *Journal of Politics* in 2013. The implications and evidence for mobilized dissent were published in the *Review of International Organizations* in 2016 after being awarded the Best Paper in International Relations at the Annual Meeting of the

Midwest Political Science Association in 2012. A public presentation of some of the arguments contained in this book were published in *the Washington Post*'s Monkey Cage Blog in 2017. We appreciate the editors and reviewers who examined, attacked, dismantled, praised, and improved these manuscripts—including at the many journals where they were rejected. Thank you, especially, to Oxford University Press, our editor David McBride, and three very helpful anonymous reviewers. Reviewing even a portion of a book manuscript is no small task, and we appreciate everyone's efforts toward making this one better.

So many of the ideas contained in this book—its concepts, interpretations, scope, alternatives, relationships, and examples—emerged from the variety of scholars to whom we have presented this project in its various forms. In addition to refining the arguments with our colleagues at the University of California, Merced, we shared it in conferences, online workshops, graduate seminars, and invited research talks, benefiting from new questions and ideas all the while. Thank you to the participants in seminars at Binghamton University; the State University of New York at Buffalo; the University of California, Berkeley; the University of California, Merced; Duke University; Emory University; Florida State University; George Washington University; Universität Hamburg; the University of Illinois; the University of Indiana; the University of Iowa; the London School of Economics; the University of Maryland; the University of Michigan; the University of Mississippi; the University of Nebraska; the University of Pennsylvania; Pennsylvania State University; the University of Pittsburgh; Princeton University; Rice University; the University of South Carolina; Texas A&M University; the University of Texas; Texas Tech University; Stanford University; Vanderbilt University; and Yale University. Thank you also to conference participants at Princeton University, the MultiRights Summer Institute at the University of Oslo, Political Economy of International Organizations, Visions in Methodology, and the annual meetings of several national and international political science organizations.

In spring 2016, we hosted a book conference at the University of California, Merced. Although we promised our participants California sunshine, it rained for the duration, including during a postworkshop visit to Yosemite National Park. Over the course of that rainy weekend, we were fortunate to have some extremely intelligent, creative, and generous scholars tear our project down and then build it back up again. Thank you to Kathleen Cunningham, James Hollyer, Yon Lupu, Heather Elko McKibben, Will Moore, Jeff Staton, and Scott Wolford for making the trip to Merced and bringing with them their very best ideas to shape our manuscript. All of our colleagues and graduate students at UC Merced went out of their way to make our guests feel welcome, especially Peter Carey, Jared Oestman, and Ae sil Woo, who took detailed notes and helped with conference logistics; Tom Hansford, who ably led our raincoat-clad group through Yosemite Valley; and Nate Monroe and Darick Ritter, who offered us logistical and psychological support in our attempts to feed and house our colleagues for several days. Book conferences are expensive; we are grateful to the Political Science Department, the School of Social Sciences, Humanities, and Arts at UC Merced, and the Tony Coehlo Endowed Chair of Public Policy for funding the workshop.

Many generous mentors and colleagues offered us their time and expertise in the form of invaluable comments, critiques, and discussions on various parts of this manuscript. Prior to the book workshop, Christian Davenport, Emilie Hafner-Burton, and Jeff Staton served as members of a book advisory committee, commenting on chapters and offering counsel about the book publishing process. In addition to the people named above—many of whom we could thank in every paragraph of our acknowledgments—we benefitted from the expertise and thoughtful suggestions of Paul Almeida, Phil Arena, Sam Bell, Tom Clark, Chad Clay, Justin Conrad, Danny Hill, Yukari Iwanami, Amanda Licht, Carolina Mercado, Amanda Murdie, Monika Nalepa, Rob O'Reilly, Hong Min Park, Cesare Romano, Beth Simmons, Jens Steffek, Chris Sullivan, Jay Ulfelder, Johannes Urpelainen, Erik Voeten, Jana von Stein, Jim Vreeland, Geoff Wallace, Jim Walsh, and Joe Young. Extra special thanks to Yon Lupu, Will Moore, and Scott Wolford, who read more bad and decent drafts of the articles and book manuscript than a person should ever have to do for a colleague or friend. We are grateful to Ellen Cutrone, Jeanette Hencken, Daniel Hoffmann, and Susan Navarro Smelcer for copyediting the manuscript at its interim stages and to Heath Sledge (http://heathsledge. com) for quick and able copyediting while we worked to meet our final deadlines. Over the course of our presentations of this work, we are grateful to have had hundreds of additional helpful conversations that improved our arguments immensely. We certainly have forgotten to list someone important by name, not because we are ungrateful, but because we are overwhelmed with gratitude for the wealth of expertise on which we have been fortunate enough to draw.

Darick Ritter (www.sequentialpotential.com), who is an incredibly talented artist, took our formal model—based on mathematical equations and social scientific jargon—and turned it into a work of art that conveys the main contributions of this book to wide audiences. We are thrilled that Oxford agreed to publish his work, Figure 3.1, in color, as it succinctly summarizes (and brings to life!) the dynamics of what sometimes feels like a very complicated story. Darick also designed and illustrated our beautiful book cover, which we love. Because our theory is based on counterfactual analysis, it is similarly challenging to locate illustrative examples of its dynamics; to that end, we are also grateful to Peter Carey, Ishita Chaudhry, Chris Medina, and graduate students at Universität Hamburg for helping us find examples to color our prose.

DEDICATION

We dedicate this book to the memory of Will Moore, whose work serves as the intellectual foundation on which we base our arguments and who was an advisor, a mentor, and a friend. Over the course of his career, Will's research tended toward two main topics: the dissent-repression "nexus" and the effect of institutions on government respect (or lack of respect) for human rights. The framework for the theory and empirical tests that we present in this book—our contention that scholars should take the conflict seriously when they investigate the effect of institutions on human rights outcomes—was born of Will's influence.

Perhaps as a result of this influence, he liked the book. At least, we *think* he liked it; he invested in it by dismantling multiple versions of it multiple times. He celebrated when we finished the first draft, and he celebrated when it was sent out for review. Will died one year ago today, the day on which we pen this dedication. He did not live to celebrate with us when the book was accepted for publication, as he had when so many of our other publications were put in print. We hope the final version of the project would make him proud.

In addition to being influenced by Will's scholarship, we were also incalculably fortunate to be the recipients of his time, his energy, and his mentorship. Will was insatiably curious and intellectually tireless. He invested heavily in both of our careers, spending hours upon hours guiding us and pushing us to improve our work. He modeled the practice of doing things not because it's how other scholars do it but because it's fascinating, bold, weird, inviting, and maybe wrong. He taught us to build institutions where none exist to solve a problem, to write non-positivist articles if you have an idea to share, and to ask questions in new and different ways. Because he was a builder of community, Will also encouraged us to be fiercely supportive of one another and of other scholars in our community. In dedication to Will, we promise to pay it forward.

PERSONAL ACKNOWLEDGMENTS: COURTENAY

I have been fortunate to have many generous mentors, colleagues, and friends to direct me in this profession and to redirect me when I wandered off course. But Will Moore stands alone as the most important driving influence in my becoming—and continuing to work as—a political scientist. Will was my dissertation advisor and my coauthor. He was an irreplaceable source of support and advice until his death; I rarely make a professional decision today without first asking myself what Will would do, what Will would say. (Asking those questions sometimes results in my doing the opposite of what he would have suggested, but I know he would understand.) Will is not simply responsible for influencing my work; I am a political scientist because of Will Moore. I miss him immensely. And I hope to one day be even half the scholar that he taught me to be.

My most important personal thank-you is tinged with professional gratitude. My husband, Nate, makes my life immeasurably better every day—by filling my days with joy and laughter, by working hard to build a Home with me, and by making me aspire to be a better scholar. I'm grateful to have his fingerprints on my life and on my work. Thank you to Abby and Will for embracing me as family and reminding me (daily!) about the importance of work-life balance. I love you both very much and cannot wait to see you with your new sister, Charlie—who, thankfully, seems to have delayed her arrival just long enough for us to complete this book. I am endlessly grateful to my parents, Bill and Charlotte, who instilled in me a great love of learning, always maintained high expectations for me in spite of my failures, and reassured me tirelessly along the way. Thank you to the rest of my family—Matt, Elaina, Mary, Keith, Amy, Dean, Dylan, Sadie, and Papa—for providing necessary diversions from my work and always seeming interested in this project, even when it felt like we might never finish it. Finally, an enormous debt of gratitude goes to Emily, who sets the bar incredibly high for coauthors. It has been *eight* years since we first started talking about this project; I cannot imagine anyone with whom I'd rather have celebrated its successes or cried about its setbacks.

PERSONAL ACKNOWLEDGMENTS: EMILY

I had been advised over and over again not to write a book before tenure because of the uncertainty of its timeline. I did so because the ideas in our heads were too big for articles. It needed to be a book. So often I wished I had taken my colleagues' advice, and so often I was glad I hadn't. Though I did not heed their warnings on this particular point, I constantly lean on mentors, colleagues, and friends for advice, reassurance, examples, and encouragement.

I have boundless gratitude for my political science colleagues at the University of California, Merced. I am moving to a new university this year after five years at Merced, and the loss of these colleagues leaves a crater in me. At Merced, I learned how to think deeply and across contexts. I learned the value of both likeness and diversity of thought. I learned how to build new institutions from scratch and disagree respectfully. I learned how to mentor others from those who mentored me. And I learned how to honor and practice work-life balance and equity of experience. I am indebted to my UCM colleagues, fine people and researchers all: Aditya Dasgupta, Daniel de Kadt, David Fortunato, Matt Hibbing, Haifeng Huang, Brad Le Veck, Melissa Sands, and Alex Theodoridis. I am especially grateful to the founders of this magnificent department, who so often bear more service, responsibility, and kindness than they should have to, so that the junior faculty can succeed, all while advancing toward a steady vision and publishing their own brilliant work. Thank you, Tom Hansford, Nate Monroe, Steve Nicholson, and (my senior mentor!) Jessica Trounstine. Your example will follow me as I develop my own role as a senior scholar.

I must of course thank the many steadfast and supportive mentors on whom I rely in making so many career decisions. Warren Rosenblum was a key supporter and critic while I was a fledgling undergraduate scholar and remains one of my loudest cheerleaders now. David Davis, Jeff Staton, Jen Gandhi, Tom Clark, Dani Reiter, and especially Cliff Carrubba continually act as academic family to me, stepping aside to watch me grow while continuing to answer my calls, long after I left the Emory nest. Christian Davenport and Will Moore identified me as a person with potential long before I would have known it, and they invited me into their fold. They shaped who I am as a thinker, colleague, mentor, and participator in academia. I hope to someday be the kind of mentor to someone else that they have been to me. Thank you especially to Scott Wolford, whose discerning eye is on everything I write. I would not be the scholar I am if not for you.

Finally, I must thank my family—those related by blood, marriage, or friendship. My mom, Jeanette, taught me fairness and respect for all people, and she passed to me the excitement of discovery and understanding. My dad, Tom, taught me how things work and the mechanisms of cause and effect in the garage. Thank you, both, for making me a scientist. Thank you to the many people who love and root for me in my family—my sister, my in-laws, my aunts, uncles, cousins, grandparents—we are a large brood of loud love. Thank you to my beautiful friends: Lindsey Barrow, Jessica

Braithwaite, Cassy Dorff, Kara Gibson, Carissa Hansford, Daniel Hoffman, Ryan Louis, Doug Mackay, Alex Main, Amie Medley, Stephanie Raczkowski, Toby Rider, Sara Schumacher, Susan Navarro Smelcer, Jakana Thomas, James Wilson, and Scott Wolford. I often need pulling up by my armpits and a trip to the outdoors to find myself again, and you are the people who find me when I am too lost to do it on my own. And to Courtenay, with whom I am so in sync that we might be of one (very detail-oriented) mind: I cannot wait for a hundred more retreats of creating, writing, laughing, and crying with you.

My greatest loves are Darick and Henry Ritter. Thank you for giving me wings, pushing me to fly, and reminding me to come back home. You are my everything.

Contentious Compliance

CHAPTER 1

✧

Do Human Rights Treaties Protect Rights?

E veryone wants to be safe from government violence. Unfortunately, billions of people experience human rights abuses as a way of life. More people die at the hands of their own government than in war. Minority groups are excluded from power, people are denied access to education, dissidents are beaten, prisoners are tortured. According to annual reports on human rights practices published by Amnesty International (AI) and the U.S. Department of State, every government violates the rights of some of its citizens in every year. During the last two decades of the twentieth century, over 70 percent of governments have engaged in torture in each year.[1] In 2012 alone, over a hundred countries were accused of limiting their citizens' rights to freedom of expression, and the security forces of fifty countries were reported to have unlawfully killed citizens.[2] The most frequent victims of repression are members of vulnerable groups: women and children, elderly persons, indigenous cultures, and impoverished populations.[3] In 2011, for example, AI reported that indigenous peoples in the Americas struggled for government recognition of their land rights, and in Europe and Central Asia, migrants, the Roma, and lesbian, gay, bisexual, and transgender (LGBT+) individuals continued to face widespread discrimination.[4] Violations of human rights can have

1. Cingranelli, Richards, and Clay 2014; Conrad, Haglund, and Moore 2013.
2. Amnesty International 2013.
3. See, e.g., Conrad, Haglund, and Moore 2013; Rejali 2007.
4. Amnesty International 2012.

widespread, dire consequences: Restrictions of individual liberties are associated with poverty and inequality, societal conflict, and nondemocratic governance.

In the face of such abuses, individuals all over the world demand the right to speak their minds and challenge their governments without fear of discrimination or violent reprisal. Groups of people who oppose existing policies or resource allocations can work together to pressure the government for change, peacefully or violently; authorities can end or deter the popular threat by repressing, accommodating, or adapting in one of many other ways. Even in democracies, majorities and other powerful groups may support repression because they derive power from maintaining the status quo.[5] As in international conflict, domestic discrimination and violence are extensions of bargaining over disputed policies and resources. Many people see government repression as a natural part of politics.

Victims, human rights advocates, and policymakers continually search for ways to end government abuses and their heinous individual and social consequences. The remedy most often suggested is law. Governments and international organizations alike turn to laws and courts to identify, stop, and prevent violations of human rights. Laws define individual rights, laying out the government's obligations with regard to people's security; courts adjudicate violations when they occur so that they can be rectified.[6] Unlike many other democratic institutions, the rule of law is intended to protect minorities from the will (and abuse) of the majority, and law and courts are thus ideal for protecting vulnerable populations from violations of human rights.[7]

This is the driving idea behind international human rights treaties (HRTs), designed in the wake of World War II to protect citizen rights from government intrusion.[8] In ratifying an international human rights treaty, national governments publicly commit themselves to protect the rights of persons under their domestic rule. These laws explicitly define the rights to which people are entitled, as well as the legal duties of the ratifying countries to protect people from the infringement of those rights. Some treaties are broad, governing a wide swath of human rights and relevant populations (like the International Covenant on Civil and Political Rights). Others are more specific, defining the rights and obligations with regard to

5. Conrad, Hill, and Moore 2017.

6. See, e.g., Cross 1999; Hathaway 2005; Keith 2002b; Moustafa 2007; Powell and Staton 2009.

7. Conrad, Hill, and Moore 2017.

8. A number of prominent scholars have written detailed, informative accounts of the historical development of the international human rights regime, including Simmons (2009, Chapter 2) and Hafner-Burton (2013, Chapter 4).

one violation (like torture, as in the UN Convention Against Torture and Other Cruel, Inhuman or Degrading Treatment or Punishment) or offering specific protections to one group (like children, as in the UN Convention on the Rights of the Child).

Government leaders face domestic and international pressure to obligate themselves to international human rights law. Domestic actors, including nongovernmental organizations (NGOs), unions, and political opposition parties, encourage heads of state to sign human rights treaties.[9] International leaders and institutions also pressure governments, using a variety of punishments and rewards to encourage them to commit to international standards based on an assumption that treaties will positively influence governmental rights protections.[10] Victims and advocates often act as if treaties have the legal and political strength to bind authorities who would violate rights. They refer to international obligations to protect in domestic court cases, in protests, in news reports, and in social movement campaigns.

But does international human rights law actually reduce government repression? Although human rights treaties clearly define obligations and are legally binding, they rarely include mechanisms for domestic or international enforcement. Signatory governments must restrain themselves and their agents, either by creating domestic institutions that punish rights violations or choosing on their own not to repress.

Without inherent enforcement, scholars, policymakers, and even dissidents expect human rights treaties to "work" only when signatories would not violate rights anyway; in other words, treaties constrain repression only in the absence of a domestic threat to power. Government authorities will allow themselves to be constrained by treaties only when they can use tactics other than repression to effectively control challenges. Institutions that allow for peaceful leader replacement, for instance, are more likely to protect rights when opposition groups push for electoral turnover.[11]

If, instead, they predominantly repress when challenged, governments ignore their international obligations. Autocratic regimes are frequently signatories to international human rights treaties while violating the treaties' terms with impunity. For example, countries including the Democratic Republic of Congo, China, Egypt, Syria, and many others have ratified

9. Hafner-Burton 2009.

10. Finnemore and Sikkink 1998; Keck and Sikkink 1998; Risse, Ropp, and Sikkink 1999.

11. Hafner-Burton, Hyde, and Jablonski 2014.

the UN Convention Against Torture (CAT) while continuing to engage in the torture and ill-treatment of their citizens at alarming rates. Syria acceded to the Chemical Weapons Convention in 2013, during its ongoing civil conflict, but in April 2017 unleashed chemical agents, killing dozens and maiming hundreds of civilians.[12] Democratic leaders do this, too, publicly denigrating international laws with the intent to violate their terms. Prime Minister Theresa May responded to terror attacks in 2017 by proposing to change Britain's human rights laws to allow authorities to deport suspected terrorists without sufficient evidence to convict. She has similarly argued that the United Kingdom should leave the European Convention for Human Rights (ECHR), saying, "The ECHR can bind the hands of parliament, adds nothing to our prosperity, makes us less secure by preventing the deportation of dangerous foreign nationals—and does nothing to change the attitudes of governments like Russia's when it comes to human rights."[13]

With frequent abuses in all regime types and public disdain for international rights treaties among state leaders, scholars and policymakers tend to be pessimistic about the ability of human rights law to limit government repression. Many argue that international human rights treaties are mere window dressing, letting states put on a benevolent image while violating rights whenever they can justify it in the interest of power.[14]

In this book, we argue that government decisions about whether to comply with international human rights obligations are directly tied to conflicts with civilians over policies; in other words, *compliance* with international human rights law is a function of *contention*. To know whether and when human rights treaties will effectively constrain governments from repression, we must understand the context of dissent faced by those governments. Most scholars studying human rights treaties focus on the extent to which authorities have the *opportunity* to repress. They assume that governments will violate rights whenever possible and international and domestic institutions limit the governments' possibilities or opportunities to do so. This approach assumes that countries with strong institutions of constraint, like domestic courts, contested elections, or democratic legislatures, are more responsive to human rights treaty constraints than those with weak institutions.[15] Yet, as with any potential law violation,

---

12. Loveluck and DeYoung 2017.

13. May, quoted in Asthana and Mason 2016.

14. Downs, Rocke, and Barsoom 1996; Goodliffe, Hawkins, et al. 2012; Hathaway 2002; von Stein 2016.

15. See, e.g., Cingranelli and Filippov 2010; Keith 2012; Lupu 2013a, 2015; Simmons 2009; von Stein 2016.

opportunity to misbehave without the motive to do so yields no crime. Popular challenges and the threat they represent to a government's hold on policies and power constitute the state's primary *motive* to repress. To determine whether international human rights treaties can meaningfully influence a government's human rights behaviors, we must first consider the incentives that motivate leaders to repress.

1.1 TREATIES AND THE INCENTIVE TO VIOLATE HUMAN RIGHTS

Posner (2014, Chapter 1) opens his controversial book with a vignette about Amarildo de Souza, a Brazilian bricklayer who in July 2013 was tortured and disappeared by members of the Unidade de Policia Pacificadora (UPP) as part of its operation to crack down on drug trafficking. Following his disappearance, protesters took to the streets in Mr. de Souza's hometown of Rocinha and throughout Brazil, calling for an investigation into the disappearance. In several instances, demonstrations were met with additional police violence. Over twenty Brazilian police officers were eventually charged with (and ten were convicted of) torturing and murdering Mr. de Souza. Based on the de Souza case and his own account of the prevalence of disappearances in Brazil, Posner suggests that international human rights treaties—institutions intended to constrain these very types of government behaviors—have failed. According to Posner, Mr. de Souza would not have been tortured and killed if human rights treaties were able to successfully constrain national authorities.

Certainly, Mr. de Souza's disappearance highlights the fact that the Brazilian government engaged in human rights abuses even after the country became party to several international human rights treaties. But perhaps Brazilian abuses would have been *worse* absent their international commitment. What would Brazilian human rights practices have been if the country were not a member of the international rights treaties to which it is a party? Would disappearances have been even more prevalent? Obviously, it is impossible to know for sure; this exercise is hypothetical. But rather than assume that one highly visible abuse of human rights means that human rights treaties have failed, we use careful deduction based on the observable characteristics of countries to *predict* what those countries would have done under a different treaty obligation status.

International commitments did not prevent the crime against Mr. de Souza, but they may have prevented other crimes from occurring. Police might have used violent tactics more openly, or against more civilians, in the absence of international obligations. Brazilian authorities may repress less overall than they would have without the constraints offered by international treaty commitments. Human rights treaties also might be responsible—either directly or indirectly, via their effect on the public's willingness to protest—for ensuring justice in Brazilian courts for Mr. de Souza and his family. Following the protests, NGO Human Rights Watch repeatedly pressured Brazil to uphold its international obligations, stating, "The Brazilian government's obligation under this body of law and norms [international human rights law] is not only to prevent torture and cruel, inhuman, or degrading treatment but also to thoroughly investigate and prosecute such acts when they occur—including by making certain that detainees are brought before judicial authorities without unnecessary delay."[16] Although treaty law may not prevent all violations of human rights, we argue that treaties affect domestic conflict and policy outcomes. A nation's commitment to the terms of international human rights—and the expectation that authorities can be held legally responsible for rights violations—can embolden popular protest, and protest itself influences government repression.

This simple example illustrates the importance of identifying the counterfactual. What would happen in a treaty-obligated country if it faced the very same institutions and conflict but *was not* obligated to an international human rights treaty? What would happen in an unobligated country if it faced the same institutions and conflict but *was* obligated under international law?

To answer these questions, we cannot look simply at human rights practices before and after a government ratifies an international human rights treaty. A decrease in violations after treaty ratification does not necessarily mean the treaty is responsible for the change, and an increase in violations postratification does not necessarily mean the treaty is failing to limit government repression. Reductions in government abuses of human rights may be the result of other institutions that constrain authorities from repression[17] or of behavioral changes in political interactions that reduce incentives to repress,[18] such that the treaty is not meaningfully constraining state behavior.[19] And while governments may violate rights more after ratifying an international treaty than they did previously, if that heightened level of repression is less than they would have chosen under

---

16. Human Rights Watch 2014.
17. von Stein 2016.
18. Ritter 2014.
19. See, e.g., Downs, Rocke, and Barsoom 1996; Simmons and Hopkins 2005; von Stein 2005.

the same conditions absent the treaty commitment, international law has successfully increased protection for human rights.

In this book, we carefully investigate two counterfactuals. First, for countries that have ratified an international human rights treaty, does that obligation improve government respect for human rights relative to the projected level of repression that would have existed absent the treaty? Second, for countries that have not committed to an international human rights treaty, would treaty ratification improve government respect for human rights relative to extant rights practices absent the treaty?

Of course, it is impossible to directly observe what would have happened in an alternative treaty status for each country. We use carefully defined concepts and mathematical theory to help us identify the most logical possible outcome for each unobserved state. We assume that all governments face a set of incentives—dissidents considering a meaningful challenge to the status quo and institutions threatening consequences—that influence their decisions to commit to international human rights law or to violate people's human rights. Domestic and international constraining institutions, and the government's strategic interaction with dissidents, determine the extent to which a government will repress. We use the observable characteristics of a country at a given moment in time to predict levels of repression and dissent for two alternative scenarios, one in which the country is committed to international human rights law and one in which the country is not committed to international human rights law. The difference in conflict activities across the two scenarios represents the treaty's effect on human rights practices.

1.2 CONTENTIOUS COMPLIANCE: THE ARGUMENT

The main point of this book—its most important contribution—is to point out that international human rights treaties work. They improve human rights outcomes. Not all the time, and not with perfect certainty. But under certain conditions—namely, when the stakes of retaining power are high for political leaders and domestic courts are relatively poor at constraining the executive—international human rights law alters the structure of the strategic conflict between political authorities and potential dissidents, significantly decreasing government repression and increasing mobilized dissent activities.

To draw conclusions about whether and how international treaty obligations affect human rights practices, we need to establish when and why a government would want to abuse human rights in the first place. To do that, we model the political conflict between dissidents and government authorities and its effects on government outcomes; this lays out the government's baseline motive to engage in repression. In addition, we incorporate into our theory the domestic institutions that would constrain those leaders from repressing. This defines the opportunity to repress, enabling us to see the extent to which government repression is domestically permitted or prevented, regardless of the government's treaty status. Finally, governments can choose whether to ratify an international HRT, which will create consequences—some marginal, some significant—for violating its terms. In whole, the theory allows us to predict what government repression would look like in a country with a particular set of characteristics and then draw predictions about how repression would differ under an obligation to an international human rights treaty.

Repression is defined as any threatened limit or coercive action levied by government authorities to control or prevent domestic political challenges that would alter the status quo policy or distribution of power.[20] Repression is motivated as a response to or in prevention of dissent.[21] It can be legal or illegal, violent or nonviolent, and it includes tactics ranging from government limits on freedom of speech and assembly, discriminatory policies, and unlawful surveillance to political arrests, mass torture, and killing. It includes both what scholars and practitioners call civil liberties violations and physical integrity violations. Any behavior used to prevent people from participating in their own governance can be considered repression, and the various forms of repression are almost always violations of human rights as defined in the Universal Declaration of Human Rights (UDHR) and a multitude of international treaties.

Our definition of government repression constitutes a narrower conceptualization than the broader legal category of human rights violations. Many scholars of human rights focus on the rights first defined as such in the UDHR. In addition to the violations that we consider repression, the larger category of human rights includes, for example, a right to education, to health care, and to one's own culture (Hafner-Burton 2013, Chapter 2). Governments may violate these rights for purposes of exclusion or control, as when women are not allowed an education or a group is denied the use of its native language; we consider those behaviors to be repression. However, these rights may also be violated due to a lack

---

20. Cf. Davenport 2007a; Goldstein 1978; Poe and Tate 1994; Ritter 2014.
21. Ritter and Conrad 2016b.

of infrastructural capacity within a given state; we do not consider such violations to be repression, although they are indeed rights violations. We focus our attention on rights violated with the intent to control or prevent domestic challenges to the political status quo, so as to correctly capture the political process of contention rather than capturing violations that occur because of a lack of capacity to protect. We refer to these government violations interchangeably throughout the book as (human) rights violations and government repression.

Governments do not violate human rights randomly or without reason; they repress during conflicts over domestic policy. Authorities want to control the status quo through policy or practice or regime, and (some) people within the state's territorial jurisdiction likely prefer a different policy or practice or regime. Governments violate human rights to retain control when they are threatened by an implicit or explicit domestic challenge. Repression can reduce political challengers' ability to threaten the incumbent government[22] or help the government determine the extent to which dissenters will go to upset the status quo.[23] To be sure, authorities also violate rights for many nontactical reasons, including bias, culture, resource limitations, or the interest of domestic security.[24] These motives are less mutable than the desire for control or power, and they produce outcomes via a different process than repression, which is explicitly connected to threat. We focus here on repression.

We define *mobilized dissent* as a coordinated attempt by a group of nongovernment actors to influence political outcomes outside of means organized by the state.[25] Government authorities are more likely to repress dissent as it becomes more violent, more multidimensional, more organized, or more threatening in its goals.[26] If there is no (threat of) dissent, leaders have little reason to repress. Some countries face little dissent and consequently have little reason to violate human rights; a country's positive human rights record is not always due to rights protections from international human rights treaties or any other institutions.

Repression and dissent are connected, in that they occur as part of a strategic interaction between the government and potential dissidents. The government engages (or not) in repression in expectation of dissent, and

---

22. Nordås and Davenport 2013; Sullivan 2016b.

23. Galtung 1969; Ritter and Conrad 2016b.

24. Hafner-Burton 2013.

25. We use the terms *dissent* and *challenge* interchangeably. For similar definitions, see, e.g., Tilly 1978; Tarrow 1991; and McAdam 1999.

26. See, e.g., Davenport 1995, 1996, 2000; Davis and Ward 1990; Francisco 1996; Gartner and Regan 1996; Moore 1998; Poe, Tate, Keith, and Lanier 2000.

dissidents mobilize and take action (or not) in expectation of repression.[27] In Part I, we present a formal theory that starts from a simple model of strategic conflict: Government authorities and dissidents choose how much to repress and dissent, respectively, in the attempt to win control over some policy outcome. Because repression and dissent choices are so intertwined, we specify a theory of simultaneous action, meaning that a leader and a group of dissidents each choose their conflict behaviors in the knowledge that the other actor is making decisions at the same time. Anything affecting the government's choice to repress—for example, a commitment to an international human rights treaty—affects not only the government's decision about repression but the entirety of the conflict. When a treaty constrains the government's ability or willingness to repress, it also influences the dissidents' choices regarding dissent, which in turn alters the government's decision about whether to respond with some form of repression. From this theory, we draw conclusions about the effects of international human rights treaties on both government repression *and* mobilized dissent—interdependent outcomes of a single conflict process.

Government authorities faced with dissent do not always repress: they are more likely to violate human rights when dissent occurs in a context that is particularly threatening to their ability to set policies or hold power.[28] When losing the conflict to a dissident group damages the leader's authority, the leader represses to avoid that outcome. The leader is also more likely to repress as the stakes of holding office increase. When holding office is particularly valuable or the consequences for losing office are terrible, dissidents are more likely to challenge the government. Thus, as the stakes of holding office increase, leaders are more likely to repress to prevent possible loss to dissidents.[29]

Some leaders who are motivated to repress are nevertheless constrained from doing so by domestic political institutions that make repression more costly. The domestic institution most consistently found to constrain

---

27. Cf. Ritter 2014.

28. Davenport 2000; Lorentzen 2013; Poe, Tate, Keith, and Lanier 2000.

29. We refer formally to this concept as a leader's *expected value for power*. We use the term "expected value" because it encompasses both how much the leader benefits from retaining power and how much they expect to remain in that position. Formally, this is a von Neumann–Morgenstern expected utility function, which multiplies the probability that the leader will remain in power at the end of the interaction (which we denote as θ, where $0 \leq \theta \leq 1$) by the value of staying in power (v_{in}) or the value of losing it (which we normalize to 0). The leader's expected value of retaining power is specified as $\mathbb{E}[U_L] = \theta * v_{in} + (1 - \theta) * 0$.

government repression is the court.[30] A leader motivated to repress dissidents has to consider the probability of incurring court-related costs for violating human rights. Individuals can bring civil and criminal cases against authorities for violating rights, and their beliefs about success in the legal process inform their propensity to litigate. Even if the courts were to ultimately rule in favor of the government, the process of litigation involves costs that leaders prefer to avoid. The potential for costly legal consequences leads authorities to repress less and remain under the court's radar,[31] and that restraint opens opportunities for dissent. [32]

When a government ratifies an international human rights treaty, the treaty is incorporated into an existing baseline of constraint, much of which comes from the domestic court. We argue that an international human rights treaty obligation adds to the baseline propensity for litigation of human rights violation, adding to existing laws,[33] increasing the visibility and legitimacy of rights claims,[34] and encouraging NGO activity supporting victims of human rights violations in bringing legal action.[35]

Existing domestic constraints therefore condition how meaningful international treaties can be for changing human rights outcomes. When a government already has laws that protect rights, police who enforce those protections, and courts that identify violations, the probability of human rights protection changes very little when a treaty is added to these existing mechanisms. In his 1970 testimony to the U.S. Senate during debate about ratification of the Genocide Convention, Richard Gardner, former deputy assistant secretary of state for international organization affairs and a law professor at Columbia University, testified, "Ratification of the convention would create no new criminal liability for American citizens, since genocide already is a crime under federal and state law."[36] Countries with few laws in place or courts that have difficulty ruling against the state can draw strength from international treaty obligations. These are the contexts where an international treaty can most change the domestic legal environment. In short, international human rights treaty obligations create new and

---

30. See, e.g., Cross 1999; Hathaway 2005; Hill and Jones 2014; Keith 2002b; Mitchell, Ring, and Spellman 2013; Powell and Staton 2009; Simmons 2009. For an argument that it is not the court but the court's litigants that constrain the government, see Rosenberg 1991.

31. Powell and Staton 2009.

32. Ritter and Conrad 2016a.

33. Hill 2015.

34. Simmons 2009.

35. Hafner-Burton, LeVeck, and Victor 2016.

36. This is a quotation from an article summarizing his statements. See "Genocide Convention." 1971.

meaningful constraints when domestic courts are relatively ineffective, but they do little to change conflict relations between governments and potential dissidents in countries with effective courts.

The crux of our argument is that international human rights treaties lead to different levels of government repression than we would otherwise expect when (a) mobilized dissent is threatening enough to motivate repression (when leaders place a high value on remaining in power) and (b) domestic courts are insufficient to constrain that abuse. These conditions lead to an overall increase in conflict: dissidents engage in dissent more to try to change the status quo, and leaders repress more to control that dissent. When a leader facing these conditions is obligated under an international human rights treaty, we find empirical evidence that the government will repress less—and dissidents will dissent more—than would have happened in the same country had there been no international treaty obligation.

1.3 CONTRIBUTIONS TO SCIENCE AND PRACTICE

Our new theory and intriguing findings result from a unique approach to the research question of whether international human rights treaties improve human rights outcomes. Our approach combines theoretical and empirical innovations to address the difficulties of studying how domestic and international institutions affect human rights protections.

Social scientists disagree about whether human rights treaties effectively reduce government repression. A wealth of empirical evidence suggests that international human rights treaties do not unequivocally improve government respect for human rights,[37] and a few studies suggest that treaty commitments could even make human rights violations worse in ratifying states, especially dictatorships.[38] Treaties may function less as constraints on repressive governments than as signals of existing values or good intentions. Governments may join treaties for their expressive benefit, signaling to the international community either that they do value human rights or that they intend to make changes in the future.[39] This behavior may be particularly common when states want to be perceived as similar to other states that value human rights protections.[40] Many of the

---

37. See, e.g., Hafner-Burton 2005; Hafner-Burton and Tsutsui 2007; Hathaway 2002; Hill 2010; Keith 1999; Lupu 2013b; Neumayer 2005.
38. See, e.g., Hathaway 2002; Hollyer and Rosendorff 2011; Vreeland 2008a.
39. Hathaway 2002.
40. Goodliffe, Hawkins, et al. 2012.

countries that join human rights treaties already have good practices when they ratify, and the treaty therefore does not meaningfully change their behavior;[41] Simmons (2009) labels these states *sincere ratifiers*. Each of these explanations suggests that many countries commit to international law with no expectation or intention of changing their human rights practices, and thus that human rights treaties are ineffective.

Yet other social scientists, international legal scholars, and advocates for the protection of human rights contend that treaties act as real limits on repressive government behavior by making it more costly for the government to repress domestic populations. Costs can accrue in a number of ways when governments violate the terms of an international human rights treaty. The cost may be normative or social; states may fear a negative reputation or public shaming if they violate the terms of a treaty.[42] The costs may also be economic, for international partners may restrict trade or aid to repressive governments conditional on human rights practices.[43] Yet there is scarce evidence that other countries provide material benefits for ratification[44] or punish noncompliance with treaty terms.[45] Instead, scholars have largely turned to investigating the extent to which domestic institutions enforce otherwise unenforceable international obligations.

Scholars tend to agree that democracies—or at least countries with democratic institutions—are more likely to actually follow the terms of their treaty obligations.[46] Countries that are obligated to human rights treaties frequently exhibit stronger rights protections when they have effective domestic institutions to enforce limits on executive behavior.[47] Legislatures, emboldened by international commitments, may set policies that protect rights or make it difficult for leaders to violate them.[48] Treaty obligations can alter the tone of political discourse to focus more heavily on the rights protected by law; under an international treaty obligation, policy-makers are more likely to shift the legislative agenda, and interested social groups are more likely to push governments for more protections.[49] Monitoring and bureaucratic efficacy allow governments to better recognize

41. Downs, Rocke, and Barsoom 1996; von Stein 2016.

42. Davis, Murdie, and Steinmetz 2012; Finnemore and Sikkink 1998; Hendrix and Wong 2013; Keck and Sikkink 1998; Murdie and Peksen 2014; Risse, Ropp, and Sikkink 1999.

43. Blanton and Blanton 2007; Hafner-Burton 2005; Lebovic and Voeten 2006.

44. Nielsen and Simmons 2015.

45. Ramcharan 1989.

46. See also Hathaway 2002, Davenport and Armstrong 2004, Neumayer 2005, and von Stein 2016.

47. Hathaway 2005; Powell and Staton 2009; von Stein 2016.

48. Lupu 2015.

49. See, e.g., Simmons 2009. Some international human rights treaties may have more influence over domestic politics than others. States that ratify the Convention

violations and facilitate implementation and enforcement of the treaty's terms.[50] And domestic courts can adjudicate violations, potentially constraining leaders who would violate the terms of an international treaty.[51] These institutions create costs for violating rights that leaders would prefer to avoid.

Social science's contradictory, inconsistent findings on the effects of international human rights law are due, in part, to a misspecified model. Typically, studies assume that government authorities and institutions are the only relevant actors in what we argue is a conflict between the government and potential dissidents. The most common scholarly narrative goes like this: If a domestic or international institution creates negative consequences for authorities that violate rights, authorities will repress less frequently (or at lower levels) to avoid those consequences.[52] In other words, the incentives informing leaders' choices are assumed to be exogenous to their decisions. Repression is the government's choice alone. This model makes it straightforward to predict how a treaty's consequences will influence human rights violations: When incentives shift, the decision should respond in kind.

However, these decision-theoretic frameworks ignore the possibility that repression affects the leader's *incentives* to repress—that it affects dissent. If, for instance, repression were influenced only by covariates like culture, demographics, ethnic fractionalization, and colonial history,[53] then government authorities could easily assess the effective level of necessary repression. If, as these theories assume, domestic threats to the regime are given or exogenous, then domestic threats can simply be included as a variable in a regression model to produce a straightforward prediction of how threat affects repression.[54]

However, if, as we assert, a government makes decisions about repression as part of a strategic interaction with another actor—dissidents—who can anticipate the government's choice and change course, then an institution's effect on repression is not so straightforward.

on the Elimination of Discrimination Against Women (CEDAW), in particular, consistently have been shown to improve women's living conditions (Hill 2010; Lupu 2013b).

50. Cole 2012, 2015.

51. Hill 2012; Lupu 2013a; Powell and Staton 2009; Sikkink and Walling 2007; Simmons 2009; Sloss 2009.

52. See, e.g., Conrad 2014; Hafner-Burton 2005; Hathaway 2002, 2007; Hill 2010; Keith 1999; Lupu 2013a, b; Neumayer 2005; Simmons 2009; von Stein 2016.

53. Hafner-Burton 2013; Hill and Jones 2014; Poe and Tate 1994.

54. Conrad and Moore 2010; Davenport 2007b; Poe, Tate, and Keith 1999.

In failing to consider the effect of institutions on incentives for dissent, the decision-theoretic approach described above ignores the insights of an entire branch of social science scholarship arguing that the government's decision to repress is part of a dynamic conflict—a strategic interaction between groups that threaten mobilized action to change the status quo and a government that threatens to repress dissidents to maintain it. In this strategic model, repression is used to deter or eliminate dissent.[55] The causal arrow can also go the other way: People may mobilize because they do not want to be repressed,[56] or they may stay home altogether in expectation of having their rights violated.[57] Thus, the government's decision to repress is a function of (expected) dissent, and dissidents decide whether to dissent in expectation of having their rights violated.[58] Human rights violations are not merely determined by the leader's assessment of the consequences of rights violations; repression is also determined in part by the leader's desire to control strategic, anticipatory, popular dissent.[59]

In assuming that international human rights treaties affect government repression (or not) without considering that they also affect dissent, analysts commit the sin of omitted variable bias. If dissent only influenced repression in one direction—say, to increase it—this would not be too problematic. Omitting dissent from empirical models would bias estimated treaty effects in one way consistently, and the direction of the prediction would be unaffected. However, dissent sometimes leads to more repression,[60] sometimes less,[61] and sometimes the direction of the relationship is not clear at all.[62] Thus, scholars cannot know the direction in which the omitted variable biases their findings, and readers of these studies cannot be sure that their conclusions are correct interpretations of the evidence.

We bring together these previously divergent literatures and take seriously the idea that leaders make decisions about whether and how much to repress not only in expectation of institutional punishment (e.g., treaty

55. See, e.g., Danneman and Ritter 2014; Davenport 2007a; DeMeritt and Young 2013; Moore 2000; Nordås and Davenport 2013.

56. See, e.g., Cederman, Wimmer, and Min 2010; Gurr 1970; McAdam 1999.

57. See, e.g., Galtung 1969; Regan and Henderson 2002; Ritter 2014.

58. Ritter and Conrad 2016b.

59. For examples of explicitly strategic models, see Lichbach 1987, Pierskalla 2010, Hollyer and Rosendorff 2011, Ritter 2014, Shadmehr and Bernhardt 2011, and Shadmehr 2014.

60. Davenport 1995, 1996, 2007a; Earl, Soule, and McCarthy 2003; Gartner and Regan 1996; King 1998; Poe, Tate, Keith, and Lanier 2000.

61. Carey 2010; Davenport and Armstrong 2004; Moore 2000; Rasler 1996; Shellman 2006.

62. Ritter 2014; Ritter and Conrad 2016b.

constraints) but also in anticipation of the dynamic, strategic decisions of potential dissidents. We argue that institutions like human rights treaties affect *conflict* between government authorities and potential dissidents. Institutions that present consequences for violations affect the expectations of government authorities as well as their opposition, and therefore also affect the conflict behaviors between the two groups. We integrate the assumptions that (1) international human rights treaties, through domestic institutions, increase the costs of repressing; (2) potential dissidents may respond to those institutions and the expectation of constrained repression with changes in dissent; and (3) authorities base decisions about repression on both the expectation of dissent and institutional constraint. Because they base their decisions about repression on both dissent and constraint, leaders are caught between a rock and a hard place: the pressures on the leader to repress less *and* respond to the domestic population are frequently at odds with one another.

The ideal way to draw conclusions about the causal effects of international human rights treaty commitment on government repression is to compare a country in a given year to the very same country in the same year, one version obligated to a treaty and the other not, while taking into account that the obligated country self-selected into its obligation status. This is the most direct and useful comparison: country compared to itself in an alternative treatment, rather than compared to a dream of perfect compliance, or to a different country altogether, or to the same country at a different point in time.

Game theory allows us to make this comparison; comparative statics analysis allows us to use clear statements of the counterfactual conditions to derive predictions. We set the observable characteristics of a country (the leader's value for their office and the probability of domestic legal consequences) at particular values and predict what levels of repression and dissent the leader and potential dissidents would choose if the country was not obligated to an international human rights treaty. Then we use the same values of the state's characteristics, changing only the state's treaty commitment status. By comparing these predicted values (across a continuum of possible state characteristics), we can identify whether and how conflict outcomes differ with changes in treaty commitment status, with an explicit understanding of the reference point on which that claim rests. The theory also addresses the selection concern described above—the fact that treaty-obligated countries have usually voluntarily opted in to their treaty status. The theory has implications as to how the treaty's likely effect should differ for states that opt into its jurisdiction as compared to those that opt out. From the formal model, we derive several nuanced and conditional implications as to when and how treaties affect repression and dissent, which allow us to do multiple critical tests of this and alternative explanations using observed statistical data. This process allows us to come as close as possible to comparing the behavior of a country *to itself* in an alternate treaty reality using observable evidence.

As a consequence of the incorporation of strategic dissent into our theory and the clear identification of the behavioral counterfactual, the argument presented in this book yields a rich set of implications not previously seen in—and even running counter to—prior international human rights treaty scholarship. We argue, supported by empirical evidence, that treaties meaningfully reduce government repression under surprising conditions: They meaningfully reduce repression when authorities are both motivated to repress most severely and are relatively unconstrained in doing so. Furthermore, we derive implications as to how international human rights treaties affect the likelihood of dissent actions supporting popular demands—novel findings that are undescribed in prior scholarship, which has focused on government repression rather than on the broader dynamic of strategic conflict between repression and dissent.

1.3.1 Human Rights Treaties and Repression

We argue that human rights treaties constrain or prevent government repression through a logic of expectations. Of course, HRTs do much more than prevent repression: They set standards, express collective goals, create institutions, and much more. And, of course, full human rights protection requires much more than simply stopping politically motivated abuses; it also requires developing and supporting individual freedoms and rights. But one of the central functions of HRTs is to stop repression, and we show in this book that they frequently do—more, even, than some scholars or analysts would suppose.

Much has been written about the "screening" effect of international human rights treaties. According to scholarship, countries with high values for human rights protection are the most likely to join treaties but the least likely to change their behavior.[63] After all, there is little to change; these countries are already on their best behavior. Most scholars identify these screening countries by institutional or state-level characteristics

63. Downs, Rocke, and Barsoom 1996; Goodliffe and Hawkins 2006; Hathaway 2002; Hill 2010; Lupu 2013b; von Stein 2016.

that make authorities more likely to protect rights, such as democratic or otherwise effective institutions.[64] We also posit that countries with strong constraining institutions should see little effect from international treaties on rights practices, and that these countries are more likely to join treaties. In particular, we find countries in which the population and authorities generally expect that repressive actors could be brought to court will not change their repression practices with treaty ratification. In these countries (which are highly likely to voluntarily join treaties), rights protection comes not because the court enforces international treaty laws, but because domestic actors already expect legal consequences for rights violations; in screening states, rights violations are already constrained by the domestic court. In other words, although international human rights treaties are correlated with rights protection in countries with effective courts, treaties do not *improve* rights protection in these countries.

In a surprising turn, we also find that countries that enjoy a lack of threat from potential dissidents behave like screening states. While it is not new to argue that regimes facing threat are more likely to repress,[65] the idea of threat has been difficult to conceptualize[66] and rarely applied to theories of human rights treaties.[67] Most scholars agree that dissent represents a threat to a government's power or policies, but not every instance of dissent elicits a repressive response.[68] We show that leaders who have low stakes in a conflict over policy are generally less threatened by dissent; repression would cost them more than it would help them. International human rights treaties do not constrain these leaders, since they would not have repressed with or without the obligations. A lack of motive means no constraint is necessary. Thus, treaties are not redundant only in countries with strong domestic institutions; they are also unnecessary and have no effect when regimes do not face threats.

Importantly, however, we show that treaty obligations can have a meaningful and positive constraining effect in countries where government repression and mobilized dissent are most likely to occur. Leaders who have the most to lose from conflict are both likely to be challenged and prone to high levels of repression.[69] These are conditions where

64. Lupu 2015; Powell and Staton 2009; Simmons 2009; von Stein 2016.
65. Conrad and Moore 2010; Davenport 2000, 2007b; Galtung 1969; Goldstein 1978; Poe, Tate, Keith, and Lanier 2000; Tilly 1978.
66. Davenport 2007a.
67. See, e.g., Goodliffe and Hawkins 2006; Hafner-Burton 2005; Keith 1999; Landman 2005; Neumayer 2005; Powell and Staton 2009.
68. See, e.g., Lorentzen 2014.
69. Ritter 2014.

institutional constraint becomes possible, because in this situation, there is repression that can be constrained. Compared to what the same government would do absent an international human rights treaty commitment, obligated governments repress less. Empirical estimates with observed data across multiple types of human rights treaties and repression support this prediction.

Our results highlight previously unstudied variation in the effects of international and domestic constraints on human rights outcomes, shifting the focus from national predictors—the state level—to leaders as decision-makers—the individual leader level. For example, it is well known that democracies are more likely to comply with international treaties than nondemocracies,[70] but within each of these regime types, the leaders vary year to year in their expectations of or benefits from holding power and consequences for losing it. Our theory suggests that leaders with the most on the line—the leaders often found in dictatorships—are more likely to respond to institutional constraints like treaties, while leaders with lower stakes in retaining office—some in democracies, some in nondemocracies—are less likely to base their decisions on treaty commitment status. The implications for predicting democratic and dictatorial responses to international treaty commitment are unexpected.

To be clear, although treaty obligations constrain leaders to repress less than they would absent such commitments, overall levels of repression often remain high. This result is key to understanding the many contradictions in scholarly and political analyses of treaty effects. Comparing repression straightforwardly across countries might lead one to conclude that treaties actually improve the rights practices in states with low-stakes leaders rather than high-stakes ones, since the former repress less overall.[71] However, when we estimate the appropriate counterfactual—what the same leader would do under a different treaty obligation status—we find that although high-stakes leaders repress more than low-stakes ones, it is the high-stakes leaders whose repressive behaviors change under treaty obligations, because those obligations change the conflict between them and domestic dissenting groups.

Our findings suggest that constraints like international human rights treaties work to improve rights practices in situations where previous research would have inferred institutional failure. International institutions are most effective at limiting rights violations when repression is

70. Hathaway 2002; von Stein 2016.
71. See, e.g., Hafner-Burton 2013; Hafner-Burton and Tsutsui 2007.

expected to be at its highest levels—they serve as a last-ditch effort to protect rights when threat motivates conflict and domestic institutions fail to constrain a powerful government. Thus, in spite of scholarly skepticism,[72] human rights treaties may play an important role in limiting violations of human rights where and when the need for institutional constraints is the most critical.

1.3.2 Human Rights Treaties and Dissent

Although numerous studies point to the social causes and societal consequences of mobilization and protest,[73] very few scholars examine the effect of international institutions on the outcomes of these domestic conflicts. This book breaks new ground in the study of social mobilization and popular dissent by arguing that international human rights treaties influence both repression and dissident challenges at the same time.[74]

Individuals face a collective action problem when deciding whether to engage in mobilized dissent activities around an issue or practice. Grievances such as inequalities, deprivation, exclusion from power, or poor economic conditions create dissatisfaction, which serves as a precondition for dissent or rebellion.[75] When actors desire change to existing policy or practice, they consider joining together, committing to exert resources and effort and assuming the risk of negative government responses.[76] Changes in the status quo (such as policy change) often take the form of a nonexcludable good (in other words, the change benefits everyone in a related group, not only the people who worked to bring it about). Individuals thus have incentives to free-ride and let others bear the costs of collective action.[77] The logical conclusion of the free-rider problem is underprovision[78]: no one joins the movement, and the desired change cannot occur. To solve this problem, institutions or actors must reduce the costs of mobilization, increase the benefits of mobilization, or provide information about each.[79]

---

72. See, e.g., Hafner-Burton and Tsutsui 2007.

73. See, e.g., Earl 2003; Earl, Soule, and McCarthy 2003; Gates 2002; Kuran 1991; McAdam 1999; McCarthy and Zald 1977; Olson 1965; Schussman and Soule 2005; Tarrow 1991; Tilly 1978.

74. See also Ritter and Conrad 2016a.

75. Acemoglu and Robinson 2006; Cederman, Wimmer, and Min 2010; Gurr 1970; Muller 1985; Weede 1987.

76. Lohmann 1994; Shadmehr and Bernhardt 2011.

77. Lichbach 1995.

78. Olson 1965.

79. Klandermans 1984; Klandermans and Oegema 1987; Kuran 1991; Lichbach 1995; Snow et al. 1986.

International treaties can provide information that helps coordinate and motivate mobilization, offering an institutional solution to the collective action problem.[80] Formal standards, especially laws, serve as focal points, creating common expectations as to appropriate government actions and violations thereof that individuals can rally around.[81] Nongovernmental organizations often refer to these international obligations when mobilizing collective demands, drawing on the law to convince dissatisfied actors of the importance of an issue and the country's obligation to respond.[82] These studies suggest that government obligation to human rights treaties may lower individuals' expected costs of solving the collective action problem, thus leading to realization of more challenges.[83]

Although previous literature examines how law influences mobilization processes, there has been little research into the effect of treaty law on dissent. Dissent is different from mobilization; whereas mobilization indicates that individuals are coordinating, dissent indicates that they have directed that coordination against the government.[84] To draw an analogy from international conflict, just because a country has an army does not mean it will necessarily fight a battle. There is thus a great deal to be learned from how international human rights treaties may or may not affect actual dissent activities.

By considering how human rights treaties affect conflict between the government and potential dissidents, we uncover a new mechanism by which these treaties affect dissent. Institutions that constrain repression have a *structural* effect on dissent, altering the incentive framework within which dissidents make decisions. Individuals and groups considering dissent look for external cues as to the likely success of their efforts, strategically acting when leaders are likely to be constrained by (international) legal concerns. A treaty commitment modifies how decisions to dissent are made based on the potential dissidents' expectations about two factors:

80. Bell, Bhasin, et al. 2014; Dai 2005; Dodson 2015; Keck and Sikkink 1998; Risse, Ropp, and Sikkink 1999; Simmons 2009.

81. Carey 2000; Dai 2005; Keck and Sikkink 1998; Weingast 1997.

82. Hafner-Burton and Tsutsui 2005; Keck and Sikkink 1998; Risse, Ropp, and Sikkink 1999.

83. Dai 2005; Keck and Sikkink 1998; Simmons 2009.

84. Mobilized dissent materializes in two stages. First, individuals decide whether to pool their resources and efforts to act collectively (mobilization). Second, dissidents threaten to or actually carry out actions that impose costs on the government in an effort to alter the status quo (dissent). Throughout this book, we refer to the process of individuals joining a group and pooling their resources as *mobilization* and the action the group takes or threatens to take against the government as *dissent*. We treat these processes as distinct (though connected) decisions.

(1) the likelihood that a treaty will create consequences that a repressive actor would otherwise not incur, and (2) the propensity of government authorities to repress. If leaders would not repress the opposition regardless of their behavior, then an institution changes neither the expectation of repression nor dissidents' behavior. However, dissidents' behavior does change as a result of treaties in certain situations: people should expect that treaty obligations have the strongest constraining effects on repression when leaders face few domestic institutional constraints and when they value office highly enough to repress at will, and under these conditions, treaties lead to more dissent. Although international treaties can act as focal points to facilitate coordination,[85] we argue that these institutions also change the structural game dissidents are playing.

This picture of mobilized dissent is consistent with both the resource mobilization and political opportunity theories of social movements. Resource mobilization theory argues that protest movements emerge and succeed when there are resources and organization to allow groups to form, expand, and act. According to this theory, when leaders or groups are able to reduce the costs of mobilization, increase the benefits of mobilization, or provide information about each, more people will join the movement and its actions will be more effective.[86] Other scholars argue that resource mobilization is not enough to predict when dissidents will act and whether movements will succeed. In addition to needing to mobilize resources, they assert, dissident groups must also look for political openings: events or institutions that weaken or constrain leaders, making them more likely to concede, accommodate, or change policies, and less likely to repress the dissidents.[87] Tarrow (1994, p. 18) writes, "political opportunity structures are 'consistent dimensions of the political environment which either encourage or discourage people from using collective action.' "

International human rights treaties represent such a dimension, encouraging people to act collectively toward changes in the status quo. Treaties open opportunities for dissent, since dissidents anticipate a lower probability that they will be repressed for their action than if the treaty were absent. Perversely, by creating space for dissidents to increase dissent, governments may be further motivated to repress dissent. Like others who combine social movement scholarship with conflict studies,[88] we argue that

---

85. Finnemore and Sikkink 1998; Simmons 2009; Vreeland 2008a.
86. Klandermans 1984; Klandermans and Oegema 1987; Kuran 1991; Snow et al. 1986.
87. McAdam, McCarthy, and Zald 1996.
88. See, *inter alia*, Chenoweth and Stephan 2011; Schock 2005; Weinstein 2007; Wood 2003.

to understand mobilized dissent—and specifically the effect of treaties on mobilized dissent—we must place it within a framework of contentious politics. Political opportunities, like international legal obligations, change the decision environment for governments as well as dissidents, whose respective decisions are strategic and intertwined. We therefore build from and extend political opportunity theory, carefully considering the role of contention in that opportunity.

1.3.3 Human Rights Treaties and the Law

In legal scholarship, most examinations of international treaties focus on the interpretation and application of law in international and domestic courts.[89] Legal standards and norms require that international laws are most often adjudicated in domestic courts (international courts are for the last resort), and that is especially the case when it comes to cases against individuals accused of violating a law. Domestic courts either invoke and support international standards or they do not; if not, conventional scholarly arguments suggest that international laws cannot influence behavioral outcomes.[90] Other scholars consider whether the international legal institution would actually be invoked by bringing violators to trial; if not, these scholars argue that the institution will have failed to meet its goals.[91]

In similar fashion, we argue that the primary mechanism by which international human rights treaties constrain leaders is through domestic legal consequences, but we argue that the courts play a different role in the international constraint process. Again, most scholars argue that domestic courts are the arbiter of international law. In practice, the domestic judiciary rarely references or implements international treaties in particular cases. Indeed, courts are often slow to constrain government discrimination and other human rights violations.[92] Nevertheless, we argue that domestic courts are important for identifying the influence of international law on government behavior because they mitigate popular expectations of constraint. The courts' effect is not on the government directly, but on the expectations of potential dissenters: in treaty-obligated nations, dissenters *think* that courts will punish repression

---

89. See, e.g., Hathaway 2007.
90. See, e.g., Sloss 2009.
91. See, e.g., Goldsmith 2003; Goldsmith and Krasner 2003.
92. Rosenberg 1991.

under international standards, so they are then more willing to engage in dissent.

Assuming simply that the international obligation increases the *expectation* (by leaders and potential dissidents) that violations will be met by litigation and court-related costs, we find that international HRTs have a limiting effect on repression, even when the domestic court system is relatively ineffective. These expectations of court constraint are often supported by behavioral evidence (more cases being brought to trial, more NGO activity around international laws, changes in domestic laws to reflect the obligation), but they need not be; expectations change even in the absence of evidence of court constraint. Early survey data suggest that people believe that international treaties are likely to create costs for authorities that violate rights, even in places where international human rights law is rarely considered in domestic policies or court decisions.

In fact, international treaties have their strongest effect on human rights outcomes when countries lack the domestic legal mechanisms to constrain leaders. This runs counter to existing scholarly research, which argues that courts need to be effective to enforce treaty obligations.[93] As we show in our formal theory, governments in countries with strong courts already repress at lower levels than those with weak courts, and a treaty obligation does little to change that constraint environment. But in low-constraint environments, treaty obligations alter expectations a great deal. Our model indicates that when all other conditions remain the same, a state with weak courts that is obligated to a treaty engages in repression less than it would if it were not so obligated. In these low-constraint states, treaty obligations affect both repressive behavior from the state and dissent behavior from the people, changing the entire conflict. It is this change in the conflict, we posit, that causes these countries to reduce violations in line with treaty terms.

In short, we approach the way in which international law affects domestic outcomes by examining not domestic law but societal and governmental behaviors. This, we argue, is because international human rights treaties can affect outcomes even if they do not directly and observably either change court behavior or the implementation of laws. To decrease government repression, treaties need only influence the expectations of those things.

---

93. See, e.g., Powell and Staton 2009; Simmons 2009.

1.3.4 Human Rights Treaties and Advocacy

While social scientists and legal scholars tend to focus on interactions between elite institutions and leaders or the application of legal processes to complex and obtuse policies, human rights activists know that the question of rights protections versus violations frequently comes down to simple interactions between dissidents and government authorities. We bring the question of constraining institutions to the ground level, giving those who design institutions a better understanding of the implications of their designs in the actual field, and enabling those advocating for rights protection to demand the institutions that best improve rights outcomes.

Our findings run counter to the dominant trend of scholarship; we find that international human rights treaties have a positive effect on rights protections when governments are most motivated to repress. International law has only a small influence on perceptions of domestic politics, but it is enough to yield a substantive, meaningful reduction in rights violations when leaders are highly invested in keeping power. This finding buttresses the efforts of those who advocate for international institutions as solutions in countries with poor domestic barriers to rights violations. In contrast to Hafner-Burton and Tsutsui (2007), we find that international human rights treaties have the strongest effects where they are most needed—where conflict and repression are most likely to occur, unconstrained by other institutions.

Because they influence both repression and dissent, international human rights treaties have potentially conflicting effects: When they are most effective at constraining government violations of human rights, they provide incentives for mobilized dissidents to take action against the government. International law creates openings for more effective dissent, which is particularly appealing when the call for change to the status quo is connected to improved human rights. Although we argue that dissent should be more likely to occur regardless of the substance of the dissidents' particular policy demands, this is a useful side effect for advocates supporting rights protections around the globe.

For all of the good news about treaties presented in the book, their effects on government repression are not always large and are limited to a subset of states. And critically, the effect of an international institution depends on the status of an extant domestic institution: the judiciary. Very consistently, our findings suggest that domestic courts are much more effective than treaties at constraining government leaders from engaging in repression. Practitioners would do well to increase the effectiveness of the domestic judiciary, but if they cannot, international treaties can help to constrain the worst violators of human rights.

1.4 ORGANIZATION OF THE BOOK

In this book, we explore when and how human rights treaty obligations affect a leader's decision to repress, focusing on the domestic institutional and behavioral enforcement of international obligations to protect people from government abuse. Institutions that create costs for violating rights do not affect government entities in isolation; instead, they change the decision-making calculus for all actors in a domestic conflict—the leader as well as dissidents within the population. As such, we shift the analytical focus of study from the more traditional concentration on government decision-making to a dynamic and innovative model of domestic conflict between government leaders and an opposing population.

The theory and empirical analyses presented in Parts I and II explain why international human rights treaties curb human rights violations under some conditions but not others. The theory is based on a formal model of conflict between government authorities and potential dissidents, which is presented in Chapter 2. Highlighting two interconnected decisions—the leader's choice to repress and the dissidents' choice to dissent—we paint a picture of how domestic conflict plays out in the absence of an international obligation to protect human rights. In doing so, we establish a counterfactual to which we can compare the same theoretical country if it were bound to a minimal expectation that violations would be punished. This conceptual exercise allows us to derive theoretical predictions related to three human rights–related outcomes, which we discuss in Chapter 3:

1. the effect of an international human rights treaty on the likelihood of government repression,
2. the effect of an international human rights treaty on the likelihood of mobilized dissent, and
3. the likelihood that a government will ratify an international human rights treaty, given its anticipated effects on conflict.

Part II presents a series of statistical analyses in support of our claims that treaties meaningfully reduce repression and increase dissent. These analyses examine several international human rights treaties and their effects on government repression and mobilized dissent. In Chapter 4, we translate our theoretical concepts into measurements and describe the methodological approach we take to analyzing the implications of the theory. Our statistical models echo the structure of the data-generating process we assume in the formal theory: Countries select into nonrandom samples of treaty obligation status, and we draw inferences as to the effect of the treaty by comparing the actors' conflict behaviors to what they would have done if they had been assigned to the other group. For example, we compare repression and dissent activity in nonsignatory countries to what our theory implies would have occurred had that same country committed to an international treaty. We also compare conflict outcomes using the opposite counterfactual, by determining what would have occurred in treaty-obligated countries had they failed to commit to a treaty.

We estimate and interpret the effect of a government obligation to the International Covenant on Civil and Political Rights (ICCPR), the UN Convention Against Torture and Other Cruel, Inhuman or Degrading Treatment or Punishment (CAT), and the UN Convention for the Elimination of Discrimination Against Women (CEDAW) on the likelihood of repression (Chapter 5) and dissent (Chapter 6). In Chapter 5, we find empirical support for the implications of our theory for government repression: Leaders committed to international treaties who are secure in power repress less than they would if they were not bound to a treaty's terms, but the international obligation has no identifiable effect on leaders who are more vulnerable to turnover. The CAT has the weakest effect on government behavior, with stronger effects from obligation to both the ICCPR and the CEDAW, but all treaties exhibit consistent, robust effects according to our conditional expectations. In Chapter 6, we examine the likelihood that the government will face mobilized dissent from one or more groups of dissidents in the population. We find that state obligation to an international human rights treaty leads to a meaningful increase in mobilized dissent when people expect it to influence repression outcomes—when leaders are secure and courts are ineffective. If the judiciary is relatively effective or the leader is vulnerable to removal, treaty obligation does little to constrain the executive beyond the constraints they would already face at home. Under these conditions, the government obligation to an international human rights treaty has no meaningful effect on mobilized dissent.

Because treaties intended to curb state repression can, in some states, have domestic political effects that perversely incentivize more conflict, we discuss in Chapter 7 the policy implications of our research for those seeking to create institutions to better protect human rights. The conclusion also highlights a number of ways in which our theory's implications could extend to elements of domestic politics that this book does not explicitly examine. For instance, we discuss what our theory has to say about the likelihood that different types of countries will ratify international treaties. We also propose an extension of the theory in which the domestic court acts as a strategic player, (perhaps) in opposition to the executive. Finally, we discuss the assumptions about institutions that explain why treaties have the effects we predict, considering how to apply the theory to various international and even domestic institutions that seek to constrain human rights violations.

In summary, this book fills a critical gap in the scholarship on international human rights law specifically and on government repression more generally, introducing dynamic, multiactor considerations to a largely state-centric literature. From a social science perspective, our approach is novel, combining two literatures on human rights questions—one focused on institutional constraints and another focused on the behavioral conflict dynamics that determine repression—that until now have remained separate from one other. Practitioners should see our approach not as the sterile creation of abstract institutions that may or may not effectively impose costs on repressive leaders, but as an accurate reflection of on-the-ground conflict dynamics. Our theory recognizes that binding leaders with domestic and international constraints is not enough to improve human rights, for doing so may also change the domestic threats that leaders face. These changes do not always reduce violations of human rights writ large, but in many important situations they help protect vulnerable citizens from being abused by their governments.

PART I

A Theory of Conflict
and Treaty Constraint

CHAPTER 2

ↂ

A Model of Conflict and Constraint

The United States is a member of the International Covenant on Civil and Political Rights (ICCPR), an international human rights treaty that aims to protect a wide variety of rights, including the right for people to express opinions and engage in assembly (Articles 19 and 21). The Bill of Rights in the U.S. Constitution also provides legal protection for the rights to speech and assembly, which the U.S. Supreme Court has generally upheld. Assembled groups—including those that involve antigovernment protests—cannot be restricted based on what they demand or say. In the United States, domestic laws establish these rights and domestic authorities administer them; international human rights treaties like the ICCPR add a layer of obligation to existing domestic protections.

Although the rights to speech and assembly are protected by both domestic and international laws and institutions, U.S. authorities violate those rights on a regular basis, with discriminatory effects. In 2017, the former UN Special Rapporteur on the rights of assembly and association, Maina Kiai, issued a report after examining U.S. police interactions with protesters from the Black Lives Matter (BLM) movement. Black Lives Matter groups actively protest the discriminatory aggression of police officers toward persons of color, as well as calling attention to broader themes related to the administration of justice and inclusion of all peoples. In his report, Kiai accused U.S. authorities of illegally and discriminatorily curtailing BLM protests, pointing out that black protesters experience more intimidation and disrespect than other groups of protesters in the United States. Relative to their treatment of nonblack protesters, U.S. police are more likely to arrest black protesters, detain them for longer periods of time, and charge them with more serious offenses.[1] Such discriminatory policing has the effect of discouraging black participation in protest activities.[2] More broadly, when government authorities violate domestic and international protections for assembly and association, they often discourage or deter dissidents from protest.

U.S. president Donald Trump, newly elected at time of Kiai's report, has to the date of this writing made no effort to correct or prevent violations against BLM protesters. The United States' ICCPR obligation to protect assembly seems to be ineffective: state authorities (i.e., police) infringe upon the right, and the U.S. obligations to international law do not appear to alter either the government's behavior toward protesters or the protesters' actions in anticipation of repression.

However, some groups have used the United States' international obligations to their advantage. For example, in 2014, a group of protesters from the Chicago-based We Charge Genocide organization attended a meeting of the UN Committee Against Torture in Geneva, Switzerland,[3] to protest U.S. police brutality and discrimination against persons of color.[4] The UN Committee Against Torture is an international body that monitors implementation of the UN Convention Against Torture (CAT) by state parties. The CAT, to which the United States is a ratifying party, defines *torture* as an act perpetrated by a public official that causes severe pain or suffering used either as punishment for a crime a person has or may have committed or intimidating the person based on discrimination of any kind.[5] We Charge Genocide, which is associated with the Black Lives Matter movement, presented a report to the committee regarding discriminatory police aggression in Chicago and stood in silent protest to encourage further examination of U.S. (non)compliance with its CAT obligations. The

1. See, Davenport, Soule, and Armstrong 2011.

2. Kiai 2017.

3. We Charge Genocide describes itself as a "grassroots, inter-generational effort to center the voices and experiences of the young people most targeted by police violence in Chicago." Additional information about We Charge Genocide is available at http://wechargegenocide.org/.

4. Berlatsky 2014.

5. The full text of Article 1 of the CAT reads: "For the purposes of this Convention, the term 'torture' means any act by which severe pain or suffering, whether physical or mental, is intentionally inflicted on a person for such purposes as obtaining from him or a third person information or a confession, punishing him for an act he or a third person has committed or is suspected of having committed, or intimidating or coercing him or a third person, or for any reason based on discrimination of any kind, when such pain or suffering is inflicted by or at the instigation of or with the consent or acquiescence of a public official or other person acting in an official capacity" (*Convention against Torture and Other Cruel, Inhuman or Degrading Treatment or Punishment* 1984).

naming and shaming of U.S. police—and of the Chicago Police Department in particular—at the United Nations creates reputational consequences for authorities accused of repression, which may affect not only police decisions regarding the issue but also protesters, who are likely to feel additionally validated in their challenge. Although the issue of their dissent was torture (hence, the decision to appear before the UN Committee on Torture), it was the protections of the ICCPR that gave the members of We Charge Genocide the opportunity to protest without fear of government reprisal. The group expected that international legal obligations were sufficiently constraining on the government that they could make demands at a lower risk than if the United States were not party to international human rights law.

These two examples—Black Lives Matter and We Charge Genocide—are in tension with one another. The Special Rapporteur pointed out that, while government authorities know how to interact with protesters under internationally defined norms, they sometimes systematically ignore their international obligations and restrict the rights of persons to assemble. Yet protesters who demand better protections for their rights continue to point to international law, seemingly with the expectation that international obligations will restrict government reprisals. Although both examples originate in the contemporary United States, one example (BLM) suggests that international rights obligations have no power, while the other (We Charge Genocide) supports the idea that international obligations can alter actors' conflict behavior.

Although these cases illustrate some dynamics of repression and dissent, they do not provide us with enough information to know whether or not commitment to international human rights influenced human rights outcomes. We cannot know, for example, whether protest policing under the current constellation of international legal commitments is the same as it would be if the United States were not party to the ICCPR or the CAT; we similarly cannot know if We Charge Genocide would have protested about discriminatory policing in the same manner in the absence of a U.S. obligation to international law. Because illustrative vignettes can only take us so far in understanding the effect of HRTs on conflict, we instead use theory to characterize the process by which governments and dissidents make decisions and to predict what those actors would have done under different circumstances. We compare these predictions about the counterfactual to what actually happened.

In this chapter, we present a model of conflict between dissidents and the government when the government faces potential domestic institutional consequences for rights violations. This allows us to predict how these actors make decisions in the absence of an international treaty. Once we establish these baseline expectations, we change one thing: the government selects into an international human rights treaty. This enables us to compare outcomes and predict the effects of international law on repression and dissent and allows us to answer a number of questions, which we address throughout this book. How does the leader balance the increased probability of paying costs associated with HRTs against the incentives to repress citizens who might challenge policies? Does the population respond differently to leaders who have adopted HRTs than those who have not committed themselves under international law? Under what conditions do human rights treaties alter the conflict behaviors of these actors? And when does a government that anticipates such changes obligate itself to international law in the first place?

This chapter establishes the conceptual definitions, relational assumptions, and decision-making framework we use to study treaty effects on conflict. We wade a bit into the weeds to be as precise as possible about what is and is not included in the scope of our theory, and we explain the applicability of the assumptions we make. Here, we lay the formal foundation for the more implications that are the central contribution of this book, which we discuss in a less formal manner in Chapter 3.

We begin with a brief discussion of our assumptions regarding decision-making in general; we use a rational-choice framework to motivate our starting assumptions, and that framework has implications for our likely conclusions that we try to address ex ante. We then describe the formal theory of conflict and constraint, explaining our assumption choices and their implications and specifying the foundational structure and payoffs of the model. Finally, we describe the equilibrium behavior we should expect to see from such a model. In the next chapter, we turn to the empirical implications of the theory, focusing on the conditions under which HRT obligation will lead to a meaningful difference in repression and dissent.

2.1 INSTITUTIONS, CONFLICT, AND DECISION-MAKING

To study, explain, and predict human rights protections and violations is to study government decision-making. When and why do government authorities violate rights? When and why do they protect them? Whether they give direct orders to attack a group or passively allow discrimination against out-groups, authorities make a choice: they can repress or not.

Leaders also make choices: they choose to repress more or less severely,[6] they choose which targets will be repressed,[7] and they choose the repressive tactics to be used.[8] Because government authorities—under superior or individual responsibility for their actions—decide whether or not (and how much) to repress actors protected by international human rights law and norms, we must first understand what influences the choice to repress in order to better explain and predict the outcome of that choice.

An individual's choices (in any context) are a function of (1) the relative values of the outcomes of those decisions and (2) the structure of the decision itself. Individuals make choices that yield outcomes, and they weigh the outcomes' benefits against their costs in order to make the best choice for them.[9] Authorities decide to repress when this decision maximizes the likelihood that they will achieve a given set of goals, whether those goals are personal or professional.

Outcomes of an individual's decisions are determined not in a vacuum but in a strategic environment. Each person's decisions combine with other people's decisions in interactions that lead to particular consequences. To predict what a person will do under a given set of circumstances, a researcher must consider not only what that person wants, but also that person's ideas about others: what they want and what they are likely to do.[10] As we discuss in detail later in this chapter, a leader who chooses to repress does so to yield particular gains in power—to control policy outcomes or to consolidate power. Whether repression will produce those desired gains depends on the persons or groups the leader wants to control; their decisions interact with the decisions of the leader, and this interaction may yield consequences the leader may not want.

These basics of strategic decision-making are further structured by institutions. We define an *institution* as a set of incentives that enable and/or limit behavior.[11] Institutions can be formally established and written down[12] or informal, evolving into convention over

6. Davenport 2000; Ritter 2014.

7. Bhasin and Gandhi 2013; Conrad, Haglund, and Moore 2013; Sullivan 2016a.

8. Conrad and DeMeritt 2011; Payne and Abouharb 2015.

9. This assumption does not necessarily imply or require that individuals make careful calculations for every decision or even that they have an accurate sense of their own costs or benefits for an outcome. The model can be useful as long as persons act, on average, as if they consider decisions according to their preferred outcomes and the strategic structure of the model.

10. Tsebelis 1989.

11. This definition draws from North 1990, Chapter 1. For alternative and often quite different definitions of institutions, see, e.g., Ellickson 1991, Knight 1992, Calvert 1995, Vanderschraaf 1998, and Diermeyer and Krehbiel 2003.

12. Carey 2000; Hardin 1989.

time.[13] Positive and negative incentives in the form of institutions encourage individuals to take certain actions over others, prohibiting some choices and permitting or encouraging others. Institutions "are the framework within which human interaction takes place."[14] They structure actors' choices, so they can constrain actors' behavior, but not necessarily determine it.[15] In practice, then, institutions are incentives that affect choices in a manner separate from the strategic choices of other actors.[16] Punishments create negative consequences for undesirable actions;[17] stigmas, social pressures, and reputations can do the same.[18] Rewards push our behavior to be more in line with society's preferences,[19] while written focal points and common expectations can help to coordinate individuals into joint behavior.[20]

These types of incentives, and the consequences that they produce, are the focus of this book. North (1990, Chapter 1) uses a sports analogy to demonstrate the point: Institutions are the rules of a sport, defining limits and incentives for play, and within those confines, the players make decisions that vary depending on who they are playing. This is why the play of any individual game differs, though the rules stay the same: The players on the field differ, as do the opponents in the strategic interaction. Here, we want to understand how institutional incentives alter the decision-making process of the various types of individuals and groups responsible for determining human rights outcomes, focusing in particular on international human rights treaties and the domestic courts through which HRTs constrain government behavior.

2.2 A MODEL OF TREATY OBLIGATIONS, COURTS, AND CONFLICT

Our formal theory includes the following basic elements: a leader and a group of dissidents, a policy conflict between the two actors, the risk that

13. Morrow 2014; Vanderschraaf 2000. Institutions are created and maintained when they are sustainable in equilibrium (Abbott and Snidal 1998; Calvert 1995); actors put and keep them in place when they would achieve no more by altering the established incentives.

14. North 1990, p. 4.

15. In game theoretic terms, institutions are the exogenously set incentives that enter the actor's utility functions as a result of their decision histories. Institutions may be exogenized to study outcomes or endogenized to study the establishment of the institution itself (Diermeyer and Krehbiel 2003).

16. Koremenos, Lipson, and Snidal 2001; North 1990; Pelc 2009; Przeworski, Alvarez, and Cheibub 2000; Stone 2011.

17. Axelrod 1984; König and Mäder 2014.

18. Downs and Jones 2002; Johnston 2001; Morrow 2014.

19. Ellickson 1991.

20. Morrow 2014; Ostrom 1990; Weingast 1997.

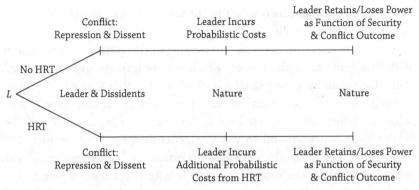

Figure 2.1 Sequence of Play

the leader might lose power, a baseline expectation of the government's consequences for repressing (e.g., potential for domestic litigation), and a state obligation (or not) to an HRT. Before elaborating on the actors' preferences and probabilistic outcomes in the following sections, we first describe the simple sequence of interactions upon which we build the theory, which is depicted in Figure 2.1.

We model an interaction between a Leader (L) and a group of dissatisfied persons within the state's population. We refer to that group as Dissidents (D). At the outset, the leader decides whether to ratify, or commit the state to, an international human rights treaty. If the state does not join the treaty (the upper sequence in Figure 2.1), the leader and the dissidents choose levels of repression and dissent in a conflict over a status quo policy. If the state does join the treaty (the lower sequence in Figure 2.1), the state receives some international or domestic benefit from joining, and the obligation increases the probability that the leader will incur consequences (i.e., litigation) for repressing, relative to the domestic baseline in the absence of an international human rights treaty. This is a model of complete information; both actors know which treaty status they are in, as well as all other information about the theoretical interaction.

Regardless of the government's treaty ratification choice, the choices that follow the respective histories are the same: a leader and a group of dissatisfied civilians enter a conflict over some status quo policy. The conflict can be over any existing policy or power distribution; it need not be rights-related or related to the substantive focus of a particular international treaty. The leader and the dissidents decide simultaneously how much to repress (r) and dissent (d), respectively, paying correlated costs for their chosen efforts. Their decisions combine in a costly lottery $\left(\frac{d}{d+r}\right)$ such that increased repression makes the government more likely to win the policy and increased dissent favors the dissidents. The victor determines the new policy.

We also need to capture how threatening or dangerous the interaction with dissidents is to the leader, which we encapsulate in the expected value for retaining power ($\mathbb{E}[U_L] = \theta * 1 + (1 - \theta) * 0 = \theta$). We alternatively refer to this as the *stakes of the conflict*. If the government wins the policy, this expected value does not change. However, if the leader loses policy ground to the dissidents as a result of conflict, the expected value for retaining power decreases to $\frac{\theta}{\kappa}$, where $\kappa > 1$. The higher the stakes, the more dangerous it is to the leader to lose to the dissidents.

Following the conflict, there is some probability that the leader incurs consequences for repressing the dissidents. This is the case whether or not the leader has obligated the state to an international human rights treaty. In the baseline context, these consequences are a function of whatever domestic and international institutional incentives are already in place. Some leaders already operate under expectations of consequences for repression, while others face weaker institutions that are unwilling or unable to impose costs on repressive leaders. We examine the legal consequences of repression. For a government that elects into an international human rights treaty, the probability that costs are imposed is (some small amount) higher than it would have been for that government in the baseline. Adding an international treaty obligation increases the likelihood that the leader will incur costly consequences for repression, for the reasons we discuss below.

Equations (2.1) and (2.2) present the actors' expected utility functions, which we describe at length below. The leader's formal payoffs are as follows:

$$
U_L = \begin{cases}
-r * \phi + \left(1 - \dfrac{d}{d+r}\right) * \theta + \left(\dfrac{d}{d+r}\right) * \dfrac{\theta}{\kappa} & \text{uncommitted to HRT} \\[3ex]
-r * (\phi + \epsilon) + \left(1 - \dfrac{d}{d+r}\right) * \theta + \left(\dfrac{d}{d+r}\right) * \dfrac{\theta}{\kappa} + \mu & \text{committed to HRT}
\end{cases}
$$

$$\tag{2.1}$$

and the dissidents' payoffs are the same for either treaty status:

$$
U_G = -d + \left(1 - \frac{d}{d+r}\right) * (1 - \theta) + \left(\frac{d}{d+r}\right) * \left(1 - \frac{\theta}{\kappa}\right) \tag{2.2}
$$

For ease of reading, Table 2.1 describes the model's notation:

Table 2.1 TABLE OF FORMAL NOTATION

Term	Assumptions	Concept
r	$r > 0$	level (and cost) of repression
d	$d > 0$	level (and cost) of dissent
ϕ	$0 < \phi < 1$	probability of legal consequences
ϵ	$0 < \phi + \epsilon < 1$	HRT boost to the probability of legal consequences
θ	$0 < \theta < 1$	expected value of retaining power
κ	$\kappa > 1$	tenure consequences of losing policy to the dissidents
μ	$\mu > 0$	state benefit of HRT obligation

2.2.1 The Effects and Costs of Repression and Dissent

A leader decides how much to repress actual or potential dissidents, expecting that there is some probability of incurring negative consequences for the choice. Heads of state and top government officials rarely carry out repression themselves. Leaders sometimes directly order police officers, prison guards, intelligence agents, and members of the military to repress, communicating orders or personally signing policies into law. Other times, repressive agents, including police officers or members of the military, violate human rights under the auspices of collecting information or maintaining order.[21] Regardless of the actual perpetrator, the leader is responsible for ordering, changing, or allowing human rights violations in policy and/or practice. This can be a single leader, a ruling party, or even the legislature, either in combination with the executive or not. Because we treat the leader as a unitary actor, the theory applies to any person or group that acts as a single decision-making entity with the authority to make decisions to protect or violate human rights on behalf of the state. We make this assumption in order to make cross-national comparisons of the effects of international human rights treaties. The theory can also apply more broadly to the decisions of a lower-level authority interacting with a dissenting group under

21. For more on the delegation of government repression, see, for example, Rejali 2007; Butler, Gluch, and Mitchell 2007; Mitchell 2009; Conrad and Moore 2010; DeMeritt 2015; Mitchell, Carey, and Butler 2014; Morrow 2014; Salehyan, Siroky, and Wood 2014; and Dragu and Lupu 2017.

expectations of domestic and potentially treaty-based consequences for the decision.

The leader's primary concern is to retain control over policies and stay in power.[22] All leaders desire power, whether for vicious or virtuous reasons. Some leaders want to hold office simply for the sake of power itself. Others value the access to resources that comes with power, such as rents or the ability to grant resources in exchange for personal favors. Still other leaders desire a position of power to set policies to benefit the public welfare. Whatever their reason, we assume that all leaders want to stay in power as long as possible.

One of the most important ways by which a leader tries to hold on to power is to control policies and their outcomes. The ability to set policies allows the leader (or ruling party, etc.) to consolidate power, collect rents, reward key constituencies, or rule benevolently, depending on what outcome is most likely to extend the leader's tenure at the lowest cost of resources and effort. In other words, a leader's stakes in the conflict are the very position of power, which depends on the control of policy. The more overt popular challenges endanger the policy, the more they endanger the leader's power.[23]

Although the leader would ideally like to set their most preferred policy and remain in power without having to repress challenges, a group of people from among the population may challenge that policy. We call the members of this group *dissidents*, even if they ultimately do not take action against the state. Dissidents prefer a different policy from the leader and consider engaging in some mobilized dissent activities to try to change the policy.[24] Because dissent activities are costly (in time, resources, risk, etc.), dissidents also want to get their best outcome at the lowest cost—without having to engage in dissent actions.[25]

22. See, e.g., Bueno de Mesquita, et al. 2003.

23. Another interpretation of the stakes of the conflict that would be consistent with our theory would be to set aside the leader's position of power and suggest that authorities receive some benefit from the policy itself and are willing to fight to keep it in place.

24. We use the terms *mobilized dissent*, *popular dissent*, and *opposition dissent* interchangeably throughout the book. Dissent refers not to the disagreement with the policy but instead to overt threats or actions taken to challenge it.

25. We focus on popular dissent, which ranges from nonviolence to violence and can be organized or unorganized. Other forms of contention include domestic terrorism or insurgency, which can be similar in concept but tend to include particularly extreme or committed membership. These individuals are likely to take action against the government no matter what and are unlikely to be swayed by the differential expectations associated with treaty status.

The actors' opposed policy preferences create a domestic conflict in which the government considers repression to control the status quo and the dissidents consider dissent to change it. Historical and current examples abound. In the late 1960s, the Republic of New Africa called for a separate nation for black Americans, where they would live outside of U.S. government rule; for this goal, they organized dissent activities and experienced both covert and overt repression.[26] In the summer of 2006, Turkish civilians demanding civil rights and possible leadership change were met with mass unemployment, political arrests, violent policing, and the government calling for a state of emergency.[27] Violent policing of nonviolent protests in South Africa has led to injuries, deaths, and counterescalation, whether protesters call for access to basic services delivery[28] or the reduction of university costs.[29] Each of these instances highlights the way that disagreement over some policy or practice is the centerpiece of conflict. The policies vary in threat and type, the dissent varies in participation and tactics, and the repression varies in scope and violence—and all of these factors combine to influence what policy emerges at the end of the day.

In our theory, the victor of the policy conflict is determined by what economists call a *costly lottery*: the actors' relative efforts combine to form the probability that the dissident group receives its demanded policy or good allocation $\left(\frac{d}{d+r}\right)$. This contest function captures the idea that dissidents are more likely to receive their demands as dissent increases and less likely to get what they want as repression increases.[30]

In an effort to "win" the contest (i.e., maintain the policy in question and stay in office without or in spite of a challenge), the leader decides how much to repress (r) the dissidents. Repression is any action or policy—legal or illegal, violent or nonviolent—taken by authorities to prevent a group or population from participating in their own governance.[31]

As such, we do not expect them to act in a way that is consistent with this theory.

26. Davenport 2015.

27. Sariyuce and Dewan 2016.

28. Eyewitness News 2014.

29. Duncan 2016.

30. The government could accommodate the dissidents' demands rather than repressing. Our specification allows the leader to choose a level of $r = 0$, which ensures that the dissident group receives its demands ($\frac{d}{d+0} = 1$). That being said, the theory primarily speaks to situations in which repression is a potential choice for the leader, which is most often the case. Most governments engage in human rights violations in most years. See, for example, Conrad, Haglund, and Moore 2013.

31. Davenport 2007b; Goldstein 1978; Ritter 2014.

It can take the form of torture or political arrests; violent policing or extrajudicial killing; limits on assembly or speech; fraudulent elections or voter intimidation, policies that discriminate by gender, race, or language; or any number of other actions or policies that violate international standards.[32]

Governments repress to undercut dissident efforts to mobilize and take action.[33] Repression can damage dissidents' capacity to mount a coercive threat: Restrictions make it difficult to assemble groups or plan dissenting actions, invasive or covert policies or behaviors can undermine group challenges before they take place, and discriminatory policies can limit resources.[34] Repressive actions also reduce people's willingness to challenge the state: Disappearances, targeted arrests, violent policing, or torture make would-be dissidents fear joining a movement and/or challenging the government.[35]

In deciding how much to repress, the leader makes a set of choices (which can include no repression at all) that determine the scope of rights violations: what tactics to use in what combination, how violent the action(s) will be, how many victims will be targeted, how many agents will participate, how public or secretive the repression will be, and so on. According to the costly lottery function we use, the more severely the government represses relative to a given level of dissent, the more likely that the dissidents' challenge will fail and the status quo policy will remain.[36]

32. Human rights protection also involves *positive* obligations to protect. Governments have the responsibility not only to not torture but also put programs or policies in place to prevent torture that might occur as a function of agency and other variations (Conrad and Moore 2010), and the absence of these protections can also serve to undermine challenges. However, their absence also can involve a lack of capacity to implement such policies, adding complication to the concept. We focus on the narrower concept of those policies or practices explicitly intended to counter or prevent dissent activities.

33. Davenport 2007b, p. 47.

34. Davenport 2015; Sullivan 2016b; Tilly 1978.

35. Galtung 1969. On the government use of torture to intimidate those who might challenge the state, see Rejali 2007, p. 23. On the killing of civilians to deter their participation in conflict, see Kalyvas 1999 and Valentino, Huth, and Balch-Lindsey 2004. On the use of repression to prevent or deter dissent before it occurs, see Lichbach 1987, Nordås and Davenport 2013, Danneman and Ritter 2014, Sullivan 2016b, and Ritter and Conrad 2016b.

36. The leader and the dissidents can choose any form or amount of repression and dissent, respectively, including not to repress or dissent at all. Selecting $r = 0$ while $d > 0$ is the same as accommodation—granting concessions to dissidents—while $d = 0$ under non-zero repression accepts the status quo.

Although repression is an important weapon in the government arsenal for maintaining the status quo, it is costly. The costs of repression increase with its severity $(-r)$. The leader has to pay the military to respond to riots, the police to enforce curfews, and the prisons to maintain holding cells. Effort is required to alter and enforce repressive policies and monitor their effectiveness. Furthermore, as we consider separately, repressive leaders risk incurring negative consequences as a result of domestic and international institutional constraints, such as international human rights treaties. The state is more likely to put down the dissidents by repressing as severely as possible, but the costs of doing so can be prohibitive; leaders are mostly limited to repressing only what they can afford to do.[37]

At the same time the leader is making decisions about repression, the dissidents decide what dissent actions (d) to take against the government.[38] We define a *mobilized dissent action* to be a coordinated attempt by nonstate actors within the territorial jurisdiction of the state to influence political outcomes outside of state institutions. Mobilized dissent materializes in two stages. First, individuals decide whether to pool their resources and efforts toward a collective threat or action (mobilization). This is the decision to join. Once able to overcome the problems of mobilization, a formed group considers actually challenging the government. Dissent is a threat or action to impose consequences the government would prefer to avoid, leveraging their collective resources in the attempt to gain concessions on some policy, resource allocation, or power arrangement. If the government does not concede the point, the dissidents may or may not carry out the threat or engage in continuing dissent.[39] To emphasize this distinction, consider the soldiers carrying out international conflict: having a mobilized and well-resourced military may make conflict more probable, but it does not mean conflict will occur. We focus here on predicting the conflict action—dissent—rather than the process of mobilization. Mobilized dissent may be legal or illegal, violent or nonviolent, with dissident actions ranging from peaceful protests to violent riots, from groups of any size or level of organization.

---

37. This idea assumes there are costs that would make the government prefer not to repress if it could keep the status quo without doing so. However, if instead it is costless or even beneficial to repress, the relationships predicted by our model would differ. This could be the case if, for instance, the population participates in discriminatory policies; this may make it more costly for the government to enforce policies to *stop* repression. If so, our model would predict a much smaller or negligible treaty effect than we find in this book.

38. For additional information on social movements in the face of repression, see, e.g., Francisco 2004, Chenoweth and Stephan 2011, and Davenport 2015.

39. For more on why and how individuals dissent, see, e.g., Gurr 1970, Tilly 1978, Grossman 1991, Kuran 1991, Moore 1998, and McAdam 1999.

The dissidents' decision calculus includes not only the expected value of changing the status quo but also the risk that the leader will repress them for their action.[40] Political opportunity arguments suggest that dissatisfaction is insufficient to cause challenges; groups considering dissent rationally weigh benefits and costs, taking risk into account.[41] Dissatisfied groups decide, based on the conflict with the leader, how severe dissent will be: what tactics they will use, how violent it will be, how public the target is, how many people to mobilize toward the action, and so on. Mobilized dissent represents a significant threat to the leader's hold on power, imposing physical and opportunity costs on the state and causing damage to their reputation as a legitimate ruler. The larger, more damaging, or more visible the dissent actions are, the more likely the dissidents are to change the status quo policy.

But dissidents also face resource constraints that bind them from excessive action: The more severely or frequently the dissident group dissents against the government, the more resources it expends $(-d)$. The choice of dissent tactic varies in its required resources, with sit-ins, strikes, nonviolent marches, and violent demonstrations all requiring different levels of investment and opportunity costs for the participants. Echoing our argument about the leader's preferences, dissidents prefer to dissent just enough to have a strong chance of receiving their demands from the leader while minimizing resource expenditures. Limited action also protects dissidents in the conflict, because they should expect that an increase in mobilized dissent activity will correlate with an increase in government repression.[42]

In our model, decisions regarding repression and dissent are made simultaneously, and there are many ways that these choices influence one another. Civilians may protest either in response to discrimination or in anticipation of it. Likewise, governments may arrest political opponents in response to a challenge or in anticipation of dissent. Put differently, these behaviors are connected through simultaneous causation—sometimes referred to as endogeneity.[43] In this formal specification, neither actor has

---

40. Cf. Moore 1995; Ritter 2014.

41. McAdam 1999; McAdam, McCarthy, and Zald 1996; Shadmehr 2014; Tarrow 1994.

42. This is implied by the contest success function.

43. The simultaneity assumption in our model means that we assume that both the leader and the dissidents choose conflict, rather than anticipating the other's action and opting out (see, e.g., Ritter 2014). This is a useful simplifying assumption, because we are interested in how HRTs affect the conflict that *does* occur, rather than in how they affect repression and dissent that are threatened but do not materialize.

a chance to see or react to the other's choice before making their own. Being in the dark about the other's actual decision, each actor makes decisions about repression and dissent, respectively, as a function of elements they *can* observe—the extent to which they are constrained by domestic and international institutions and the leader's expected value for staying in office. These state- and leader-centric characteristics help them forecast what their opponent will do, and they behave accordingly.[44]

2.2.2 The Expected Value of Power and the Consequences of Policy Control

As the government and the dissidents increase their conflict efforts, each increases the probability that they will determine the policy outcome at the end. Policy outcomes are important because they influence the possibility that the leader will lose office. We argue that the leader and dissidents believe the likelihood of leader turnover to be a function of two elements: (1) the leader's expected value of retaining power ex ante (or prior to) conflict and (2) the outcome of the conflict with the dissidents. Leaders have an expected value for remaining in their position of power, and this value varies over time and across leader. We use the term "expected value" because it encompasses both how much the leader benefits from retaining power and how much they expect to remain in that position. Formally, this is a von Neumann–Morgenstern expected utility function, which multiplies the probability that the leader will remain in power at the end of the interaction (which we denote as θ, where $0 \leq \theta \leq 1$) by the value of staying in power (v_{in}) or the value of losing it (which we normalize to 0). The leader's expected value of retaining power is specified as $\mathbb{E}[U_L] = \theta * v_{in} + (1 - \theta) * 0$.

The leader's expected value for office increases, intuitively, as their value (benefit) for keeping it (v_{in}) increases. This might be because a leader has

---

44. The simultaneity assumption represents a snapshot of an interaction that is, in most cases, a string of back-and-forth dynamics between the state and unsatisfied dissidents. Although this setup substantively captures both response and anticipation, it limits the strategic behavior of whichever actor might have moved first. If, for instance, dissidents acted first and were responded to by the government, the dissidents could set equilibrium behavior in their interest, and the government would then be constrained in its best response. The reverse would be true if the government moved first, setting the tone of the interaction. In other words, sequential action allows the first mover to be strategic in a way that favors it over the opponent, which is not an option in simultaneous choice frameworks. In practice, dissidents and authorities both initiate interactions, and aggregating these various advantages approximates the simultaneous setup we present here.

policy goals that are personally meaningful, or because they expect to receive high rents while in power, or because the ego is disproportionately tied to the position. Heads of oil-rich states, for instance, are often among the world's wealthiest people, garnering their personal wealth from the state's resources.[45] The value for retaining power, v_{in}, also increases as it becomes more costly or dangerous for the leader to *lose* office; we think of gained benefits and avoided losses as two sides of the same concept. Leaders who leave office to start foundations and influence policies in other ways do not mind losing office as much as those who face jail, exile, or death upon removal. For ease of computation, we set $v_{in} = 1$, but the concept is, in theory, variable (i.e., $v_{in} \in [0,1]$). The concept of value is also intentionally vague: it can refer to emotional attachment to the office, monetary or resource benefits, personal rents, policy preferences, and more. We use the terms *value* or *benefit* here because they allow us to slip between these meanings without choosing one.

Leaders also have some expectation of how likely they are to keep holding power, aside from the conflict interaction we model here. We call this expectation the leader's ex ante job security, formalized as $0 \leq \theta \leq 1$.[46] Many elements inform a leader's likelihood of retaining power, including observable personal characteristics like age and experience, the institutional means available to remove them from office, and policy outcomes during their time in power. Is the leader sick, untested in office, subject to a called election, or overseeing a weak economy? These characteristics (and others like them) set the stage for the conflict with a potential dissident group. A secure leader by this expectation will be one likely to hold power based on personal characteristics and policy outcomes outside of repression and dissent, whereas an insecure leader will be likely to lose it even in the event of a victory over the dissidents.

The *probability* of retention and the leader's *value* for holding power thus combine into the leader's *expected value for holding office*. Assuming $v_{in} = 1$, the function reduces to $\mathbb{E}[U_L] = \theta * 1 + (1 - \theta) * 0 \Rightarrow \theta$. This captures their attachment to the position: Are they likely to keep it, no matter what they do? Are they likely to lose it, regardless of control? Are they committed to keeping it, or will they be fine without it? With the leader's expected value for power in mind, they enter a policy conflict with dissidents, which threatens that position. Control over the disputed policy is in service to

---

45. Taylor 2017.

46. Because so many of the dynamics included in this model are endogenous to one another, for tractability, we conceptualize ex ante job security as exogenous to conflict. See also Cheibub 1998 and Young 2009.

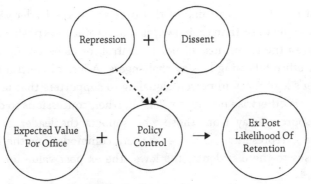

Figure 2.2 How conflict choices affect leader turnover

staying in power. Thus, we also refer to the expected value for power as the leader's *stakes in the conflict*.

The outcome of the policy conflict modifies the compound (i.e., ex post) expectation for holding office. Figure 2.2 illustrates how the actors' conflict choices indirectly affect a leader's ability to remain in power.

To recapitulate, we assume that losing control of the disputed policy in a conflict with dissidents reduces the leader's expected value of retaining power. Repression combines with dissent in a costly lottery that determines who will set the policy. If the government retains control over the status quo policy, even after facing dissent (recall that the government wins the policy conflict with probability $1 - \frac{d}{d+r}$), there is no change to the leader's expected value of retaining power (θ). The policy outcome remains in the leader's favor, so they expect the same benefit or likelihood of retention as prior to the conflict.[47] In January 2018, following antiregime protests across Iran, Revolutionary Guard brigadier general Mohammad-Ali Jafari claimed that protests had been unsuccessful: "Today, I can say, is the end of this sedition... Our [good] security status and people's prudence caused the enemy to experience another failure."[48] The victory over protests protected status quo policies and the secure position of the regime.

If instead the government loses policy control to the dissidents (with probability $\frac{d}{d+r}$), the expected value of holding office decreases. Formally, a winning leader's expected value is $\mathbb{E}[U_L](win\ policy) = \theta * 1 + (1 - \theta) * 0 \Rightarrow \theta$, and one that loses receives $\mathbb{E}[U_L](lose\ policy) = \frac{\theta}{\kappa} * 1 + (1 - \frac{\theta}{\kappa}) * 0 \Rightarrow \frac{\theta}{\kappa}$,

---

47. Using repression in the conflict does deplete the government's pool of resources, which we discuss in additional detail below.
48. Bozorgmehr 2018.

such that $\kappa > 1$. We can think of this decrease as the leader valuing the dissident's policy less than their own, as valuing office less postconflict than before given the recent loss of policy control, or as becoming less likely to retain office following loss to challengers. A loss of control threatens the leader's legitimacy in power, signaling to supporters that he sets bad policies or is otherwise not fit to rule.[49] Further, concessions to dissidents move resources away from those who support the leader in power.[50] The value κ represents the scope of the accommodation; the more the leader loses to the dissidents, the lower the ex post value for retaining power.[51]

In specifying the model as in Figure 2.2, we assume that is not the use of repression or the experience of dissent that damages the leader's chances of remaining in office; it is the outcome of that conflict that is the key mechanism. We make this decision because there is no commonly accepted relationship between repression or dissent and leader tenure. To our knowledge, very few studies have looked directly at the effect of these behaviors on either retention or turnover as the dependent variable. Several scholars have found correlations between job security and repression choices, with Young (2009) finding that increasing security makes leaders less likely to repress and Ritter (2014) finding that increased security makes repression less likely but more severe when it does occur. Gandhi (2008) argues that authoritarian regimes repress and co-opt opposition groups for the same reasons—to end challenges and retain power, but she does not directly examine this assumption. In a rare study that directly asks this question, Escribà-Folch (2012) finds that authoritarian regimes are more likely to remain in power as they repress more. In short, there is no scholarly consensus as to whether the choice to repress makes a leader more or less

---

49. Davenport 1995.

50. See, e.g., Bueno de Mesquita, Smith, et al. 2003.

51. Lohmann 1993 argues that leaders want to retain office and so want to side with the majority of the general population; the size of a protest group tells the leader whether the majority is likely to agree with the dissidents. The larger the social movement, the more likely the leader should be to accommodate protesters. Shadmehr and Bernhardt 2011 make a similar argument. We posit that protest has a similar effect on the leader's prospects, such that the more a group dissents or the larger it is, the more likely the leader is to lose office because she will lose the conflict. Importantly, however, the implications of our argument for repression differ from those of Lohmann 1993 due to the difference in the mechanism. We argue that giving dissidents the policy will make the leader worse off in the eyes of his winning coalition; Lohmann argues that the accommodation will please the masses. Where we would predict repression, she would predict accommodation. This is essentially a difference in perspectives as to how a leader holds power: Is it by the support of powerful groups or the consent of the masses?

likely to retain power, so we hesitate to assume one or the other. Instead, we assume that *losing policy control* hurts a leader in the eyes of supporters, who may reduce or withdraw their support, as is often assumed when leaders lose resources in international conflict.[52] In so doing, we assume that repression and dissent influence leader tenure only through a mechanism that is solidly grounded in extant scholarship—conflict outcomes and their effect on support.

In our thinking, the concept of the leader's expected value for office—their stakes in the conflict—captures the core idea of threat that is so central to scholarship on repression. Leaders repress when their power or wealth is threatened. Some scholars operationalize threat as a function of group characteristics, like size, tactic, or claim.[53] Instead, we argue it is a leader's vulnerability to loss that determines how threatening a challenge is. When they have more to gain by being out of power than in, or when, for other reasons, they are extremely likely to lose office anyway, leaders are less vulnerable to policy change and conflict advocating policy change. Such leaders have little incentive to repress. In contrast, leaders who use their position to extract wealth from the country or who expect to hold office far into the future (e.g., Syria's al-Assad or the Saudi royal family) have every incentive to repress dissidents.

Our discussion so far establishes the behavioral conflict that is the core of repression/dissent interactions. It is a bargaining model: Two actors disagree over an allocation or policy, and they threaten to fight over it. Leaders choose how much to repress and civilians choose how much to dissent, and those decisions interact to produce policy and turnover outcomes of some relative value to each of the actors. The next subsection introduces institutional structure to this basic interaction, considering the incentives that do or do not constrain leaders from repression and how they may additionally affect the strategic choice to dissent.

2.2.3 Institutional Consequences for Government Repression

International human rights treaties are not the only institutions that can influence or constrain authorities from violating rights, and predicting repression for the baseline or control case requires an understanding of the domestic institutions already in place. Countries vary a lot in their

52. Bueno de Mesquita, Smith, et al. 2003; Chiozza and Goemans 2004, 2011.
53. See, e.g. Davenport 2000, 2007a; Poe, Tate, Keith, and Lanier 2000.

institutional structure: Some have legislatures, others do not, and those legislatures vary in competitiveness and actual power. The same goes for variation in judicial independence, electoral quality, media freedom, civil society strength, and mechanism for regime replacement. Some of these characteristics create consequences for leaders who would repress their population, while others allow or even facilitate repression.[54] Understanding the *domestic* consequences that leaders and dissidents expect to occur as a function of extant institutional constraints allows us to estimate a baseline to predict whether and, if so, how a treaty would affect human rights outcomes.

According to scholars, domestic law and courts are the institutions that are most useful in preventing or punishing government violations of human rights.[55] Moreover, it is straightforward to conceptualize how treaty law complements domestic legal institutions. Therefore, we use a legal baseline—the existing expectations, held by both leaders and dissidents, that authorities would experience legal consequences for repression—for comparison, and we investigate the extent to which the addition of international human rights treaties changes government repression and dissident choices.

Authorities incur consequences that they would prefer to avoid when victims allege in court that the government's repressive action is a violation of the law. Going to trial requires resources to build and defend a case, diverts attention and resources from other matters, and generates negative publicity of the government as a repressor. U.S. president Donald Trump's

---

54. A wide range of scholarship examines the ways in which varieties of domestic institutions affect human rights outcomes. Among many excellent and citable studies omitted here, these include examinations of democracy and democratic institutions (Davenport 1995, 2007a, 2007b; Davenport and Armstrong 2004; Poe and Tate 1994; Poe, Tate, and Keith 1999; Regan and Henderson 2002); elections and electoral systems (Bueno de Mesquita, Downs, et al. 2005; Conrad, Hill, and Moore 2017; Davenport 1997, 1998; Hafner-Burton, Hyde, and Jablonski 2014; Hill 2016; Richards 1999); legislatures, parties, and veto points (Cingranelli and Filippov 2010; Conrad 2011; Conrad and Moore 2010; Davenport 2007b; Kim and Gandhi 2010; Lupu 2015; Richards and Gelleny 2007; Simmons 2009; Tsebelis 2002; Vreeland 2008a); the media (Conrad and Moore 2010; Whitten-Woodring 2009; Whitten-Woodring and James 2012); and nongovernmental organizations (Bell, Clay, and Murdie 2012; Clark 2010; Davis, Murdie, and Steinmetz 2012; Hendrix and Wong 2013, 2014; Murdie and Davis 2012; Ron, Ramos, and Rodgers 2005; Wong 2012).

55. See, for example, Cross 1999, Keith 2002b, Hathaway 2005, Moustafa 2007, Powell and Staton 2009, Keith 2012, Lupu 2013a, Hill and Jones 2014, and Conrad 2014. Judicial independence has more predictive power when it comes to estimating the likelihood of reduced repression than almost all other commonly posited empirical indicators, suggesting the importance of domestic law and courts in constraining repressive behavior (Hill and Jones 2014).

executive order prohibiting immigration of any persons into the United States from several predominantly Muslim countries was challenged as discriminatory in federal courts. Although the Supreme Court ultimately allowed an amended version of the ban—ruling, essentially, in support of the government's position—the administration had to defend the policy through several levels of appeals, which was a costly and onerous process even though the basic order was implemented into policy.[56] The president's displeasure with the process could be seen in his online attacks of the courts and the legal challenges themselves, again, despite the Court ultimately ruling with the government.

The consequences are even higher if a court is likely to rule against a repressive leader.[57] Independent or effective courts limit the power of the executive to violate civil rights and liberties guaranteed in a country's constitution.[58] Leaders often obey domestic court rulings when there is institutional or popular support for the court or its decisions.[59] Other times, a government may ignore the court's decision, but its ruling serves as precedent and catalyst for others to bring suit with similar claims, chipping away at the government's violations. This happened during the civil rights era in the United States, when federal and state governments largely ignored the order to integrate schools after the *Brown v. Board of Education* ruling; continued legal efforts by the NAACP eventually forced the government's hand.[60]

In short, authorities who would repress would like to avoid litigation over that repression. Whether they settle, win, or lose in court, the process of undergoing litigation is costly for repressive government authorities. One way to avoid those costs is to prevent victims and advocates from litigating in the first place; another way is by maintaining a court so weak

56. In January 2018, the U.S. Supreme Court agreed to hear the case on appeal; see Wolf 2018.

57. Not all institutions are created under the auspices of reducing violations of human rights. Even when an institution, such as a domestic court, is not created with the explicit goal of protecting citizen rights, the incentives that it establishes can have that unintended consequence. For example, although Egyptian authorities created the Supreme Constitutional Court (SCC) with the express goal of attracting international investment, civil society groups used the court as a forum to bring human rights cases against government officials (Moustafa 2003, 2007).

58. See, e.g., Keith 2002b; Mitchell, Ring, and Spellman 2013. Constitutional protections can help limit government actions first by stating the clear substantive expectations for behavior, within which authorities tend to act just because the expectations are so delineated (Carey 2000; Davenport 1996; Elkins, Ginsburg, and Melton 2009).

59. Carrubba 2009; Gibson, Caldeira, and Baird 1998; Staton 2010a; Vanberg 2005.

60. Rosenberg 1991; Supreme Court of the United States 1954.

that victims would not see it as a place to find remedy.[61] Another, more common reaction to a constraining domestic court is for a leader to repress less as the likelihood of incurring litigation increases.[62]

Leaders considering repression take into account how likely they will be to face domestic litigation for violating human rights, which we formally define as ϕ, where $0 < \phi < 1$. That probability varies depending on several factors: the court's independence, which enables it to rule against the leader and accept challenging cases; litigants' willingness to bring suit; the prevalence of domestic legal referents for the right in question; and so on. This probability represents the baseline expectation that state authorities will be held accountable for violations of human rights by incurring the litigation costs associated with the domestic court, outside of international obligations to protect rights.[63] The value ϕ is multiplied by $-r$ such that if a case is brought against the government, authorities pay a cost commensurate with the extent of the violations.

How do human rights treaties fit in this story? The primary role of human rights treaty law is not in enforcement but in *standard-setting*. The Universal Declaration of Human Rights (UDHR) established the first written comprehensive list of rights: "a common standard of achievement for all peoples and all nations ... every individual and every organ of society."[64] This document and the legally binding treaty standards that followed the UDHR represent norms of correct government behavior with regard to human rights.[65] International human rights law establishes

61. Note, however, that we assume the probability of litigation costs to be exogenous in our model, as described above. We discuss implications of this decision below and the potential for relaxing the assumption in our Conclusion.

62. Conrad 2014; Cross 1999; Keith 2002b; Moustafa 2007.

63. We assume the probability that repression will incur court-related costs to be exogenous. By doing so, we assume that the leader and citizens have a common expectation about the judiciary's effectiveness, willingness to accept cases, etc. In many cases, however, authorities·can and do exercise control over the judiciary and can influence this probability of litigation. If we were to allow L to set or influence ϕ, we assume the leader would set it as low as possible to minimize his risk. In such a case, we would be far less likely to see the judiciary constraining state repression. As long as there are empirical instances of the judiciary constraining the state rather than the state constraining the judiciary, however, our theory can be used to explain state behavior.

64. United Nations 1948.

65. Norms alone can be powerful constraints (Risse, Ropp, and Sikkink 1999): The simple knowledge that others expect you to behave in a certain way is a powerful motivator for conformity, even at the level of the state. Moreover, observers can impose consequences when states breach these common standards of behavior. Violating norms can lead to public shame (Clark 2010; Hafner-Burton 2008; Hendrix and Wong 2013; Krain 2012; Lebovic and Voeten 2006; Risse, et al. 1999), damage to a state's

the expectations to which governments must adhere to avoid societal or institutional sanctions. Formal, legal obligations to protect rights deepen the expectations of protection beyond informal norms of appropriate behavior. Laws set official standards to which governments are—at least in theory—organizationally bound. Explicit limits on government action are then used as a benchmark by which to assess overreach, at which point other actors or institutions potentially punish leaders with institutional or collective action.[66]

The most direct mechanism by which to punish governments that violate treaties is domestic litigation. International human rights treaties represent new legal obligations to which the government can be held accountable in a domestic court.[67] Several countries, such as the Netherlands, have constitutional conditions specifying that international treaties automatically become domestic law upon ratification.[68] Other countries adjust their laws to meet the new standards. Colombia, Estonia, Finland, the Philippines, Russia, and South Africa, for example, borrowed language directly from human rights treaties in their national constitutions.[69] Different domestic institutions—the courts, the legislature, and executive offices—are responsible for the implementation of treaty standards in both policy and practice.[70]

Even in cases where domestic law is not modified as a result of treaty ratification, human rights law enters into obligated states' jurisprudence. In many systems, international court rulings and precedent add to the domestic canon, increasing the legal referents and case law from which claimants can draw.[71] In common-law legal systems, countries that commit to HRTs can adopt precedents from human rights cases decided in international courts,[72] and international human rights law is cited by judges in domestic judiciaries. In countries with dualist legal systems (i.e., countries where treaties do not have the force of law domestically), courts often apply treaties indirectly by interpreting domestic law to "conform

---

reputation as an appropriate or legitimate state (Finnemore and Sikkink 1998; Hawkins 2004; Risse, Ropp, and Sikkink 1999), and direct behavioral responses to violations of expectations (Keck and Sikkink 1998).

66. Elkins, Ginsburg, and Melton 2009; Keith 2002a, 2012; Keith, Tate, and Poe 2009; Weingast 1997.

67. Sikkink and Walling 2007; Sloss 2009; Staton and Moore 2011.

68. Simmons 2009.

69. Hafner-Burton 2013.

70. Simmons 2009.

71. Helfer 2002; Pelc 2014.

72. Hill 2012; Simmons 2009.

to international obligations codified in unincorporated treaties."[73] The Indian and South African Supreme Courts have gone further, allowing international law to increase domestic judicial costs for rights violators; both use international law to aid in their interpretation of their domestic constitutions on issues ranging from gender equality and privacy rights in India[74] to the death penalty, corporal punishment, sodomy punishments, and deportation in South Africa.[75]

International human rights treaty obligations also increase the likelihood that someone will bring a case challenging state practices. Treaty ratification shifts the agenda,[76] focusing domestic and international attention on the extent to which governments respect (or fail to respect) the human rights of their populations and increasing legitimacy for rights-related grievances.[77] The obligation represents a commitment to respecting particular rights under legal force, and this leads victims to *presume* that they are more likely to find redress in the courts than they would without said government commitment.[78] Therefore, victims (and their advocates) are more likely to litigate when a country is committed to an international human rights treaty than in the absence of such a commitment.

Nongovernmental organizations (NGOs) and nonstate legal entities also use international laws as a talking point to highlight rights violations, mobilize dormant dissatisfaction, and help bring cases against repressive practices.[79] Obligation to a human rights treaty encourages NGOs to train lawyers to bring cases against the state under international law.[80] For example, the Association for the Prevention of Torture (APT), a Geneva-based NGO, conducts regular training workshops intended to educate domestic judges and attorneys on the use of the UN Convention Against Torture (CAT) in domestic adjudication. Upon CAT commitment,

---

73. Sloss 2009, p. 7. In courts in Australia, Canada, and the United Kingdom, judges often "interpret statute to conform with treaty obligations" (ibid., p. 17), while the United States and Israel sidestep this with judicial procedure (ibid., p. 8).

74. Ibid., p. 25. "For example, the Indian Supreme Court has invoked the Convention on the Elimination of Discrimination Against Women to support its interpretation of gender-equality provisions in the Indian Constitution. Similarly, it has invoked Article 17 of the ICCPR to support its holding that the constitutional guarantee of personal liberty includes a right to privacy, and Article 9(5) to support its holding that surviving family members of individuals killed in police custody have a constitutional right to monetary compensation" (ibid., p. 25).

75. Ibid., p. 27.

76. Simmons 2009.

77. Finnemore and Sikkink 1998; Keck and Sikkink 1998.

78. Simmons 2009.

79. See, e.g., Moustafa 2003; Simmons 2009.

80. Merry 2006; Smith, Pagnucco, and Lopez 1998.

APT also works to support victims in their attempts to bring allegations of human rights violations before domestic courts and submits "shadow reports" to the Committee Against Torture regarding the human rights situation in CAT-signatory countries.[81] On their own or with the help of NGOs, aggrieved citizens whose rights have been violated are more likely to bring suit against authorities when the government is obligated to international law than in the absence of such obligation.

In these ways, international legal obligations increase the probability that government authorities will face litigation-related costs for violating rights. Rights treaties increase the probability of sustaining court-related costs for violating rights by adding legal referents to the domestic canon, bringing NGOs into the conversation, and motivating victims to litigate. More importantly, the obligation increases the *expectation* that the leader will face legal costs, thereby affecting both the government's and the dissidents' behavior. Victims are likely to believe the treaty helps their claim and so seek redress. Both the government and potential dissidents should expect increased litigation under a treaty as compared to without. In other words, commitment to a treaty increases the baseline (domestic) probability of incurring legal consequences by a small amount. Formally, the probability that the state will pay resource costs for violating rights increases by ϵ when the state is obligated to a human rights treaty, where $0 < \phi + \epsilon < 1$.[82]

Although the higher likelihood of costs creates incentives for a strategic government *not* to commit to treaties in the first place, governments receive some benefits ($\mu > 0$) that can incentivize ratification. A wealth of literature argues (or assumes) that there are international benefits that drive states to ratify HRTs, even if the treaties bring the potential for negative consequences. Some of these benefits—like foreign aid—are tangible, while others—like international praise—are less so. Material rewards can include increased foreign investment or international trade,[83] as well as "positive political relationships."[84] States may commit to human

---

81. For more details on the APT, see www.apt.ch/en.

82. It is worth noting that the model is specified such that the leader will incur the negative cost $-r$ *only* if litigation occurs, which is probabilistic (ϕ or $\phi + \epsilon$). While this seemingly implies that the leader can repress without consequences, that does not have to be true. Instead, this specification captures the role that institutions play in adding consequences to some existing baseline costs that we assume to be unchanged in the course of play. If there are situations where there could be higher consequences for repressing if there is no legal claim than if there is one, the implications of our theory would not apply.

83. Hathaway 2004.

84. Goodliffe and Hawkins 2006.

rights treaties to express that the government supports the protection of rights in principle.[85] Leaders may also receive domestic benefits from commitment to rights treaties.[86] These could include leaders delegating to international law to decrease uncertainty over future outcomes,[87] to please opposition groups,[88] or to send a costly signal to the opposition that the government is willing to violate rights at will.[89] All that is necessary for our theory to hold is that governments receive some positive utility for commitment.

In summary, an obligation to an international human rights treaty increases the expected probability the leader will incur litigation-related costs above the baseline probability that derives from extant domestic legal institutions. That baseline probability may be low, such that the treaty obligation essentially creates possibilities for litigation where very few existed, or high, such that the treaty adds to an already strong system of legal rights enforcement. The increased expected probability of consequences, however small, alters the structural environment of incentives in which leaders and dissidents make conflict decisions.

2.2.4 Summary of Theoretical Assumptions

Leaders and dissidents enter a conflict over policy. The more a government represses, the more likely it is to win the conflict and maintain the status quo policy, which means it maintains the ex ante value of retaining power. The more a dissident group engages in dissent activities, the more likely it is to win the conflict, and the more likely the leader is to lose policy control and, with some increased probability, power. If the state *is not obligated* to a human rights treaty, the leader and dissidents make their tactical choices based on (a) the leader's expected value of retaining office *prior* to conflict outcomes and (b) the baseline probability of consequences—litigation—for repressive behavior. If the state *is obligated* to an HRT, actors make their conflict decisions expecting the probability of domestic consequences like litigation to be marginally greater than in the absence of the obligation. As

85. See, e.g., Hathaway 2002; Risse, Ropp, and Sikkink 1999.
86. Nielsen and Simmons 2015.
87. See, e.g., Moravcsik 2000.
88. See, e.g., Vreeland 2008a.
89. See, e.g. Hollyer and Rosendorff 2011.

we show in Chapter 3, the addition of the treaty modifies both repression and dissent behaviors in surprising ways.

2.3 EQUILIBRIUM BEHAVIOR

Before turning to the empirical implications of this theory in the next chapter, we first describe the equilibrium behavior implied by the solution.

We use the concept of Subgame Perfect Equilibrium to identify the possible solutions. For this particular specification, there is a unique equilibrium such that there is one optimal choice for any given combination of parameter values. Proposition 1 states the equilibrium solution; proofs of all propositions can be found in the Appendix.

Proposition 1 *The following strategies constitute the Subgame Perfect Equilibrium: (1) when L is not obligated to a treaty, G dissents at level d_U, and L represses at level r_U, defined as*

$$d_U \equiv \frac{(\kappa - 1)\theta\phi}{\kappa(1+\phi)^2} \quad and \quad r_U \equiv \frac{(\kappa - 1)\theta}{\kappa(1+\phi)^2};$$

(2) when L is obligated to a treaty, G dissents at level d_C, and L represses at level r_C, defined as

$$d_C \equiv -\frac{(\kappa - 1)\theta(\epsilon + \phi)}{\kappa(1+\epsilon+\phi)^2} \quad and \quad r_C \equiv \frac{(\kappa - 1)\theta}{\kappa(1+\epsilon+\phi)^2};$$

and (3) L commits to the treaty when

$$\mu > \frac{\theta}{2\kappa}\left(-1 + \frac{2(\kappa - 1)}{(1+\phi)^2} + \frac{2}{1+\phi} - \frac{2(\kappa - 1)}{(1+\epsilon+\phi)^2}\right).$$

In sum, whether or not a country is obligated to an international human rights treaty, the leader and dissidents engage in conflict simultaneously, conditioning their choices on what each expects the other to do. The more that dissidents engage in dissent, the more damage it causes to authorities, and the more likely authorities will be to concede the policy. Higher levels of dissent require more resources. Dissidents engage in just enough dissent activity to have a strong chance of receiving their demands while minimizing resource costs. Similarly, the leader can best control the dissidents and keep them from changing the status quo, by repressing severely and widely, but the costs of doing so limit state authorities to repressing only what they can afford.

Each party makes these conflict decisions without knowing the other actor's choice by looking to the exogenous variables that condition that choice: the probability of domestic litigation (ϕ), the treaty's effect on the likelihood of consequences (ϵ), and the leader's expected value of leader power prior to the conflict (θ). These observable characteristics of the state allow both actors to "solve" the model as we analysts do, using them to inform their expectations of the opponent's optimal choice and their own simultaneously.

Each actor chooses a level of repression or dissent to maximize their returns in the costly lottery over the policy while minimizing resource costs. The actors further consider the probability that authorities will incur the costs of being brought to court for violating rights. As stated in Equation 2.1, repression becomes more costly as both the level of repression (r) and the probability of litigation (ϕ) increase. In states that are obligated to a human rights treaty, the probability of litigation against government actors is even higher. To counter the increased probability of being brought to court, authorities can repress less and reduce the consequences of institutional punishment. The leader must therefore navigate a balance in the equilibrium decision: increase repression to maintain the status quo or decrease it to avoid litigation costs?

Authorities thread this needle as a function of their stakes in the conflict. If the leader emerges from the policy conflict with control over the status quo, the expected value of power remains the same. But when a leader submits to a challenge and accommodates dissident demands, the policy loss undermines the expectation and/or value of continuing in power. Leaders with high stakes in the conflict thus have to prioritize potential threats to their removal, whereas leaders with low value or probability of retention has little incentive to repress. This is the key variable that conditions both dissent and repression choices; in Chapter 3, we discuss at length the conditioning role and the effects of the expected value for holding office on the other variables.

The two actors thus select conflict levels that reflect the tradeoffs implied by their particular structural circumstances; the expectation of these costs and their policy, judicial, and power outcomes influence the leader's choice over treaty ratification. As we discuss further, many leaders who expect the treaty to be particularly binding will select out of the obligation; those who expect to be less affected will opt in and commit to international law. Nevertheless, as we contend in the next chapter, the treaty obligation creates a meaningful change in conflict behavior for a significant range of cases.

2.4 APPENDIX 1: PROOFS OF FORMAL THEORY

2.4.1 Proof of Equilibrium Behavior

Proof. In the final stage, L and G simultaneously choose levels of repression and dissent.

When the state is not committed to an HRT:

The first order conditions (FOC) of the players' respective utility functions are $\frac{\partial U_L(\neg C)}{\partial r} = \frac{d\theta(\kappa-1)}{\kappa(d+r)^2} - \phi = 0$, which ensures r_U will be a maximum because $\frac{\partial^2 U_L(\neg C)}{\partial r^2} = -\frac{d\theta(\kappa-1)}{\kappa(d+r)^3} < 0$ when $\kappa > 1$, which is true by assumption, and $\frac{\partial U_G(\neg C)}{\partial d} = -1 + \frac{r\theta(\kappa-1)}{\kappa(d+r)^2} = 0$, which ensures d_U will be a maximum because $\frac{\partial^2 U_G(\neg C)}{\partial d^2} = \frac{2r\theta(\kappa-1)}{\kappa(d+r)^3} < 0$, in both cases when $\kappa > 1$, or when L is more likely to lose office if he loses the conflict with G, which is true by assumption. Solving simultaneously for d and r yields G's and L's optimal choices to be

$$d_U = \frac{(\kappa-1)\theta\phi}{\kappa(1+\phi)^2} \quad and \quad r_U = \frac{(\kappa-1)\theta}{\kappa(1+\phi)^2}.$$

When the state is committed to an HRT:

The FOC of L's utility function is $\frac{\partial U_L(C)}{\partial r} = \frac{(\kappa-1)d\theta}{\kappa(d+r)^2} - \phi - \epsilon = 0$, which ensures r_C will be a maximum because $\frac{\partial^2 U_L(C)}{\partial r^2} = -\frac{2(\kappa-1)d\theta}{\kappa(d+r)^3} < 0$ when $\kappa > 1$, which is true by assumption. The FOC of G's utility function is $\frac{\partial U_G(C)}{\partial d} = -1 + \frac{r\theta(\kappa-1)}{\kappa(d+r)^2} = 0$, which ensures d_C will be a maximum because $\frac{\partial^2 U_G(C)}{\partial d^2} = \frac{2(\kappa-1)r\theta}{\kappa(d+r)^3} < 0$ when $\kappa > 1$. Solving simultaneously for d and r yields G's and L's optimal choices to be

$$d_C = -\frac{\theta(\epsilon+\phi)(\kappa-1)}{\kappa(1+\epsilon+\phi)^2} \quad and \quad r_C = \frac{(\kappa-1)\theta}{\kappa(1+\epsilon+\phi)^2}.$$

The optimal d and r in both committed and uncommitted states are positive given the defined constraints of all parameters.

Commitment stage:

Finally, L commits to the HRT when $U_L(C) > U_L(\neg C)$. Substituting the optimal levels of repression and dissent into the original utility functions, L will commit to an HRT when

$$\frac{\theta + \kappa\mu + \dfrac{(\kappa - 1)\theta}{(1+\epsilon+\phi)^2}}{\kappa} > \frac{\theta(1 + 2\kappa + \phi(4+\phi))}{2\kappa(1+\phi)^2},$$

which holds true when

$$\mu > \frac{\theta}{2\kappa}\left(-1 + \frac{2(\kappa-1)}{(1+\phi)^2} + \frac{2}{1+\phi} - \frac{2(\kappa-1)}{(1+\epsilon+\phi)^2}\right).$$

☐

2.4.2 Comparative Statics

2.4.2.1 *Proofs of Propositions 2 and 3*

Proofs of Propositions 2 and 3 are included in the propositions themselves.

Comparative statics demonstrating the relationships stated in Implications 1 and 2 are presented in Figures 2.4.2.1(a) and (b). This figure plots the *equilibrium* levels of repression and dissent across the range of executive job security under two scenarios: (a) a high baseline probability ($\phi = 0.8$) of incurring litigation costs for repression and (b) a low baseline probability ($\phi = 0.2$) of incurring litigation costs. These figures assume that commitment to a treaty increases the expectation of litigation by $\epsilon = 0.2$.

Black lines indicate equilibrium predictions for repression, while gray lines indicate equilibrium predictions for dissent. Solid lines represent actors' behaviors when the state is *not* obligated to a human rights treaty, and dashed lines represent optimal behavior under treaty commitment. The *difference* between the solid and dashed lines represents the effect that obligation to a human rights treaty has on the actors' respective behavior.

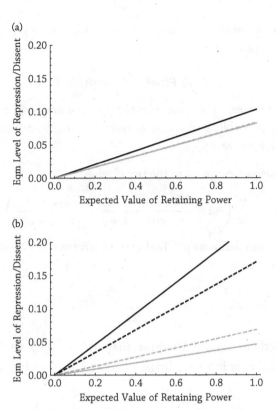

In Figure 2.4.2.1(a), the gray lines indicating dissent cover the dashed black line that represents HRT-obligated repression. In this scenario of an effective judiciary or strong extant domestic rights protection, obligation to a human rights treaty causes a relative drop in the state's optimal level of repression. That difference widens as the executive's job security increases.

By comparison, when the probability of experiencing domestic adjudication is low (Figure 2.4.2.1(b)), authorities repress at higher levels across the board than they would if the court were more effective. Nevertheless, the difference between repression without a treaty (black solid) and repression under a treaty (black dashed) is larger than under more effective domestic legal systems, suggesting the treaty effect is greater for these states. This is the foundation of Implication 1.

The gray lines for dissent overlap one another in the upper figure, such that the equilibrium suggests there is no meaningful difference in a group's optimal behavior as a function of treaty obligation when domestic courts are already fairly strong. In the lower figure, there is a clear treaty effect, with the dashed gray line indicating groups will dissent more in these obligated, weak-court states as the leader's job security increases. This underlies Implication 2.

2.4.2.2 *Proof of Proposition 4*

Proposition 4 states, "The state is less likely to commit to a human rights treaty as the probability of leader survival, θ, increases, but this effect attenuates as ϕ increases."

Proof. Recall that L commits to the treaty when

$$\mu > \frac{\theta}{2\kappa}\left(-1 + \frac{2(\kappa - 1)}{(1+\phi)^2} + \frac{2}{1+\phi} - \frac{2(\kappa - 1)}{(1+\epsilon+\phi)^2}\right),$$

a cutpoint we can define as μ^*. Taking the derivative of μ^* with respect to job security, θ, yields

$$\frac{\partial \mu^*}{\partial \theta} = \frac{\frac{2(\kappa-1)}{(1+\phi)^2} + \frac{2}{1+\phi} - \frac{2(\kappa-1)}{(1+\epsilon+\phi)^2} - 1}{2z} > 0,$$

which is strictly increasing. However, that effect, $\left(\frac{\partial \mu^*}{\partial \theta}\right)$, decreases in the extant probability of incurring litigation costs for repressing, ϕ:

$$\frac{\frac{\partial \mu^*}{\partial \theta}}{\partial \phi} = \frac{-\frac{4(\kappa-1)}{(1+\phi)^3} - \frac{2}{(1+\phi)^2} + \frac{4(\kappa-1)}{(1+\epsilon+\phi)^3}}{2z} < 0.$$

□

CHAPTER 3

⤸

Empirical Implications of Treaty Effects on Conflict

This chapter explores the equilibrium behavior of the model we defined in Chapter 2. Having established what decisions can be made and the potential consequences thereof for government leaders as well as dissidents, we use this chapter to understand the comparative statics: How does change in one variable or another affect the outcomes of repression and dissent? Why does that effect occur, and what does it look like?

To predict how obligation to an international human rights treaty (HRT) affects government repression and mobilized dissent, we must first identify the theoretical counterfactual: What conflict behaviors would the leader and dissidents choose if they were not obligated under an HRT? How do these behaviors change as domestic government and leader characteristics change? We then compare those expectations to how the same leader and the same dissidents under the same domestic conditions would act if the country were obligated to international human rights law. We conclude by considering how the expectations of these conflict outcomes affect the leader's propensity to commit to an international human rights treaty in the first place.

We focus primarily on the relationship between our main independent variable—HRT obligation status—and dependent variables—government repression and mobilized dissent. The relationships between these variables are a consequence of a number of assumptions and theoretical linkages. For example, the formal model yields a number of implications as to how the leader's value for the retention of power affects government repression, which is a key prediction for understanding how treaties alter that connection. Yet the effect of the leader's conflict stakes is not the main variable of interest to us, so we treat this implication as interim, forming the basis of the connection between treaty obligations and conflict outcomes. To make clear how we derive the implications that we evaluate as hypotheses in later chapters, we state a number of formal results as *claims* below. Because they are not the main focus of the book, we do not subject these claims to empirical analysis. Instead, we think of the claims as the axioms on which our implications of interest are built: If the claims are true, then our hypotheses of interest—those related to the effect of human rights law on domestic conflict—logically follow.

3.1 ESTABLISHING THE BASELINE: CONFLICT BEHAVIORS IN THE ABSENCE OF A TREATY

In our theory, mobilized dissent and government repression work against one another in a probabilistic interaction that determines who sets a given policy, the leader or the dissidents. For potential dissidents, "winning" the conflict means altering the status quo policy. For the leader, more is at stake than just a policy outcome: "losing" to dissidents reduces the leader's expectation or value of remaining in power. Beliefs about this expected value for power determine the stakes of the conflict to the leader and influence how much the leader is willing to repress to retain political office.

Authorities condition their use of repression on their expected value for remaining in power. The value that a leader places on the retention of power may be high under several different conditions: when governing is particularly resource-valuable (e.g., the Saud family), when the leader holds centralized power (e.g., Vladimir Putin), or when the leader's position is secure long into the future by law or practice (e.g., Kim Jong-il), for instance. The higher the leader's expected value for office, the more a leader has to lose in the conflict over policy. Consequently, leaders who highly value the retention of political office have greater incentives to repress in order to control policy outcomes.

Imagine middle-aged leaders who expect to be in power until they are well into their nineties, with no concerns about illness, electoral challenge, or lack of resources. For these hypothetical leaders, losing policy ground to dissenting groups—and the attendant dip in publicly perceived legitimacy or resources to disburse to winning coalitions—has a major effect on what would otherwise be a sure retention of power. Leaders who have a high value for remaining in power thus prioritize potential threats to their removal over the short-term consequences associated with domestic pressures not to repress.

To think through this formally, recall from Equation (2.1) that dissidents "win" their demands with probability $\frac{d}{d+r}$, such that the leader will remain in power with the diminished *ex post* probability $\frac{\theta}{\kappa}$. The greater the leader's value for office (θ), the more damage κ does—the more the leader stands to lose as dissent increases and makes defeat more likely. Consequently, the more secure a leader is in office prior to a policy conflict, the stronger incentives they have to quash dissent and maintain control over the status quo. This is the case even when repression is costly.

By contrast, if leaders have a low expected value for retaining power—perhaps they expect to be removed from office for some reason besides dissent, like a term limit or poor economic outcomes—the potential payoff from repression is not as high. Repressing dissidents under these circumstances does little to help our hypothetical leader stay in power, since they expect to lose office regardless of the outcome of the conflict. Because it does little to increase their tenure prospects and is costly, a leader with a low valuation for office represses a given level of dissent less than a similarly situated secure leader. In short, we expect that leaders repress *more* as their expected value for power increases and repress *less* as they become more vulnerable to political turnover.[1]

The current Chinese president, Xi Jinping, whose position both as the president and as leader of the Communist Party is now more secure than ever,[2] provides a good example. In addition to pushing through a constitutional amendment removing a two-term limit on ruling the party,[3] he has purged hundreds of potential challengers from government service to ensure the security of his office. His is a position of particularly high value, as he rules the most populous country in the world and benefits from extremely high economic output. On the personal side, he and his family are quite wealthy, partially due to his political position, and that wealth would likely make him a future leader's target if he were to leave office.[4] These are precisely the sort of conditions under which we would expect a leader to repress frequently and severely, even though it seems that popular protest would be unlikely to undermine his secure position. There is little

---

1. This is consistent with extant empirical studies on leader vulnerability and turnover, e.g., Ritter 2014.

2. Babones 2018.

3. Xinhua News Agency 2018.

4. Wallace 2018.

room for error in defending such a valuable office. Xi has indeed increased repression of dissidents and media as compared to the prior leader, and he has maintained this increased level of repression until the time of this writing.[5]

Claim 1 *As a leader's expected value for retaining office increases, government repression increases.*

In our theory, increased repression correlates with increased dissent. Dissidents wish to remain competitive in the fight over policy while minimizing expended costs and efforts, and they therefore do not want to engage in too little or too much action. Dissenting at low levels or with few participants is unlikely to achieve policy change against a very repressive government, but massive social movements are unnecessary against a government that does repress severely. For each optimal level of repression, there is an optimal level of dissent that maximizes the dissidents' probability of winning and minimizes their cost of action. Because these behaviors are set in a simple contest function (i.e., $\frac{d}{d+r}$),[6] the optimum levels of repression and dissent move in tandem—if leaders expect more dissent, they repress more to match it; as repression increases, optimal dissent increases monotonically.

This is not to say that repression and dissent "match." Often repression occurs before dissent can be realized, or dissent occurs in the absence of repression. However, we expect that, on average, realized dissent and repression tend to move together.[7] The conditions that make a leader more likely to repress lead to similar increases in the frequency or severity of dissent. When leaders highly value the retention of power, low levels of dissent will not change the contested policy: dissidents' efforts will be subsumed by government repression. Dissidents must increase their actions as they expect the leader to engage in more repression; they must make the most efficient use of dissent in order to "win" the interaction. Because leaders violate rights more as the expected value for power goes up, dissent also increases as the expected value for power rises.

The Democratic Republic of the Congo (DRC) provides an illustration of these dynamics. Joseph Kabila has ruled the DRC from 2001 to the time of this writing. His constitutionally mandated two-term limit ended in December 2016, but he remains in power as of June 2018. In January

5. Cook 2015.
6. Blattman and Miguel 2010.
7. Pierskalla 2010; Ritter 2014.

2015, the legislature passed a bill requiring a national census before an election could be held, which would delay Kabila's replacement for several years. Although the bill was eventually amended, its passage in the lower house incited large peaceful demonstrations. A series of actions and rulings—including efforts to amend the constitution, court rulings against opposition leaders, and the passing of the term limit without an election—increased Kabila's ability to hold power.[8] With every new action or announcement that continued to extend Kabila's rule beyond the constitutional mandate, popular demonstrations increased. Largely peaceful nationwide protests have occurred consistently since 2015, increasing in scope and participation with each move to retain Kabila in office. At the same time, repression has increased. Government authorities and hired security agents have violently attacked protesters, exiled human rights workers, arrested organizers without charge, and killed peaceful protesters, including children. In the competition between the government and dissidents over the status quo, as Kabila's expected value for power increased, so did repression and dissent.[9]

Claim 2 *As a leader's expected value for retaining office increases, mobilized dissent increases.*

The other mediating concept in our theory is the expectation of domestic consequences for repression—more specifically, the probability of domestic litigation costs.[10] When authorities repress members of the population, they open themselves to the possibility of negative consequences from a domestic court of law. Many domestic characteristics can influence the probability of litigation: the number and clarity of rights-related laws in the domestic canon, precedent for similar situations coming to trial, the presence of NGOs to advocate for victims, laws allowing citizens to have standing in constitutional courts, and so on. As potential litigants become more likely to bring cases against repressive authorities, the leader will repress less to avoid that cost.

Claim 3 *As the probability of domestic litigation costs increases, government repression decreases.*

8. Kabila's value for holding power is also very high, as he benefits from reported and unreported incomes from mining and agricultural holdings that place his family's estimated net worth in the hundreds of millions of dollars (Kavanagh and McCarey 2017).

9. Human Rights Watch 2016.

10. We refer to this concept interchangeably as the probability of *adjudication* or *litigation* costs.

A leader is likely to expect more severe penalties for repression as the probability increases that they will experience legal consequences—consequences that they expect will intensify with the severity of the repressive behaviors. As repression increases, more victims may bring lawsuits before the court, evidence is more likely to emerge, and more laws are likely to be broken. This puts leaders in a tight spot: they can repress more in an attempt to hold on to their preferred policies (and office), but in doing so, they increase the risk of incurring legal consequences for their behavior.

The tension between the costs and benefits is most salient for leaders who face the strongest incentives to repress: leaders repress more as their expected value for retaining office increases (Claim 1). The leader's incentive to repress more severely is reinforced by the expectation stated in Claim 2, such that they also face increasing dissent. The heightened motive to repress—more dissent—means that leaders are more likely to face legal action for the violation of human rights. Comparatively, leaders with low expected values for power will be less concerned with the possibility of litigation costs, both because they repress less and because they are unlikely to be in power to incur those costs. Thus, we expect the effects of domestic litigation costs to be conditional on the leader's expected value for office.

Claim 4 *As a leader's expected value for retaining office increases, a greater probability of domestic litigation costs will be more likely to constrain government repression than a lower probability of litigation costs.*

Leaders with high expected values for power are more constrained by domestic consequences (i.e., by the probability of facing litigation costs) than vulnerable leaders, and these constraints create opportunities for dissidents to take action. Dissent is more likely to yield policy success while the leader is constrained from repressing as much as they would prefer. Since potential dissidents expect this constraint to restrict the leader's behavior more as the probability of litigation costs increases, a stronger court is related to an increased likelihood of dissent. The constraint becomes irrelevant as the leader becomes prone to losing office outside of the conflict interaction, so dissent is also not affected by the possibility of consequences under these conditions.

Consider the case of African Americans in the United States following World War II. During this period, the white majority had a firm hold on power all over the United States, and especially in the South. U.S. leaders at both the federal and state levels of government had a higher expected value for retaining power than prior to the war, having emerged from the conflict as a global economic power with fierce domestic support for the victorious leaders. This is a critical period in the demand for African Americans' rights, with victorious black soldiers returning home to face repression, humiliation, and violence endemic (but not limited) to the South. This period of American strength is characterized by major increases in both black dissent and local and state repression. From the early fifties through the sixties, popular dissent increased in severity and scope, drawing more participants and spawning two distinct branches, the nonviolent civil rights protest movement and the violent Black Power movement.[11] Increases in dissent under secure U.S. leadership coincided with increased action in state and federal courts. During this period, NAACP lawyers became more active than ever, especially as courts increasingly began to support plaintiffs on issues related to civil rights. While leaders were similarly secure throughout this period, the increased litigation and judicial action constrained authorities from increasing repression proportional to the increased dissent.[12] Government leaders certainly engaged in repression, but they were more limited in overt action than they had been during the immediate postwar period.

Claim 5 *As a leader's expected value for retaining office increases, a greater probability of domestic litigation costs incentivizes more mobilized dissent.*

Claims 1 through 5 establish the theoretical baseline of domestic constraints and conflict behavior for governments that are not committed to international human rights treaties. Both government repression and mobilized dissent increase as leaders' expected value of retaining power increases. These are also the conditions under which the probability of incurring domestic consequences most influences those decisions, causing leaders to repress less than they otherwise would prefer and dissidents to take more direct action against the government. Although we do not test these claims, they represent a snapshot of equilibrium behavior that tells us what we should observe in an institutional baseline or counterfactual—a status quo of conflict within an existing structure of consequences from a domestic court absent treaty obligation. We now turn to how these behaviors differ if the very same countries commit to international human rights law.

11. Joseph 2006.
12. Rosenberg 1991.

3.2 A FORMAL COMPARISON: CONFLICT BEHAVIORS UNDER A HUMAN RIGHTS TREATY

In what follows, we consider how the actors' choices differ from the above baseline if a country is obligated to a human rights treaty. We assume that obligation to international human rights law increases the expectation, shared by both leaders and potential dissidents, that leaders will face litigation costs when they violate human rights. Although HRTs affect only the leader's utility function, government repression and mobilized dissent are endogenous. As a result, treaty obligations directly affect the likelihood of government repression and indirectly affect the likelihood of mobilized dissent actions.

International human rights treaties affect the domestic legal environment such that leaders who violate the terms of an HRT by repressing will be more likely to be brought before a court than leaders who repress but are not similarly obligated. Unlike many other domestic and international constraints, human rights treaties are not institutions with long arms, and other governments are often unwilling to enforce them. Instead, HRTs add to some probability of litigation already in place in a given country, altering to some extent the domestic environment of constraint. More importantly, though, treaties change perceptions about human rights constraints. In the presence of international HRT obligation, persons considering dissent and those considering repression operate with beliefs that the government is bound to protect rights more than in the law's absence.

We compare baseline repression and dissent behaviors to behaviors under HRT obligation where observers perceive that obligation to be constraining. When the domestic consequences for government repression are high enough, obligation to an additional institution does little to change that already high probability. An HRT's terms add some (but not many) new legal referents to extant law, NGOs are already active but receive some new resources from international NGOs, and so forth. The country's existing laws and institutions already hold the government to strong standards of rights protection. Adding another layer of legal protection is like putting a bandage on a plaster cast; the bandage certainly does not make things worse, but it is not the main form of protection. Neither dissidents nor authorities are likely to change their behavior much in the face of an international obligation if the domestic situation already minimizes repression on its own.

We expect leaders under such a domestic legal situation to only minimally alter their repressive strategies under obligation to an HRT.

Furthermore, when dissidents already expect to be able to act against a constrained government, adding a treaty does not alter those expectations. Put together, these dynamics mean that as the domestic environment becomes more favorable to rights protection, obligation to a treaty yields an increasingly small effect on repression and dissent.

Claim 6 *As the probability of domestic litigation costs increases, the effect of obligation to an HRT on repression and dissent decreases in magnitude to the point of negligibility.*

Claim 6 implies that domestic circumstances that limit government repression are ones where a treaty will do little to change common expectations about conflict. Similarly, the kinds of leaders who have little motive to repress will not differ in their repression behavior based on treaty status. Following the same logic, these leaders already repress little, so treaty constraints do alter their behavior.

The more the leader and their agents repress, the more vulnerable they are to the consequences of accountability. Because leaders with a higher expected value of remaining in power will repress more to retain that security, the expectation of consequences has a greater restraining effect than it does on leaders who would repress less. By comparison, insecure leaders have little to fear in terms of consequences, both because they repress at lower levels and because they do not expect to be in power to bear the costs. Logic implies that any increase in the likelihood of litigation costs that HRT obligation brings with it will have no effect on the repression decision of a leader who has a low expected value for power. Dissidents considering actions against the state follow suit: their dissent does not depend on treaty status, because the treaty does not alter the leader's already-limited repression. HRTs (and their associated increase in the domestic probability of litigation) therefore will have no effect on dissent when the common expectation of the leader's security in power is low.

Claim 7 *As the leader's expected value for retaining power decreases, the effect of obligation to an HRT on repression and dissent decreases in magnitude to the point of negligibility.*

Obligation to an international human rights treaty has the greatest constraining effect on repression when (a) the baseline probability of litigation consequences for repression is *low*, and (b) the leader's expected value for power is *high*. Formally, the actors choose different conflict behaviors under the constraint of an HRT than they do in the less constrained baseline scenario. For all defined values of the parameters,[13] $r_C < r_U$: a leader in the baseline, unobligated condition represses more than a leader under the same conditions who is obligated to a human rights treaty. For the same parameter values, $d_C > d_U$, such that dissidents engage in more dissent when the leader is constrained by the treaty obligation. Obligation to international human rights law thus increases popular dissent and decreases state repression in tandem.

The *magnitude* of the differences defining those inequalities depends on the value of θ, the leader's expected value for remaining in power. As this value increases, the treaty leads to a greater difference in conflict behaviors. In line with Claim 6, the HRT effect attenuates as the baseline expectation that the leader would experience court consequences for violating rights (ϕ) increases. The stronger the domestic judiciary, the less of an effect the treaty will have on conflict behaviors, even when the leader would otherwise be motivated to repress severely. The leader is already likely to repress far less in a country with strong, or many, institutional consequences for rights violations; adding an HRT to this already repression-limiting environment has a smaller effect on both actors' behaviors than adding a treaty does in a relatively unconstrained environment.

Thus, obligation to a human rights treaty reduces repression for leaders who would repress the most—those with low chances of going to court and high expected values for retaining power—and this reduction opens space for increased dissent. When a leader has a strong incentive to retain power, state obligation to a human rights treaty is associated with a meaningful increase in mobilized dissent. Interestingly, this is especially the case when domestic courts are unlikely to hear cases against the government. Formally, as $\phi \to 1$, the effect of θ on the difference between baseline dissent and dissent under obligation to an HRT approaches 0.

Proposition 2 *The difference between r_U and r_C increases as the probability of leader survival, θ, increases as a function of the probability of litigation costs, ϕ. $\frac{\partial r_U - r_C}{\partial \theta} = \frac{\kappa - 1}{\kappa (1 + \phi)^2} - \frac{\kappa - 1}{\kappa (1 + \phi + \epsilon)^2}$, which is greater than 0, but as $\phi \to 1$, the effect of θ on the difference between baseline repression and repression under obligation to an HRT approaches 0.*

---

13. That is, $1 > \theta > 0, 1 - \phi > \epsilon > 0, 1 > \phi > 0$, and $\kappa > 1$.

Proposition 3 *The difference between d_C and d_U increases as the probability of leader survival, θ, increases as a function of the probability of litigation costs, ϕ. $\frac{\partial d_C - d_U}{\partial \theta} = \frac{(\kappa-1)(\epsilon+\phi)}{\kappa(1+\phi+\epsilon)^2} - \frac{(\kappa-1)\phi}{\kappa(1+\phi)^2}$, which is greater than 0, but as $\phi \to 1$, the effect of θ on the difference between baseline dissent and dissent under obligation to an HRT approaches 0.*

3.3 UNDERSTANDING TREATY EFFECTS

A key implication of the theory is that obligation to international human rights law will lead to the greatest difference in leader and dissident behavior when it alters the expectations of leaders and potential dissidents, moving them away from the baseline expectations about litigation costs and constraint. Effective, independent courts, individual standing to bring suit, existing laws protecting rights and freedoms, a low standard of proof: all of these domestic conditions already make it straightforward for a victim of repression to find remedy in the judiciary—even without an international obligation to protect rights. While these are ideal conditions for the carrying out of international laws, these conditions also mean that a human rights treaty creates a small rather than a substantial shift in the legal environment. HRTs might create new laws or supporting activities, but international commitments are not likely to change behavior very much when existing domestic law already provides protections and courts are willing to implement them.

Conversely, when the domestic court cannot constrain a leader on its own, committing to a human rights treaty leads to higher expectations that a leader will experience litigation costs—an increase that affects conflict behaviors a great deal. In this situation, the domestic system is insufficient to impose consequences on repressive leaders, and this produces a comparatively larger change in the structural environment than under strong courts. Hill (2015) finds a similar pattern: HRTs only alter behavior when there are not similar rights protections already encoded in domestic law. Similarly, when countries who already have strong judicial systems in place join the International Criminal Court (ICC), they see almost no effect from adding a level of oversight, but countries with insufficient judicial systems are more likely to see the Rome Statute invoked—an expectation that can prevent them from joining the ICC at all.[14] In short, a treaty commitment leads to the greatest change in the leader's and dissidents' decision-making

---

14. Simmons and Danner 2010.

structure when the baseline probability of consequences is otherwise relatively low.

But how do treaties constrain behavior when courts are ineffective or unable to rule against authorities? Why would treaty obligations encourage people to bring cases when the court is weak—when they expect it would not be able to work in their favor? According to Carrubba (2009), during the early stages of change in judicial institutions' legitimacy, there is a meaningful opportunity for litigants to push boundaries, as often the court is then willing to rule in ways that it previously would have avoided. When courts lack independence and legitimacy, they must operate in close alignment with the executive's preferences.[15] As a court builds its independence and legitimacy through the development of jurisprudence, however, public support and adventurous lawyers and litigants can push a relatively young or weak court to foray into new waters.[16]

Egypt provides an illustrative example. At its inception, Egypt's Supreme Constitutional Court lacked independence and was unable to bind government behavior in any area. The Egyptian government found it needed to make credible commitments for international financial relations, and it ceded some limited power to the very weak constitutional court for the enforcement of property rights protections. Domestic human rights organizations, seeing a small opening, began to bring human rights–related cases before the court, although there was no evidence that the judiciary would rule in their favor. Not only did rights litigation increase, but the court occasionally ruled against the state in cases of accused government repression.[17] This example and others suggest that small shifts in the incentive structures surrounding even very weak courts can lead people to seek redress and thereby increase the litigation costs incurred by the state.[18] Kenneth Roth, executive director of Human Rights Watch, made the point clearly in a debate with legal scholar Eric Posen, writing, "Treaties are effective even when courts are too weak to enforce them because they

15. Helmke 2002, 2005.

16. Carrubba 2009; Rosenberg 1991; Staton 2010b; Vanberg 2005.

17. Moustafa 2003, 2007.

18. See, e.g., Carrubba 2009; Helmke 2005; Hilbink 2007; Staton 2010b. If courts accept cases but continually rule in favor of the state, people should no longer expect restitution and should eventually stop bringing cases before the court. This would mean the treaty's effect on actors' expectations—and their behavior—would attenuate over time. We would expect to see a spike in the treaty's constraining effect in the first few years after ratification that then diminishes. Empirically, we do not find this pattern. Controlling for the effects of time with cubic splines and counters does not alter the strength of the findings we report in the following empirical chapters (Beck, Katz, and Tucker 1998; Carter and Signorino 2010).

codify a public's views about how its government should behave. Local rights groups, working with their international partners like Human Rights Watch, are able to generate pressure to respect these treaties by contrasting a government's treaty commitments with any practices that fall short. The shame generated can be a powerful inducement to change."[19]

An HRT-related shift in the probability of consequences for human rights violations reduces the repression the leader would otherwise choose. This dampening effect occurs for any repressive leader. This constraining effect occurs for any repressive leader, but it increases as incentives for authorities to repress increase. To illustrate this idea, we can think of the level of repression as the number of victims targeted by the action. Imagine, hypothetically, that commitment to a constraint like a treaty makes it 1 percent more likely that the leader will be brought to court for these violations. To offset the higher likelihood of litigation costs, the leader should decrease repression by 1 percent. If the leader would otherwise violate the rights of ten people to win the conflict, this reduction is very small, and it would not save a single person from repression. However, if the leader would otherwise violate the rights of one hundred people, the treaty obligation would save one person from rights violations; if a thousand, it would save ten. Because higher levels of repression are more likely to lead to litigation, a treaty obligation that makes litigation more likely to occur—even the slightest bit—will have a greater constraining effect at this end of the violation scale. To be sure, this scenario illustrates that overall repression may still be quite high when the treaty "works." This is part of why many scholars claim treaties do not protect rights—because many obligated states have very severe repressive practices. But it is in these very states where treaties change behavior (as compared to the same repressive states in the absence of a treaty).

Leaders who expect that they would remain in power if they retain policy control but who would have a lot to lose in conflict are the leaders who repress the most. It is these leaders who are most impacted by the higher probability of costs associated with a treaty. Insecure leaders do not repress much, since doing so will not save them from an ouster, and the likely loss of office reduces the likelihood that they will spend their political, social, and economic capital to defend policies that will probably not benefit them once out of office. A comparatively higher likelihood of facing repression-related costs will not change these leaders' level of repression—it is already quite low. When two identical states with leaders at identical low expected values for power are compared, one

19. Posner and Roth 2014.

committed to an additional constraint like an HRT and the other not, the difference in their repression activity is negligible. But as a leader's expected value for holding power increases, they repress at higher levels to fight off increasing dissent, and these additional human rights violations create more opportunities for consequences. When two identical states with leaders at identical high expected values are compared, the leader obligated to a treaty will repress less than the leader in an uncommitted state.

For example, high-ranking civilian and military members of U.S. president George W. Bush's administration designed and executed a program of imprisonment and enhanced interrogation techniques outside of legal jurisdictions that extended from 2001 to 2007. The U.S. war on terror was in full swing from 2001 to 2004, public approval for the president and government was steadily strong, and the administration was in the high-value position of enjoying public support and the potential for reelection. In circumstances such as these, we argue, leaders have strong incentives to repress to hold on to that position—and the Bush administration did torture in their attempt to win the conflict over the policy at issue (the war on terror) and retain power. However, these are also the circumstances in which we expect treaty obligations like the Convention Against Torture and the Geneva Conventions to constrain the government from doing what it would most prefer to do. The 2011 Congressional Report detailing the program, its outcomes, and the process of defending it in the U.S. domestic legal system reveals that there were many governmental attempts to avoid the legal purview of the treaties.[20] Memorandums, speeches, and legal defenses redefined torture so that the interrogation techniques would not fit the definition, classified the victims as noncombatants to move them into legal gray zones, and conducted the activities away from U.S. territory so as not to be subject to territorial courts. And in the absence of the treaties, the legal standards they provide, and the public interest in those treaties, the government might have acted much differently, perhaps torturing more openly or on a wider scale.

HRT obligation also increases opportunities for dissent, since potential dissidents expect governmental restraint. We assume that human rights treaties do not change the relative costs or benefits of dissent directly but indirectly, via their effect on repression. In the presence of the obligation, the increased expectation of repression-related consequences constrains repression more than in the absence of the obligation, and this creates space

20. CNN 2017.

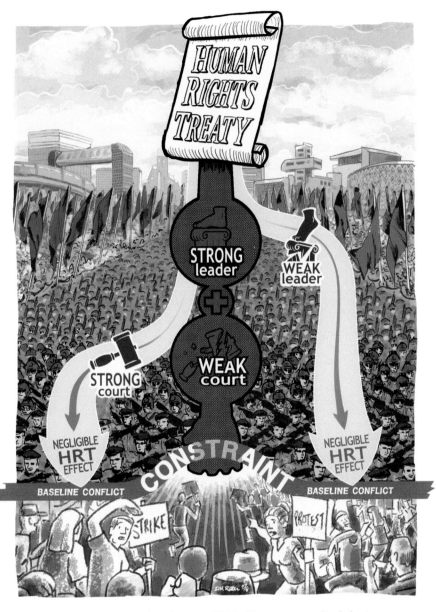

Figure 3.1 The theory: Conditional predictions of HRT obligation on conflict behavior

for dissidents to demand their desired change. Dissidents expect treaties to constrain repression at times when the leader would have otherwise repressed the most. That large change occurs when the domestic legal baseline is low, and so under this condition, a treaty has the greatest effect on dissent.[21]

As described earlier, the Chinese Communist Party and its leader, Xi Jinping, enjoy positions of significant power under a weak judiciary, which we associate with significant and severe repression. Yet China has ratified a number of human rights treaties, including the Convention Against Torture and treaties protecting the rights of women, racial minorities, children, and persons with disabilities.[22] Although the government represses openly, in violation of these treaties, dissidents use the treaty terms as referents, and this implies that they expect that these treaties are potentially constraining the government's action. Nobel Laureate Liu Xiaobo wrote the Charter '08 document demanding improved political rights for the Chinese people. The document, which cites a number of human rights treaties that China has signed and/or ratified, was released on the anniversary of the UN adoption of the Universal Declaration of Human Rights. The Charter '08 document, signed by two thousand other activists, suggests the importance of international law in the signees' impetus to dissent for democracy, although democratization is largely outside the scope of the treaties to which China is party.[23]

Building on the claims derived from the formal model and interpreted informally above, we present the main implications of our theory with regard to the effect of international human rights treaties on conflict behaviors:

Implication 1 *As a leader's expected value for retaining power increases, a human rights treaty obligation has an increasingly negative effect on repression. This effect decreases in magnitude as the probability of domestic litigation costs increase.*

Implication 2 *As a leader's expected value for retaining power increases, a human rights treaty obligation has an increasingly positive effect on dissent.*

---

21. Although individual citizens may not be aware of a state's HRT obligation status, they can respond to a change in popular expectations about repression. NGOs and other norm entrepreneurs often play a vital role in providing information to citizens about their rights and about HRT ratification status, influencing citizen expectations of state repression and thus dissent decisions.

22. *Ratification of International Human Rights Treaties—China* n.d.

23. Xiaobo 2009.

This effect decreases in magnitude as the probability of domestic litigation costs increase.

To further clarify the conditional predictions of our theory, Figure 3.1 provides a visual depiction of the effects of treaty obligations on conflict behaviors. The treaty obligation has the largest constraining effect—as compared to the counterfactual condition—when the likelihood of domestic litigation is low (i.e., when the court is weak, as per the figure) *and* when the leader would have otherwise been very repressive (i.e., at high expected values for retaining power—a strong leader in the figure). In this domestic context, a treaty obligation will lead to less repression than we would predict in its absence. Essentially, these are the conditions where leaders have the highest incentives to repress and would expect to get away with doing so, yet these are the conditions when the government is more vulnerable to potential consequences and the expectation thereof. Under these same conditions, the treaty creates an opening for dissidents to take more direct action and possibly win policy concessions. Expecting the treaty to constrain an otherwise repressive leader, dissidents may act when they would have otherwise done less.[24]

In summary, an international human rights treaty will have no meaningful effect on government repression or mobilized dissent if the domestic court is likely to place litigation costs on repressive leaders or the leader has low expectations for retaining power. When the court is weak *and* the leader is strong, an obligation to international human rights law reduces repression and increases dissent as compared to the same domestic conditions without such a treaty.

3.4 COMMITMENT TO HUMAN RIGHTS TREATIES IN EXPECTATION OF CONSTRAINT

We have argued that government obligation to HRTs can make the leader and their agents repress less than they would otherwise prefer, particularly when the leader has a high value for remaining in power, in response to changed popular expectations and anticipated conflict. Treaty obligation leads to increased dissent under the same conditions, putting conflict

---

24. Importantly, these implications rest on the assumption that repression can be costly for the government with some probability. If, instead, repression is costless to the government, or if it would be more costly to *stop* repressing than to continue it, we would expect to see very different behavior.

pressure on the leader precisely when their hands are tied from repressing at will. If HRTs shift conflict behavior in this way, constraining leaders and simultaneously increasing dissent, why do leaders ever commit to them in the first place? In countries where relatively secure leaders face an otherwise low probability of litigation costs for repressive behaviors, do the costs of commitment to an HRT always outweigh the benefits? More generally, are the governments most likely to be constrained by HRTs the very ones most likely to avoid them completely?

To learn more about the conditions under which a country will likely commit to an HRT versus opting out, we used simulated data of the theoretical parameters discussed in Chapter 2. We assigned a series of values to all of the model parameters to represent their full theoretically defined limits, yielding a dataset of over one hundred thousand different possible country scenarios of domestic legal consequences, expected value for power, treaty benefits, and expected treaty constraint. For each observation, we determined whether countries with those particular sets of conditions would commit to a human rights treaty—or opt out—in equilibrium. This yielded a set of country-types that we expect to select into commitment to international law in equilibrium, and a set that we expect to select out of commitment to international law. Taking the mean parameter values for each country-type, we then performed comparative statics analysis for those types, varying the parameter for expected value for office. We present the results of these theoretical simulations in Figure 3.2.

When leaders expect international human rights treaties to constrain their repressive behavior, they are less likely to ratify them, retaining rather than delegating their sovereign authority over rights protection. The figure on the left illustrates a meaningful difference between repression in the absence of the treaty (solid line) or in obligation to one (dashed line). Although the distance between the simulated conditions represents a significant expected treaty effect, these are countries that, in equilibrium, would opt out of treaty obligation. Secure leaders should expect to be more constrained by international human rights treaties, and they are therefore less likely to commit in the first place than their insecure counterparts. Further, leaders who face low probabilities of adjudication and the attendant litigation costs should be less likely to obligate themselves to HRTs. Our theoretical simulations show that the governments most likely to be constrained by HRTs are the least likely to commit to them.

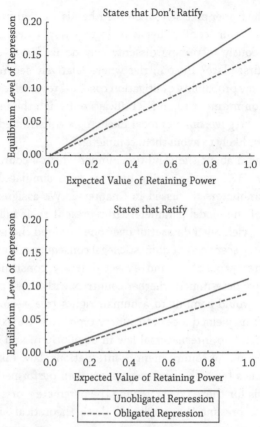

Figure 3.2 Simulated values to predict expected treaty effects for states that commit to a treaty or not in equilibrium

Proposition 4 *A government is less likely to commit to a human rights treaty as a leader's expected value for retaining power, θ, increases, but this effect attenuates as φ increases. Proof in Appendix 1.*

Implication 3 (HRT commitment) *A government is less likely to commit to an HRT as a leader's expected value for retaining power increases and more likely to commit as the probability of domestic adjudication costs increases.*

In addition to being less likely to commit to human rights treaties in the first place, leaders who expect to be constrained by international law may consider reneging on previous commitments to HRTs. In January 2017, the *Washington Post* released a draft Trump administration executive order (EO) intended to place a "moratorium" on U.S. commitments to international treaties, specifically those that "purport to regulate activities that are domestic in nature." As we argue elsewhere, "The EO proposes adding an extra step to the treaty ratification process. A new executive committee would review treaties before they come to the president's desk for signature."[25]

Despite the selection effects, which should remove a number of potential cases of constraint from the pool of HRT-committed countries, we should still observe governments committing to and then being constrained by international treaty obligations for two reasons. First, government authorities will ratify a human rights treaty when they will receive a benefit (which we formalize as $\mu > 0$) that outweighs the expected consequences for that particular leader. If the perceived benefits of ratification outweigh the perceived costs, leaders will commit even when they expect constraint. Second, leaders continue to be subject to the constraining effects of a treaty obligation *after* it is initially ratified. As a result, leaders who would never commit to an HRT themselves may still experience increased repression costs as a consequence of a previous leader's ratification decision, which we see in Figure 3.2 in the right-side graph.

Importantly, the theory presented here is a snapshot of a single interaction that includes HRT obligation, government repression, and mobilized dissent. To translate this snapshot into the empirical world, we assume that the game in our theory is played anew in every time period under observation, and that the leader and dissidents make new repression and dissent choices in each period. In practice, however, the ratification decision is typically made only once.[26] We therefore need to consider what the theory predicts about when a government would ratify in the first place and what that means about the potential for constraint on future leaders and in future periods.

According to our theory, for an unobligated leader to be willing to ratify a treaty in a particular period, the benefit of HRT ratification ($\mu > 0$)—whether short- or long-term in nature—must outweigh the expected consequences of constraining the leader *in that same period*. If a particular leader expects the likely consequences for repression and dissent to be small, then the benefit need not be large to make them willing to ratify the treaty and get the benefit. Leaders with low expected values for power or leaders facing a high probability of litigation from domestic courts will have

---

25. Conrad and Ritter 2017.

26. As we discuss in additional detail in Chapter 4, we assume that the government does make the ratification decision in each period in the empirical estimations, since it could indeed remove itself from HRT obligation. In practice, governments very rarely secede from HRT obligation.

little problem joining human rights treaties. Leaders who are secure in a particular period, though, will be quite unlikely to join a treaty, as suggested in Implication 3. Notably, while the probability of domestic litigation can be institutional and slow-moving, a leader's job security is quite variable from year to year and even month to month. It is quite feasible to imagine a leader being willing to join a human rights treaty to gain its benefits in the current period, during a time of relative insecurity for the leader, and to expect that the treaty obligation's consequences would not come due until a later period, when the leader may be out of power.

Simmons (2009, Chapter 3) argues that governments that ratify international human rights law are of one of two types: (1) sincere or (2) strategic. *Sincere ratifiers* are those governments who sincerely value human rights protection. These governments already protect human rights (at least for the most part) and so expect the legal obligation to be a relatively small or shallow shift in their already strong domestic legal environment.[27] These are the countries where we would expect that a high probability of domestic consequences was already in place; our theory implies that these countries need little benefit, whether expressive[28] or material,[29] to convince them to ratify. *Strategic ratifiers*, by contrast, join treaties to obtain short-term benefits when they expect to be able to violate the terms of the treaty with little repercussion.[30] These short-term benefits might include the expectation of foreign investment, aid donations, or increases in international trade,[31] as well as positive international press coverage, support from NGOs, or support from domestic groups concerned about human rights.[32] Leaders may also ratify international human rights law to "buy off" or signal some sort of cooperation to their domestic populations.[33] Regardless of whether the benefits are international or domestic, they are often enough to make leaders of states like North Korea and the Sudan prefer HRT ratification to inaction. We would expect that this would be the case when leaders have relatively low expected values for retaining power, desiring the short-term

27. Downs, Rocke, and Barsoom 1996; Hathaway 2002; Simmons and Danner 2010; von Stein 2016.

28. Hathaway 2002; Hawkins 2004; Lutz and Sikkink 2000; Wotipka and Ramirez 2008.

29. Goodliffe and Hawkins 2006; Hathaway 2004; Nielsen and Simmons 2015; Posner 2008.

30. Simmons 2009.

31. See, e.g., Boockmann 2001; Hathaway 2004; Smith-Cannoy 2012.

32. See, e.g., Goodliffe and Hawkins 2006.

33. Hollyer and Rosendorff 2011; Vreeland 2008a. Nielsen and Simmons (2015) fail to find robust empirical support for the international benefits associated with commitment to HRTs and suggest that benefits are likely to accrue at the domestic level.

benefits more than they fear the risk of incurring consequences under the obligation. Such a situation is consistent with the conception of a strategic ratifier developed by Simmons (2009).

These ideas imply selection bias within the pool of countries that ratify HRTs: The leaders who are more likely to ratify are the ones who do not expect to face large consequences for that obligation. Yet conditions and governments change. The leaders who make the decision to ratify may see changes in the conditions that led them to do so, or they may lose power. Regardless, future leaders are still obligated,[34] and thus can be constrained from repression by the treaty's continuing effects, even when they value office more highly than their predecessor did, per Proposition 1. Former prime minister Tony Blair committed the United Kingdom to the European Convention of Human Rights (ECHR) in the 1999 Human Rights Act, prior to British involvement in the war on terror in 2001. In other words, his government committed to the ECHR when it had little incentive to repress. In 2016, however, Prime Minister Theresa May faced significant pressure to contain terror attacks and said as part of her election campaign, "And I mean doing more to restrict the freedom and movements of terrorist suspects when we have enough evidence to know they are a threat, but not enough evidence to prosecute them in full in court. And if our human rights laws get in the way of doing it, we will change the law so we can do it." She went even further, saying that she supported leaving the ECHR toward this end—a move consistent with a preference for opting out of constraining international laws.[35] Indeed, Moravcsik (2000) suggests that states ratify HRTs under the expectation that future leaders will be constrained by the international legal obligations. Thus, leaders in time t may commit to the treaty not expecting to be constrained themselves, due to their particular domestic conditions, but more secure leaders who succeed them will be motivated to repress and yet be constrained in time $t + x$.[36]

3.5 SUMMARIZING THE THEORY

International human rights treaties affect domestic conflict under surprising conditions, changing the expectations of governments as well as dissidents who choose their conflict actions. As a result, some governments repress less and dissidents take more direct action under treaty obligations

---

34. In theory, and even occasionally in practice, leaders can exit or disband such institutions.
35. BBC News 2017.
36. We return to a discussion of strategic selection in Chapters 4 and 7.

than in their absence. Leaders must consider the potential for consequences for repression precisely under the conditions that most incentivize them to repress: when they have a high expectation of power and face challenges that threaten that security. It is the most repressive leaders who have to consider consequences, since it is their behavior—not the actions of leaders who repress less—that invokes those consequences. Furthermore, HRTs only constrain leaders who are otherwise relatively unconstrained in the domestic environment. Adding or improving an institution when a leader already tempers their behavior to avoid existing structural consequences will not change repression outcomes; introducing a treaty obligation into a context where a leader acts without consequence can have a more meaningful effect on the conflict. Although leaders in both of these contexts will be prone to repress more than more vulnerable or constrained leaders, the overall level of repression belies the value of an HRT: The effect of the constraint is much stronger in these cases than in cases with a baseline of lower repression. Dissidents also respond to the HRT obligation, but again, only when they expect it to lead to a meaningful change in the leader's repressive behavior. In short, we may see the most conflict in the very countries where treaties will make the greatest difference in behavior. In the empirical analyses that follow in Part II, we move away from vignettes and test the implications of our theory using large-N data and an empirical strategy that allows us to capture the counterfactual effects of HRTs on human rights outcomes across a wide variety of countries over time.

An Empirical Investigation of Conflict & Treaty Constraint

CHAPTER 4

cwɔ

Analyzing the Effect of Treaties on Repression and Dissent

I n Part I, we presented a theory that describes how human rights treaties—international institutions that are typically argued to have little to no independent enforcement power or influence on human rights outcomes—affect government decisions to repress and popular decisions to engage in mobilized dissent. We turn now to the evaluation of the theory. How can we know that human rights treaties, and not some other unobserved factors, affect domestic conflict outcomes in the manner we suggest in Chapters 2 and 3? How can we determine the usefulness of the theory for understanding government and dissident behavior? We cannot "prove" our theory—or any theory—to be correct. Instead, in Part II of this book, we examine systematic data on human rights treaty obligation, government repression, and mobilized dissent and see if we uncover nuanced patterns consistent with the implications of the theory described in Part I.

To quickly recapitulate, we argue that international human rights treaty (HRT) obligation has a variable effect on government repression and mobilized dissent as a function of the leader's expected value for retaining political office. When that value is low or the leader is insecure, repression is neither deterred nor encouraged by the domestic effects of an international human rights commitment, nor is dissent dependent on treaty status. As a leader's value or expectation of holding office increases, incentives to repress intensify, as do pressures to dissent and compete for policy change. Obligation to a human rights treaty affects actors' expectations in this context of heightened conflict, shifting their behaviors. Governments repress less, and dissidents take more direct action, than they would have in the absence of an international human rights treaty.

These effects are mitigated by the probability that the government may incur domestic legal consequences. HRT obligation increases the likelihood that authorities will incur litigation costs should they repress. However, dissidents will only expect this change to meaningfully affect authorities' behavior when extant domestic institutions would generally fail to constrain rights violations in the absence of a treaty obligation. If authorities are already relatively constrained—as they may be if the leader already faces an effective domestic court, for example—the addition of small consequences associated with an HRT will not alter their behavior. Dissatisfied groups expect treaty obligations to have the strongest constraining effects on repression when leaders face few extant domestic institutional constraints; these are the conditions under which we expect the largest conflict effects from treaty obligation.

In what follows, we shift from a theoretical understanding of the relationships between institutions and political behavior to an empirical one, using observed data to empirically examine the implications of our theory. To consider the usefulness of the theory for understanding the empirical world, we must translate the theoretical model into an understanding of the process that generates the data we observe. We first present a theory of measurement, translating the theoretical concepts into measures that are observable and quantifiable. We then discuss what the structural assumptions of our model imply for an empirical estimator we would use to assess the hypotheses. Finally, in Chapters 5 and 6, we present an analysis of empirical estimates of the effect of treaty obligation to three human rights treaties—the Convention Against Torture and Other Cruel, Inhuman or Degrading Treatment or Punishment (CAT); the International Covenant on Civil and Political Rights (ICCPR); and the Convention on the Elimination of Discrimination Against Women (CEDAW)—on government repression and mobilized dissent. We examine the effect of each of these treaties on the forms of repression they are intended to limit and the extent to which they provide incentives for dissent actions. Our empirical strategy is oriented around answering a simple question that is unanswerable without the tools of social science: How would government repression (and mobilized dissent) differ if the same country were able to simultaneously obligate itself and fail to obligate itself under a human rights treaty?

4.1 MOVING FROM CONCEPTS TO MEASURES

The theory that we present in Part I suggests that international human rights treaties *cause* leaders to change strategies with regard to repression and *cause* dissidents to change strategies with regard to mobilized dissent. Showing causation is difficult; correlation between two things—like international human rights treaties and repression—does not mean that one caused the other. In their discussion of causation, Shadish et al. define *internal validity* as the "validity of inferences about whether observed covariation between A (the presumed treatment) and B (the presumed outcome) reflects a causal relationship from A to B as those variables were manipulated or measured."[1] Without the ability to directly observe causation, social scientists make do by developing theory, arguing that the application or presence of *A*—in our case, a human rights treaty—could effect a change in *B*—in our case, repression and dissent—via a series of logical connections like ours.

But theory is not enough. To test the implications of a theory—to be able to make a claim that *A* causes a change in *B* in the empirical world—we need a theory of measurement. A theory of measurement is a way of moving from theoretical concepts to data representing those concepts. In our case, it answers questions like: What does it mean to "commit" to an international human rights treaty? What is government repression? How do we know it when we see it? What do we mean by mobilized dissent? Under what conditions is a leader more likely to incur domestic adjudication costs? Why would a leader be more or less secure in power, or value it more or less? Shifting from theoretical concepts to concrete measures in this way requires some assumptions. We want to be clear about those assumptions—both for the initial testing of the argument and for replicability, should other scholars decide to examine or extend our work. If a measurement is not a close approximation of a particular concept, we cannot draw conclusions about the concept—or about the causal effect of *A* on *B*—based on observation of the measure.[2]

In this section, we present and defend the operationalization of our theoretical concepts. An empirical analysis of the theory requires operational indicators for five key concepts: international human rights treaty obligation, the level of government repression, the probability that authorities incur domestic adjudication costs, the expected value of leader retention, and the level of mobilized dissent. In what follows, we describe what we

---

1. Shadish, Cook, and Campbell 2002, p. 38.
2. Carmines and Zeller 1979.

mean by each of these theoretical concepts and explain the advantages and drawbacks of the data we use to measure each of them for use in our empirical models. We then posit operational hypotheses that substitute the *measures* discussed here for the *concepts* presented in Chapters 2 and 3.

4.1.1 International Human Rights Treaty Obligation

Our main independent variable of interest is *a national government's binding legal obligation to an international human rights treaty.* Countries become obligated to an HRT by ratifying the legal document through whatever method is required under their respective domestic laws. Domestic ratification processes differ significantly from country to country. In the United States, the president can sign international treaties on his own accord,[3] but the Senate is responsible for their ratification, establishing the status of international treaties as law. In many dictatorial states, the power to sign and ratify international law is consolidated into one individual or group of individuals.[4] Once a treaty has been ratified, a national government is legally bound to it in all periods that follow ratification unless the government formally secedes from the international commitment.[5] It is not the process of ratification that alters state and dissident behavior; it is the *obligation*. HRT obligations alter the structure of government—and

---

3. The signing of an international treaty does not on its own imply that a government is bound to the terms of the treaty: "Where the signature is subject to ratification, acceptance or approval, the signature does not establish the consent to be bound. However, it is a means of authentication and expresses the willingness of the signatory state to continue the treaty-making process. The signature qualifies the signatory state to proceed to ratification, acceptance or approval. It also creates an obligation to refrain, in good faith, from acts that would defeat the object and the purpose of the treaty" *(Vienna Convention on the Law of Treaties (with Annex)* 1969, Articles 10 and 18).

4. A large number of dictatorships with uncomplicated domestic ratification processes have acceded to international human rights treaties without first signing onto their terms.

5. The Vienna Convention on the Law of Treaties defines ratification in the following manner: "Ratification defines the international act whereby a state indicates its consent to be bound to a treaty if the parties intended to show their consent by such an act. In the case of bilateral treaties, ratification is usually accomplished by exchanging the requisite instruments, while in the case of multilateral treaties the usual procedure is for the depositary to collect the ratifications of all states, keeping all parties informed of the situation. The institution of ratification grants states the necessary time-frame to seek the required approval for the treaty on the domestic level and to enact the necessary legislation to give domestic effect to that treaty" *(Vienna Convention on the Law of Treaties (with Annex)* 1969, Articles 2 (1) (b), 14 (1) and 16)).

thus potential dissident group—incentives, and it does so as long as the government remains obligated to the international agreement.

Because we are interested in obligation under international human rights law, we require a measure indicating whether or not a country is party to (i.e., has ratified or acceded to) a given international human rights treaty in a given year. In each of our empirical models, HRT OBLIGATION is coded "1" in the year in which a country ratifies or accedes to an international human rights treaty and "1" every year thereafter that it remains obligated under the law.[6] In theory, government leaders have the opportunity to renege on some of their commitments to international human rights law at any time; for example, Venezuela and Trinidad and Tobago ratified the American Convention on Human Rights but later denounced it, relinquishing themselves from the legal obligation of the treaty after several years of obligation.[7] Although this type of secession behavior is rare, the availability of the option and its occasional exercise suggests that national governments that have ratified HRTs decide whether to remain obligated to them each year thereafter.[8] There is, however, no formal process by which to withdraw from some treaties, such as the International Covenant on Civil and Political Rights (ICCPR).[9] In August 1997, the Democratic People's Republic of Korea (DPRK) notified the United Nations of its intent to secede from the ICCPR.[10] Although the DPRK was not permitted to formally secede, we consider international notification of *intent* to secede to be similar to actual secession in practice.[11]

In the theory, we examine the effects of any international human rights treaty that alters a country's domestic legal environment by increasing the probability that the government will experience domestic litigation for violating its terms. Importantly, the applicability of our theory is not

---

6. It is possible that a treaty alters state behavior from one year to the next much less after it has been committed for many years than it did in the years immediately after ratification. If so, pooling the data in the estimated models biases against finding support for the argument. Our theory does not account for such changes over time, but such processes are inherent in the data-generating process. We account for the possible attenuation of effects over time by empirically controlling for temporal dependence, which we discuss in additional detail below.

7. United Nations 1969.

8. This conceptualization is consistent with the interpretation of the formal model as modeling the decisions for a single period that would be replayed in the next period.

9. *CCPR General Comment No. 26: Continuity of Obligations* 1997.

10. Sub-Commission on the Promotion and Protection of Human Rights 1999.

11. We code the DPRK as not being party to the ICCPR post-August 1997 in the empirical models presented in Chapters 5 and 6, although our results are robust to the coding of North Korea as a party to the ICCPR post-August 1997 as well.

limited by the substantive focus of any particular treaty. Instead it applies to a wide variety of HRTs—everything from those that focus primarily on ending physical integrity violations like government torture and disappearances to those that focus on improving the quality of empowerment rights for the general population or for a specific group of individuals.[12] As long as the actors expect that the treaty will affect consequences for the state's violations of treaty terms that could be used in interactions with potential dissidents, the treaty is likely to affect government repression and mobilized dissent in the process we have suggested.

We therefore analyze the implications of the theory using data on obligation to a variety of HRTs, including the UN Convention Against Torture and Other Cruel, Inhuman or Degrading Treatment or Punishment (CAT); the International Covenant on Civil and Political Rights (ICCPR); and the UN Convention on the Elimination of Discrimination Against Women (CEDAW). These three treaties are representative of a number of international human rights laws that focus on physical integrity violations and/or empowerment rights violations. The United Nations General Assembly (UNGA) adopted the text of the CAT in December 1984 to limit government use of torture and ill-treatment. The CAT entered into force in June 1987. The ICCPR, which was adopted by the UNGA in December 1966 and entered into force in March 1976, is broader in its purview, committing state parties to respect civil and political rights writ large. These include the right to speak and assemble freely, the right to vote for one's government representatives, and the right to enjoy due process and a fair trial. While the CAT and the ICCPR are intended to protect the rights of all persons, the CEDAW, which came into force in September 1981 following its adoption by the UNGA in 1979, is intended to protect a wide variety of physical integrity and empowerment rights directed at a particular group: women.

Using information from the United Nations, we generated data on country ratification dates for each of these international human rights treaties. In our empirical models, which are conducted at the country-year unit of observation for government repression in Chapter 5,[13] The relevant measures, ICCPR OBLIGATION, CAT OBLIGATION, and CEDAW OBLIGATION, are coded "1" in the year in which a country ratifies or accedes to the ICCPR, CAT, and CEDAW, respectively, and "1" every year thereafter unless

---

12. Following Goldstein 1978, Davenport refers to empowerment rights as "first amendment-type rights," and physical or personal integrity rights as those concerned with "individual survival and security" (Davenport 2007a, p. 2).

13. When we conduct analyses at the country-month unit of observation in Chapter 6, we identify the month in which a country ratifies or accedes to a given HRT.

a country formally secedes or announces intention to secede from the obligation. Because each of these human rights treaties was created to limit different rights violations, we discuss in the next subsection the operationalizations of government repression that we use to test the effects of each treaty.

Although the theory implies that each of these international human rights treaties will limit the government's use of repression, we expect that broad treaties that focus on constraining the state from violating multiple rights (e.g., the ICCPR and the CEDAW) will have the largest effect on the probability of mobilized dissent. This is the case for two reasons. First, a more specific treaty like the CAT attempts to constrain governments from using one particular tactic of repression, which authorities and their repressive agents could easily substitute with another.[14] Dissidents who expect this substitution of repressive tactics may be less likely to alter their dissent choices as radically as they might after commitment to broader treaties. The broader ICCPR prohibits many civil and political rights violations that are common forms of government repression; if obligation to the ICCPR constrains government behavior, then it should constrain it broadly, such that dissidents might expect that direct action against the government would meet with a lower likelihood of repressive response.

Second, the ICCPR and the CEDAW represent restrictions on a wide variety of different rights issue areas, governing both the protection of individual and collective empowerment rights (e.g., the rights to freedom in voting and engaging in assembly and speech) and of physical integrity rights (e.g., the right to be protected from torture and political imprisonment); these rights are protected for all people in the case of the ICCPR and all women in the case of the CEDAW. Although we conduct empirical analyses in Chapter 6 on the effect of all three treaties on mobilized dissent against the government, we expect the Convention Against Torture to have a weaker substantive effect on mobilized dissent than either the International Covenant on Civil and Political Rights or the Convention on the Elimination of Discrimination Against Women.

4.1.2 Government Repression

To estimate the effects of human rights treaty obligation on government repression, we need a measure of repression that captures the government's

---

14. On government substitution of human rights violations, see, for example, Payne and Abouharb 2015.

chosen pattern of human rights abuse. Goldstein defines government repression as "the actual or threatened use of physical sanctions against an individual or organization, within the territorial jurisdiction of the state, for the purpose of imposing a cost on the target as well as deterring specific activities and/or beliefs perceived to be challenging to government personnel, practices or institutions."[15] This definition aligns with our concept of actions taken by a government to undermine individuals' or groups' ability or willingness to participate in political life (Chapter 1). We largely focus on physical sanctions in our empirical analyses, as these are the most dangerous concerns for potential dissidents considering direct action against the government. However, human rights treaties also govern civil and political rights whose violation may reduce dissent actions, and these are also relevant to the mechanisms that drive our theory.

Importantly, an obligation to a particular international human rights treaty does not necessarily constrain a leader from repressing in any or all ways; HRTs can only limit the types of repression described by the substance of a particular treaty. The CAT, for example, endeavors to limit government torture. It has no effect on government restrictions of popular assembly or freedom of speech. For our measure of government repression to match the concept described above, we require data on government repression that (a) capture a pattern (rather than a single incident) of human rights violations that are (b) relevant to the particular treaty under study.

Since the publication of Poe and Tate (1994), political scientists have generated several cross-national datasets of national governments' respect (or lack of respect) for human rights. Government repression and human rights violations are not necessarily the same thing. Government repression is as defined above; it is an intentional act on the part of the government and may or may not be contrary to international and domestic law. Human rights violations, on the other hand, are often discussed as government actions that are contrary to international human rights law. Imagine a government that is party to the Convention on the Rights of the Child (CRC), for example, that failed to provide primary education to its citizens. If that government did so to prevent women's empowerment, the act is both a violation of human rights and an act of government repression. If that government did so because it could not afford to build schools, that is a human rights violation, but not necessarily government repression. Because of the distinction between state repression (our concept) and

15. Goldstein 1978, p. xxvii.

human rights violations (our data), we focus attention on government acts that are likely to be both (i.e., torture, disappearances, and empowerment rights). One of the most well-known and frequently used datasets measuring such a concept is the CIRI Human Rights Data Project.[16] Based on content analysis of Amnesty International (AI) and US Department of State reports, the CIRI Data Collection Project generated annual data from 1981 to 2011 on the overall environment of global human rights violations. Researchers collected data from 195 countries—all the countries whose populations reached or exceeded one million people during the data collection period. The data are disaggregated by type of repression (e.g., torture, political imprisonment, women's economic rights) and measure the overall level of government human rights violations, encompassing both the government's choice to violate rights *and* the extent to which they do so.[17] We collapse the CIRI trichotomous measures of government human rights violations—no reported violations of human rights, some reported violations of human rights, and widespread reported violations of human rights—to create binary measures of SYSTEMIC REPRESSION. The final measures used in our empirical models are coded "1" if a government is reported to have engaged in "a lot" of a particular human rights violation in a given year and "0" otherwise.[18]

We prefer the dichotomization of this measure—and believe it to be a better match to the theoretical concept we wish to operationalize—over the original trichotomous CIRI measures of human rights violations for several reasons. First, CIRI's measures of human rights violations are coded as "1" if there is even a single incident of abuse in a given country-year; we wish to draw inferences about what affects common, systematic repression rather than more isolated rights violations, in large part because we recognize that human rights violations are subject to principal-agent problems. Coding SYSTEMIC REPRESSION as "1" only in cases that CIRI codes as "2" better captures country-years that repress as part of an overall pattern.[19] The

16. Cingranelli, Richards, and Clay 2014.

17. Like all measures of government repression, the CIRI measures employed here are likely to undercount actual human rights violations because the government has incentives to hide its repressive behavior (e.g., Conrad, Haglund, and Moore 2013, 2014). This means our results should be biased toward true or false negatives in the form of null findings (i.e., not finding support for the implications of our theory; G. King, Keohane, and Verba 1994, p. 130. See also G. King 1989, Chapter 9).

18. To capture government violations of human rights rather than government respect for human rights, we invert the scale of each of the CIRI measures.

19. All ordinal scales suffer from truncation. Because truncation in the dependent variable biases inferences toward null findings (King, Keohane, and Verba 1994, p. 130), the empirical results presented using our dichotomous measures provide a conservative estimate of predicted effects.

formal model assumes that the government will choose a level of repression from a continuous range, such that obligation to an international human rights treaty should lead to a lower level of repression under certain conditions. Dichotomization allows us to predict the latent likelihood of systematic government repression, which represents a continuous proxy of abuse that mimics the concept we employ in the theoretical model.[20]

Second, the sources from which CIRI codes allegations of government repression, Amnesty International and the U.S. State Department, are strategic actors that may face incentives to report more (or less) against certain countries for political or organizational reasons.[21] The measures of state repression are not measures of "actual" violations per se, but of allegations of human rights violations made by AI and the U.S. State Department;[22] in other words, this data may be subject to a cross-sectional measurement error. This distinction provides an additional reason for dichotomizing the CIRI indicators of human rights violations to create measures of systemic repression; although we cannot account in the empirical estimates for all of the reporting strategies of international and nongovernmental organizations like Amnesty International and Human Rights Watch, we believe that while they may ignore or miss *low*-level repression, they are less likely to erroneously or strategically report *high* levels of abuse.[23]

Finally, international human rights data based on allegations of violation are also subject to temporal measurement error. Fariss (2014) argues that international human rights standards of accountability have increased over time, and that as rights practices have improved, expectations or standards around human rights have also increased. This change biases data that are based on *allegations* of violations. Government respect for human rights has become significantly better, but international nongovernmental organizations continue to report violations at high levels, as if violations of human rights have not decreased in scope, magnitude, and intensity over time. Because we expect that this time measurement error's effects will be reduced with a categorical rather than continuous measure of human rights

20. For a discussion of the conceptual difference between likelihood and level of conflict events, see Ritter 2014.

21. Fariss 2014; Stroup and Wong 2017.

22. Conrad, Haglund, and Moore 2013, 2014.

23. Empirical models where we dichotomize the Cingranelli, Richards, and Clay (2014) data to create measures of any violations of human rights—rather than systemic violations—are available in our Online Appendix. Note, however, that this measurement decision represents a very different concept of conflict than the one we assume; it suggests that the institutions under study would have a meaningful effect on even one act of repression, rather than on systemic practices.

violations, we continue to prefer the dichotomized measures of the original CIRI indicators.[24]

Each of the international human rights treaties we examine—the CAT, the ICCPR, and the CEDAW—was created to limit different types of state repression. Although we could investigate the effect of each of these treaties on any of the rights violations they cover, we first examine treaty effects on a single violation—government torture—across all three treaties for comparability. Investigating government torture is obviously relevant to assessing the effects of the CAT, but it is also a suitable approach for examining the effects of broad human rights treaties like the ICCPR and the CEDAW. Torture is an action specifically intended to undermine potential dissidents' capacity and willingness to dissent via intimidation and fear,[25] and scholars commonly consider torture to be representative of the larger category of repression of physical integrity rights.[26] In addition, because torture is a prevalent repressive tactic, it constitutes a difficult test of the influence of HRT commitment on government respect for human rights. Authorities commonly justify it as a necessary evil for the maintenance of order,[27] and most national governments are accused of engaging in torture in most years;[28] Amnesty International (AI) documented allegations of torture and ill-treatment against ninety-eight countries in 2011 alone.[29] In short, if there were a form of repression resistant to legal intervention, it would be torture.

We begin by investigating the effect of obligation to the CAT on the likelihood that the state engages in systematic, widespread torture. The CIRI Project, following the language of the CAT, defines government torture as "the purposeful inflicting of extreme pain, whether mental or physical, by government officials or by private individuals at the instigation of government officials." This operationalization includes cruel, inhuman, and degrading treatment, as well as deaths that are reported to have

24. Our empirical results are robust to using data from Fariss (2014) that account for these temporal changes. We do not use the Fariss measure as our main indicator of government repression because it is a broad measure of physical integrity violations that does not allow us to look at the effect of international human rights treaties on specific violations of human rights. Results using the Fariss measure (dichotomized at its mean) are available in the Online Appendix.

25. Rejali 2007.

26. See, e.g., Conrad 2011; Hathaway 2002; Powell and Staton 2009; Simmons 2009; Vreeland 2008a.

27. Rejali 2007.

28. Conrad and Moore 2010.

29. Conrad, Haglund, and Moore 2014.

occurred in state custody.[30] Using the CIRI data on government torture, we follow the procedure described above and create a measure of SYSTEMIC TORTURE that is coded "1" if a government is reported to have engaged in "a lot" of torture in a given year and "0" otherwise.

Compared to the CAT, the ICCPR is a broad international human rights treaty; governments that commit to its terms promise to respect a wide range of their citizens' civil, political, and physical integrity rights. Since the right to freedom from torture is listed among a government's obligations under the ICCPR, we also use SYSTEMIC TORTURE as our main dependent variable when focusing on obligation to the ICCPR. In addition, we investigate the effect of ICCPR obligation on political imprisonment by the government. Cingranelli, Richards, and Clay (2014) define *political imprisonment* as "the incarceration of people by government officials because of: their speech; their non-violent opposition to government policies or leaders; their religious beliefs; their non-violent religious practices including proselytizing; or their membership in a group, including an ethnic or racial group." The measure of political imprisonment that we use in the empirical models is similar in structure to the measure of government torture: SYSTEMIC IMPRISONMENT is coded "1" if a government is reported to have engaged in "a lot" of political imprisonment in a given year and "0" otherwise.

When we examine the effect of the CEDAW on government repression, we also use two dependent variables: SYSTEMIC TORTURE and SYSTEMIC VIOLATION OF WOMEN'S SOCIAL RIGHTS. The measure of government torture is as described above. Although torture is not explicitly named in the CEDAW, many physical integrity rights are included, and most scholars and practitioners consider torture a violation of this treaty.[31] But the CEDAW is not only intended to protect women's physical integrity rights; it also commits the government to respect female social, economic, and cultural rights. For our purposes, CIRI (2014) provides data on women's social rights, considering a number of individual rights to participate equally with men in social environments, including rights to an education, birth planning, marriage by choice, and participation in the community. These are policies and practices the government can put in place to allow women to participate in social and political life, including dissent. Using these data, we create a measure of SYSTEMIC VIOLATION OF WOMEN'S SOCIAL RIGHTS, coded as above: "1" if a government is reported by AI and

---

30. *Convention against Torture and Other Cruel, Inhuman or Degrading Treatment or Punishment* 1984.

31. We extend this discussion in Chapter 5.

the U.S. State Department to have engaged in "a lot" of discrimination in a given year and "0" otherwise.

4.1.3 Mobilized Dissent

We argue that treaty obligation also increases the likelihood that a government will face non-state actors[32] engaged in mobilized dissent actions. Although there are several cross-national measures of mobilized dissent available at the country-year unit of observation, many of these measures are inappropriate for use as an indicator of the concept, because they often include information on government repression in combination with information on dissent. For example, data from the Political Risk Service and the World Governance Indicators combine information on opposition challenges and the government's response. Our theory requires separate empirical indicators of the two concepts. Other indicators of dissent are highly aggregated, with high standards as to what constitutes a mobilized dissent event; for example, the frequently used Cross-National Time Series dataset requires that an event have at least one thousand participants to be considered a protest event.[33] Still other data include detailed information about events but are limited spatially to particular regions or just a few countries.[34]

To measure mobilized dissent actions, we use data from the Integrated Data for Events Analysis (IDEA) Project,[35] which coded events from daily reports of the Reuters Global News Service between 1990 and 2004. We aggregate these data to the country-year in Chapter 5 and to the country-month in Chapter 6. The IDEA framework provides information on many types of events and identifies targets and sources of violent and nonviolent behavior, allowing us to create a count of incidents in which a domestic nonstate group took a conflictual action against the government. A conflictual event is one where the source of the action threatens or imposes negative consequences on a government target. IDEA data include over 10 million events, from conflict to sporting events to elections to natural disasters. From the raw event data, Ritter (2014) extracted

---

32. We use the term *nonstate actor* to refer to persons or groups that are not members of the ruling government. We generally are referring to persons within the state's jurisdiction, but that need not exclusively be the case.

33. Banks 2010.

34. See, e.g., Davis, Leeds, and Moore 1998; Salehyan, Hendrix, et al. 2012.

35. Bond et al. 2003; King and Lowe 2003.

conflictual events using as a guide the Conflict-Cooperation Scale for Inter- and Intrastate Interactions, developed by Taylor et al. (1999). To develop this scale, Taylor et al. asked scholars to rank the IDEA event categories on three scales: (1) contention-accommodation, (2) coercion-altruism, and (3) physical violence. From these rankings, Taylor et al. developed a scale that ranges from −11.033 (most conflictual) to 5.813 (most cooperative). Ritter (2014) weighted each conflictual event according to its Taylor et al. index coding.[36] All conflict events with a civilian source and government target are coded as mobilized dissent. In the sample that we used to create an indicator of mobilized dissent, events are limited to those occurring between sources and targets within the same country.[37]

Although using the IDEA data sidesteps the conceptual measurement issues for dissent, the decision to use data that rely on international news reports comes with its own bias that could potentially influence the results. Some countries have a larger media presence than others, and stories from these countries are more likely to be reported than stories from countries with just as much dissent but fewer reporters. International reporters also tend to focus on larger, more violent events, meaning that minor events are less likely to be reported. Although this measure of dissent includes very low-level events, it may miss smaller local events. Nonetheless, because these concerns should bias the estimates toward finding no effect of HRT obligation on dissent outcomes, we prefer the IDEA measure to other measures of mobilized dissent.[38]

To create a valid and representative measure of mobilized dissent for use in empirical models, we selected three dissent event forms to represent the range of severity of each of these activities. These event forms represent

36. That is, each event that is relevant to intrastate conflict short of civil war. We dropped any event that did not have a Taylor et al. coding, such as sporting events, health articles, natural disasters, etc.

37. The Taylor et al. scale places conflictual events on an ordinal scale with a linearlike relationship, which may not be an appropriate approximation of the actual relationship between and among these behaviors. While the scale was developed to assign each event a weight rather than a ranking, the weights are still based on the (informed) opinions of scholars. Weights suggest a sense of equality among events that could be seen as very qualitatively different. How many sit-ins are the equivalent of one riot? These kinds of events are difficult to compare. The scale seems increasingly ambiguous in the small differences, as it is difficult to assess qualitatively whether a beating (weighted -8.689) is more or less severe than an abduction (weighted -8.532), though this index suggests they are quantitatively similar yet different. While using such a scale ranks among the most reliable and valid ways to quantify such a concept as the severity of conflict, basing the scale on scholarly opinions introduces ambiguity to any weighting system.

38. As shown in the Online Appendix, the empirical results are robust to the inclusion of a control variable for the access of international media outlets to a given country.

a varied range of violence, coercion, and disruption.[39] The variable we ultimately include as a dependent variable in the empirical estimates of MOBILIZED DISSENT ACTIONS is a dichotomous indicator that is coded "1" in a given country-year (or country-month) if a domestic nonstate actor engages in armed hostilities, nonarmed physical force against human targets, or nonarmed protests targeted at a state actor; it is coded "0" otherwise.[40] This operationalization allows us to estimate the continuous, latent likelihood of observing mobilized dissent against the government in a given country-year or country-month.[41]

4.1.4 Expected Value of Leader Retention

Potential dissidents and government authorities choose their tactics as a function of their expectations. More specifically, leaders make decisions about how to handle threats from dissidents based on their expectations of their job security and the benefits they receive from holding power, as well as how they expect a policy loss to a dissident group to affect their position. We need to capture the former—the leader's predecision expected value of remaining in power—to operationalize this important cue, which authorities and dissidents use to anticipate one another's decisions about repression and dissent. Like the leader and the opposition group, we use observable characteristics and policy outcomes to generate an estimate of the leader's preconflict staying power; we contend that executives make decisions about repression—and that dissidents act in expectation of those decisions—based on the leader's expectations about remaining in office.

---

39. The Online Appendix lists the selected event forms and their respective severity weights.

40. As noted above, our preferred empirical estimator does not allow us to use a trichotomous or a count measure as our dependent variable. In addition, the IDEA measure of mobilized dissent is highly skewed toward zero; in cases where there is reported dissent, there is often only an instance or two of dissent in each country-year. In such a context, we are hesitant to employ a typical count model, which assumes a much more uniform distribution across the count, or a zero-inflated count model, which assumes an abundance of 0s rather than an abundance of 1s.

41. Although we include a wide range of event types we believe to be representative, the binary coding treats any dissent event of any size or level of violence as the same. The formal theory assumes the group will choose a level of dissent from a continuous range, such that obligation to a treaty should lead to a lower level of dissent under certain conditions. For purposes of empirical estimation, however, we translate this concept as the continuous likelihood of observing a dissent event. These data are described in more detail in Ritter 2014 and its online materials.

In the utility functions of the formal model, the term θ captures the leader's expected value for retaining power,[42] which decreases if he loses policy control to the group. This expected value is the combination of two concepts: the benefits the leader receives from holding power (we sometimes call this their *value for power or office*) and the likelihood that the leader will retain that power (we sometimes call this their *job security*). If the leader is very likely to lose office, or if holding that office does not have many benefits relative to losing it, the leader will repress less and then not be constrained by the court or the treaty. If holding power is extremely beneficial, either because the leader expects to retain it for the foreseeable future or because it comes with meaningful emotional or material rewards, they will repress more to control the policy and thereby retain that position.

We need a measure that (a) captures the leader's expected value for retaining power and (b) is something that observant dissidents could also estimate. We therefore assume for purposes of measurement that the benefits of holding power are constant across leaders but that the probability with which power is held varies by leader. In doing so, we implicitly assume all leaders prefer having power to losing it, but they differ in how likely they are to hold on to it.[43]

To gauge how vulnerable a leader is, both sides do some calculations using observable facts. Dissidents think about things like whether the leader is old, inexperienced, embattled, or sick, as well as whether their policies have been economic or political failures; such negatives add up to make a leader increasingly vulnerable. When vulnerable, leaders do not fight for their policies, so dissidents do not have to work hard to change the status quo. Leaders also think about how vulnerable they are; if they are on the way out anyway, they have little incentive to repress. Because both actors are using observable facts besides the repression/dissent dynamic to decide whether to repress and dissent, our statistical model has to include measures that stand in for these calculations about how vulnerable the

42. Expected value is a game theoretic term referring to the fact that a person considers not only the material benefits of an event but also the probability with which they will receive those benefits. The idea is partially akin to a lottery, in that one considers not only the payout but also the likelihood of receiving that payout.

43. Alternatively, we could measure the expected value with a continuous measure of resources, postturnover fate (Debs and Goemans 2010), or the expectation of continued policies (Licht 2010, 2015; Mattes, Leeds, and Matsumura 2016). We could also multiply these concepts together: the probability of retention times the value for retention. Any of these permutations would function in the theoretical and empirical models in the same way as what we have chosen here: as either of these concepts increase, we expect leaders to repress more to protect their position and to therefore be more likely to face institutional constraint.

leader is—calculations that predate, and are therefore exogenous to, the conflict event.

Both the leader and the dissenting group share a common expectation of the leader's security. While the task of measuring such an assumption may seem heroic, it is a necessary assumption for any theory that assumes complete information. The theoretical model assumes that both the government and the group look to the same set of observable elements and draw estimates with some amount of error. It is possible that leaders may have more information about their true chances of removal, which could alter conflict choices from what we have posited. However, this asymmetric information should not mean that their chances are systematically better or worse than the group's estimates. In other words, leaders could have information that reduces the *variance* of their own estimate, but that should not necessarily bias the average estimate away from that of the group.

Although it is difficult to measure actors' beliefs or expectations, we follow Cheibub (1998), who argues that political and economic factors affect the executive's actual probability of remaining in power. He uses parametric survival models to create empirical measures of job insecurity based on the leader's time in office, previous trends in leadership change, and annual economic growth. Because Cheibub's measure is limited, both geographically and temporally, we follow Young (2009) and estimate our own hazard models of executives' risk of turnover. The result is an estimate of executive job insecurity, modeled as a function of time-to-date in office,[44] previous trends in leadership change,[45] and economic growth.[46] Converting the hazard estimates to a probability of turnover yields a range from 0 (lowest probability of leadership turnover) to 1 (highest probability of leadership turnover). We reverse the scale to create the measure of EXECUTIVE JOB SECURITY used in the empirical models. Because, on average, leaders face a low probability of losing office in any given year (in Chapter 5), and especially, in any given country-month (in Chapter 6), the data are highly right-skewed (i.e., trend toward 1).

---

44. Goemans, Gleditsch, and Chiozza 2009.

45. Ibid. The measure accounts for previous leadership turnover, not the institutions that led to that turnover per se. This means that democratic leaders do not face lower values of executive job security in election years than in nonelection years. We do, however, run the estimates on samples distinguished by democracy and nondemocracy and present the results in the Online Appendix.

46. Using estimates as an independent variable introduces the measure's own error structure into the primary model. To adjust the variance-covariance matrix, we bootstrap the standard errors in our estimates.

The measure of EXECUTIVE JOB SECURITY captures expectations about the likelihood of the leader remaining in power. We prefer this operationalization over using one of the constituent measures (e.g., economic growth) on its own as a measure of expectations of security. To do so would be to suggest that factors like economic growth affect the likelihood of repression directly, rather than through the leader's expectation of remaining in power. In order to use this measure, however, we must assume that estimates of executive job security track with leaders' own beliefs about their likely tenure in office. We believe this to be a reasonable assumption, since each of the constituent measures that we use in the survival model—time-to-date in office, previous trends in leadership change, and economic growth—are fully observable to both government officials and potential dissidents.[47]

4.1.5 Probability of Domestic Litigation Consequences

International human rights treaty obligation increases the probability that a repressive government will incur costs via the domestic judiciary. The increase in consequences can occur because the treaty alters the content of domestic law, encourages more litigation, or empowers a judiciary to accept more cases or rule against authorities more frequently. If we do not find the patterns of evidence implied by the theory, this would suggest human rights treaties do not affect domestic politics in the way we have assumed—that perhaps they do not "boost" the probability of domestic consequences in this manner. We do not need an empirical measure of the increase; it is assumed in the theory. Importantly, however, the implications of the theory are conditional on the *extant* probability that the government will incur costs associated with a legal claim. If the court is not a place for remedy in their state, the treaty is an important change, but if the government is already constrained by a court, the treaty makes little difference. Treaty effects depend on existing judicial constraints.

We require a measure of the probability that the government will experience adjudication for repression. As described in Part I, the government

---

47. Following Young (2008), we also created an additional measure of job insecurity. Because leadership change in democracies is arguably different than leadership change in autocracies, our alternative measure of job insecurity accounts for previous trends in irregular leader change, the age of the leader, and the state's level of democracy. Our results are robust to the use of this alternative measure; we show some of these results in Chapter 6 and include the rest in the Online Appendix.

incurs costs simply by having to defend itself in court. Even if the court sides with the government, the process of a trial involves effort and resources to mount a defense, and the trial can create negative publicity and attention. Therefore, we need a measure that captures the probability that a suit—either civil or criminal—will be brought against a government actor. The majority of cases charging repression will be brought against government agents rather than leaders, but we assume that the leader (the decision-maker) incurs costs when agents are brought to trial, even if their costs are less than those of the agent under judicial scrutiny.

To measure the probability of experiencing litigation consequences, we use DOMESTIC JUDICIAL RIGHTS PROTECTION from Hill (2015). This measures the extent to which existing domestic laws encode civil, political, and personal integrity rights protection, which are the rights advanced by the HRTs we study here. To create the measure, Hill identifies constitutional provisions related to the protection of civil, political, and physical integrity rights using data from the Comparative Constitutions Project (CCP), which covers the years from 1805 to 2008.[48] He creates a summary measure of the underlying propensity to protect rights via domestic law, arguing, "One could treat the provisions listed above as functions of some unobserved characteristic of a country's legal system (*de jure* protection of civil/political/personal integrity rights) and derive estimates of the level of formal protection provided based on the presence/absence of such provisions."[49]

Hill employs an item response theory model to generate an estimate of an unobserved concept (i.e., extant judicial rights protection) as a function of observed characteristics (i.e., information on the constitutional protection of rights), noting that the model is *not* intended to measure constitutional protection: "The point is rather to treat various provisions as indicative of the protection provided by the domestic legal code generally, including non-constitutional law. The only assumption necessary to treat this as a valid indicator of the protection created by the broader domestic legal code is that the more extensive is *de jure* legal protection in domestic law, the more likely certain provisions are to appear in a nation's constitution" (ibid., p. 1139). The model produces a measure that ranges from -0.75 to 0.71, where higher values indicate domestic protections more in line with those of international law.[50]

48. Elkins, Ginsburg, and Melton 2009.
49. Hill 2015, p. 1139.
50. In Chapter 6, we also present several models in which we instead use a measure of JUDICIAL EFFECTIVENESS that accounts for several concepts: (1) whether judges are permitted to rule without interference (Keith 2002b; Staton and Moore 2011); (2)

This measure captures the baseline expectation of de jure rights protections: those protected by domestic law, outside of the treaty's legal obligations. Using this as an indicator of our concept assumes that people considering litigation use cues like constitutional protections, legislative policies, and legal rulings to form their expectations of how responsive the domestic legal environment will be to their claims of violation. We cannot be certain which type of indicator is closer to the information that potential litigants consider, but DOMESTIC JUDICIAL RIGHTS PROTECTION is a general and inclusive approximation of the existing legal environment before treaty obligation is undertaken.

We argue that as domestic consequences for repression increase, governments are less likely to choose to repress and dissidents are more likely to choose to dissent. The greater the domestic baseline for legal consequences, the smaller the treaty's effect will be on the government's already constrained behavior. In other words, we should observe smaller and smaller treaty effects on repression and dissent as domestic judicial rights protections increases. Therefore, we interact the measures of the probability of extant adjudication costs with EXECUTIVE JOB SECURITY in expectation of a decreasing magnitude in treaty effects as this probability increases.

4.1.6 Operational Hypotheses

By translating the concepts described in the theory into the measures described above, we can restate Implications 1 and 2 as operational hypotheses. Empirical estimations using observational data allow us to

---

whether judges' rulings are translated into policy (Cameron 2002; Staton and Moore 2011); and (3) whether the population believes the court is effective according to points (1) and (2) and is inclined to use it (Powell and Staton 2009). These concepts capture the likelihood that litigation will occur, as well as how likely it is to be costly to the government. The measure, which comes from Linzer and Staton 2015, was created using a heteroskedastic graded response item response theory model to cull information from eight existing measures of judicial independence, power, activity, and overall popular confidence in the rule of law to capture the underlying latent concept of JUDICIAL EFFECTIVENESS. It draws on data from Tate and Keith 2007, Howard and Carey 2004, Cingranelli, Richards, and Clay 2014, Marshall and Jaggers 2009, Clague et al. 1999, Feld and Voigt 2003, PRS Group 2009, and Gwartney and Lawson 2006, 2007. The information from these constituent measures means the final continuous indicator of JUDICIAL EFFECTIVENESS (which ranges from 0 to 1, where higher values represent higher levels of effectiveness) captures both what the court does and what the population expects it to do.

attempt to falsify these statements and learn more about the validity of our theory in the empirical world.

Hypothesis 1 (Government Repression) *As executive job security increases, HRT obligation has an increasingly negative effect on the likelihood of systemic repression. This effect decreases in magnitude as domestic judicial rights protection increases.*

Hypothesis 2 (Mobilized Dissent) *As executive job security increases, HRT obligation has an increasingly positive effect on the likelihood of mobilized dissent actions. This effect decreases in magnitude as domestic judicial rights protection increases.*

4.2 STRUCTURAL REQUIREMENTS
OF EMPIRICAL ANALYSIS

The structure of the formal theory presented in Part I provides guidance as to the structure of the data-generating process; that process informs how we should proceed with testing hypotheses using empirical models. In what follows, we discuss two issues that make assessing the empirical implications of our theory more challenging—counterfactual comparison and selection bias—and then describe the econometric models that we use to evaluate our operational hypotheses in the face of these challenges.

4.2.1 Counterfactual Comparison

Our theory provides predictions about two counterfactuals—alternatives to actual events, alternatives that did not occur. The term "counterfactual" was coined by Goodman (1947) to describe an if-then statement where the "if" is contrary to fact. The formal model yields predictions over the repression chosen by a government that selects into a treaty obligation. As discussed in Part I, comparative statics analysis of varying treaty status suggests what that government would have done if its institutional environment had differed. First, how would government repression and mobilized dissent differ if an unobligated government had actually committed itself to an HRT? Second, how would an obligated government differ in its conflict outcomes if it were *not* committed to the treaty?

We began this book by pointing out that if we want to examine the conditions under which international human rights treaties "work," we need to have a clear standard as to what that means. To develop this clear standard, we must have a concrete idea about what a positive effect would mean, as well as a reference point to which we can compare practices. Many people might agree with us that a statistically significant improvement in rights protection should be considered a positive effect, suggesting that a treaty is working the way it was intended. But positive as compared to what? This reference point differs quite a bit from scholar to scholar, leading to different and even conflicting conclusions regarding the effectiveness of international rights treaties on political conflict.

Posner succinctly characterizes the dominant approach used by social scientists studying human rights treaties: "For every state, one examines the state's treatment of the population before it enters into the treaty and after it enters into the treaty. If the Convention Against Torture (for example) has a causal effect, then a state's use of torture should decline after it ratifies the treaty (or possibly even before ratification if the government takes steps to reduce torture in anticipation of its future legal obligations to do so)—and the decline should be meaningful rather than trivial."[51] Indeed, social scientists often try to determine whether commitment to an international human rights treaty leads to a change in repression. Keith (1999) and Neumayer (2005) look for changes in repression patterns in the same year that a state ratifies a human rights treaty. Neither finds evidence of immediate improvement. Nor does Hafner-Burton (2005), who analyzes changes in rights protections one year after ratification. Others suggest that treaties are unlikely to change outcomes within short time horizons, and that we must examine whether states change their behavior over the long term.[52] Studies that examine the length of time it takes states to improve rights protections after ratification find no evidence that practices ever meaningfully improve relative to preratification practices.[53]

Other analysts compare countries to other countries, rather than to their former selves. When researchers include an indicator for treaty obligation in a regression model, they can draw conclusions by comparing observations of countries that are not obligated to observations of countries that are obligated. Matching processes also do this, looking for observations with a similar propensity to be obligated to a treaty in order to compare one that is obligated with one that is not. The idea is that comparing observations with similar propensities to ratify means the difference between them is as-if random.[54] The problem with these approaches is that HRT

51. Posner 2014, p. 72.
52. Hafner-Burton and Tsutsui 2007.
53. Hafner-Burton 2005; Hafner-Burton and Tsutsui 2007; Hathaway 2002.
54. Hill 2010; Lupu 2013b.

obligation is not random; it is chosen. A researcher cannot control for all the reasons that a leader might decide to obligate themselves—reasons that are correlated with their human rights records. Comparisons across states that are fundamentally different in their decision-making processes—no matter how similar in characteristics—are likely to be biased.[55]

The ideal way to draw conclusions about causal effects would be to compare a country in a given year to the very same country in the same year—one obligated to a treaty and one not obligated to a treaty—not to a dream of perfect compliance, not to a similar state, not to itself at a different point in time. Unfortunately for social scientists, once a government has decided to ratify or not to ratify a treaty, it has entered one pool of subjects or another, and the counterfactual is unobservable.[56] It is impossible to observe the repression and dissent that would have occurred in an uncommitted state if the same state had instead been obligated to an HRT; similarly, we cannot know what conflict outcomes would have occurred in a committed state if the obligation had not occurred in the first place. And since no two countries are identical on every relevant dimension of variance, we cannot estimate the effect of HRT obligation on conflict outcomes by comparing countries that committed to HRTs with those that did not; there are simply too many factors affecting repression and dissent on which to match countries for comparison.

Randomization is often used to solve the causal inference issues inherent in the counterfactual problem. By randomizing subjects (as in a medical trial, for example), researchers can assure balance or equality *on average* across two (or more) randomly assigned groups of subjects; by then offering some (but not all) of the subjects the "treatment," scholars can determine whether treatment has a causal effect on groups that are, on average, similar.[57] To pursue randomization in the context of our theory, we would need to recruit hundreds of countries and assign them randomly to groups that vary by domestic legal environments, leader security, and treaty status—at least eight different assignment groups. Unfortunately, absent the ability to assign varying characteristics of legal environments, leader security, and treaty obligation, we cannot study treaty effects as if they are

55. In addition, we prefer a two-stage model because we have a theoretical expectation that selection into the treatment has errors that are correlated with errors in the outcome stage. Matching models account for nonrandom treatment assignment, but not selection bias. A two-step process allows us to account for the extent to which errors in the outcome stage are strictly associated with the selection process, approximating exogeneity for errors that remain.

56. Holland 1986; Imai, King, and Stuart 2008.

57. Gerber and Green 2012; Holland 1986; Imai, King, and Stuart 2008.

randomly assigned. We are left to move beyond the laboratory in search of a research design that uses observational data, but preserves our ability to draw causal inferences and compare a treated environment to an untreated environment and vice versa. We do this by estimating counterfactuals with statistical models.

4.2.2 Selection Bias

In theory and in the observed world, countries are not randomly assigned treaty status; they select into it. Leaders (and, in many cases, legislatures) have great discretion about whether or not to obligate their governments to the terms of HRTs, and decisions about membership are based on both domestic and international considerations.[58] Helfer (2002), for example, acknowledges this when he argues that governments may select out of treaty commitments entirely if they worry about being subject to supranational adjudication for violations of human rights. Because governments *decide* whether or not to commit to international human rights law, it is much more challenging to determine the effect of HRTs on domestic political outcomes like government repression and popular dissent; the factors affecting the conflict behaviors also affect the decision to commit to international law in the first place. Although this point is made often in research related to the effect of human rights treaty obligation on government repression,[59] it is equally relevant for investigating the effect of HRTs on opposition dissent.[60] If the connection between international human rights treaties and conflict is one of self-selection, rather than treatment effects, then we cannot claim the treaty caused the changes in repression.[61] To state it differently, if governments enter a treaty because they expect it cannot say that the treaty is doing the work if that state does not repress.

In several studies, scholars argue that other factors affect both commitment to international human rights law and government repression, such that treaties are spurious or external to the true cause of repression. Vreeland (2008a), for example, argues that leaders who face organized domestic oppositions respond to antagonism with torture—and at the

---

58. See, e.g., Goodliffe and Hawkins 2006; Nielsen and Simmons 2015.
59. See, e.g., Conrad and Ritter 2013; Hill 2010; Lupu 2013b; Powell and Staton 2009; von Stein 2016; Vreeland 2008a.
60. Ritter and Conrad 2016a.
61. Cf. Downs, Rocke, and Barsoom 1996; Hill 2010; Lupu 2013b; Simmons and Hopkins 2005; von Stein 2005.

same time with concessions in the form of obligation to the CAT. In this argument, the presence of an organized domestic political opposition group affects both the government decision to repress *and* the government decision to ratify an HRT; HRTs are not argued to have a causal effect on human rights practices. Other scholars have argued that governments wishing to attract foreign aid may commit to international human rights law[62] and decrease repression,[63] not because international obligations influence rights violations but because the desire for foreign aid influences both commitment and compliance.

These examples help us to illustrate a key point: the factors affecting domestic conflict also influence the government's decision regarding whether or not to commit to an HRT.[64] States join treaties in two primary cases: when they already have good practices[65] and when they explicitly expect to continue to violate rights despite being legally bound to protect them.[66] States do not join treaties when they expect the costs of compliance to be high or uncertain.[67] This creates a process of self-selection: obligated states have particular institutional or behavioral characteristics that are correlated with a certain type of rights protections, while unobligated states do not have these characteristics. The governments that would have to change their behavior most radically tend not to ratify international human rights treaties, and those that do ratify tend not to change their behavior much following ratification. These decisions result in a set of nonrandom tendencies that can bias observers into thinking that international human rights law has little or no effect on government behavior.

If there is self-selection at work, it becomes difficult to disentangle whether international human rights treaties (1) have a real effect on human rights outcomes, or (2) are spurious, in that something else codetermines obligation status and conflict outcomes. Importantly, this self-selective process implies that the effect of an international human rights treaty on government repression and popular dissent will differ across the states that have ratified HRTs and those that have not. This is explicitly what we expect from the strategic model presented in Chapter 3. Countries that expect that committing to an HRT will lead to a large difference in their repression behavior will tend to opt out of the obligation, whereas

---

62. See, e.g., Goodliffe and Hawkins 2006; Oberdorster 2008; Posner 2008.

63. See, e.g., Lebovic and Voeten 2009.

64. See, e.g., Hill 2010; Lupu 2013b; Powell and Staton 2009.

65. Downs, Rocke, and Barsoom 1996; Hathaway 2003; Simmons 2009.

66. Hafner-Burton and Tsutsui 2007; Hollyer and Rosendorff 2011; von Stein 2016; Vreeland 2008a.

67. Hathaway 2003; Simmons 2009.

countries that expect less constraint will be more willing to commit themselves to a treaty. The two samples of governments—HRT-obligated and HRT-unobligated—should exhibit different patterns of effects.

Most social science scholarship now takes this self-selection process into account when using observed data to estimate the effect of treaties on rights practices, and most rely on methodological innovations to compensate for the bias before predicting behavioral outcomes for governments that choose to ratify. For instance, many scholars use the workhorse of a two-stage, instrumental variable regression model. This approach models the likelihood that a government would decide to ratify a treaty, given that the decision is a function of the expected compliance. The process accounts for the fact that obligated countries are not randomly selected to ratify HRTs; using a standard selection model allows social scientists to "correct" the likely bias from selection and focus on the effect of ratification on compliance.[68] Other researchers have used matching techniques to establish the propensity of a given country to be a ratifier or a nonratifier, allowing scholars to draw inferences by comparing the human rights behavior of two countries with similar propensities to ratify—one that did join and one that did not.[69]

These methodological approaches to accounting for bias (two-stage models or matching techniques) tend to treat selection bias as a nuisance rather than a process to be understood; they strip out the errors that are correlated across stages and discard them rather than studying the selection process. Two-stage least squares approaches model the correlation of errors across the selection and compliance stages,[70] allowing the researcher to focus on the treaty's effect on compliance for cases that are *not* correlated across the two stages.[71] Some models, such as the most common selection model by Heckman (1979), look only at observations that select into the pool of ratified states, dropping from the analysis those that select out of ratification. For scholars who are not interested in the ways ratification is connected to compliance, dropping these cases and sets of correlated errors is fine for analyzing treaty effects. Matching techniques account for the nonrandom nature of ratification, but the comparison between similar countries with different statuses essentially assumes ratification status to be as-if random, when we know that not to be true.[72] Consequently,

68. Examples of studies that use this approach include, inter alia, Cole 2012, Landman 2005, and Simmons 2009.

69. See, e.g., Hill 2010; Lupu 2013b; Simmons and Hopkins 2005.

70. Imbens and Angrist 1994; Wooldridge 2002.

71. Dunning 2008; Keele and Morgan 2016; Sovey and Green 2011.

72. Cole 2015; von Stein 2016.

most scholars recognize and account for the methodological problems of selection bias without theorizing, understanding, and modeling the selection process itself.

In contrast to the dominant social science approaches to the study of treaty outcomes, we examine the selection process theoretically and estimate empirical relationships in accordance with our expectations, allowing us to draw inferences about treaty effects. First, we use a concept of effectiveness that considers the ramifications of treaty obligation for both committed *and* uncommitted states. Second, we derive theoretical implications conditional on the state's choice to select into one sample of states or the other, so that we have explicit expectations as to how those samples should differ in treaty effects. Finally, we use an empirical estimator to account for the correlated errors that plague statistical analyses of selection problems, but we still examine how these errors affect the members of each sample, rather than treating the bias as a nuisance.

We use a broader concept of treaty effects than simple *compliance*.[73] Compliance occurs when a government's behavior is in line with the explicit rules and agreements it is obligated to obey.[74] In contrast, we are concerned with *effectiveness*, or whether a country's human rights practices do or would improve if the country is or were obligated to a human rights agreement. Importantly, a treaty can have an effect if a state conforms to prescribed behavior[75] (the focus of common understandings of compliance) or if the state would have had to alter its practices if it had ratified the treaty. The latter requires us to look at countries that do not ratify treaties and estimate the difference between their human rights practices and what their behavior would have been under the opposite counterfactual. If countries systematically select out of the obligation in a pattern consistent with avoidance of constraint, that would suggest that the treaty has (or would have) a meaningful effect even in those cases.

The formal theory has a structure that suggests particular conflict behaviors for particular state characteristics in equilibrium. Moreover, given

---

73. This discussion may cause some confusion, given that the title of the book is *Contentious Compliance*. We selected this title because we argue that the decision to protect rights (considered compliance with international obligations) is a process of contention, as defined by McAdam, Tarrow, and Tilly (2004). Further, the question of whether countries generally do or do not comply with their human rights obligations (as well as why) is a matter of contention among scholars. Nevertheless, the concept of interest to us is effectiveness, not merely compliance.

74. Simmons 1998, p. 77.

75. Young 1979.

the countries' beliefs about how obligation would constrain their current conflict behaviors, we determine which countries would, in equilibrium, opt in to international treaties. Comparative statics analysis enables us to look deeper. We derived precise predictions as to the expected differences in government repression and mobilized dissent behavior in the two kinds of states, using the selection process to understand more details about whether and how international human rights treaties alter political outcomes.

To do so, we use an empirical model that allows us to think carefully about the HRT ratification process, identify its differential effects on human rights behavior, and draw inferences about treaty effects under the concept of effectiveness or difference rather than compliance. We build on a treatment model described by von Stein (2005), which estimates the probability that a country will ratify a treaty in expectation of its effects and then estimates the effect of the treaty on both ratifiers and nonratifiers. This model enables us to estimate predicted differences in repression behavior if a country that ratified a treaty had not been able to do so *and* if a country that did not ratify were made to do so. We are able to analyze the behavior of governments in accordance with many of the implications of our theory, providing a stronger and more insightful analysis than other methodological approaches to the problem of selection bias.

4.2.3 The Solution: A Two-Stage Treatment Estimator

The empirical implications of the theory concern the causal effect of an international human rights treaty obligation, as conditioned by two other factors—the probability of litigation costs and ex ante expectations about the leader's security in office—on two outcomes: government repression and mobilized dissent. One-stage statistical models do not allow us to deal with the counterfactual and selection issues. We need an empirical estimator that (1) accounts for the lack of independence across the decision to commit to an HRT and the decisions to repress and dissent, and (2) allows us to estimate effects of differential treaty status on both samples of states, those that select into a treaty commitment and those that do not.

We use a two-stage treatment model based on von Stein (2005) to estimate the average treatment effects of commitment to international law on repression and dissent. The estimator is similar to a traditional selection model in that it accounts for observed factors that affect HRT membership decisions and correlated errors across the selection and outcome stages.[76] For our purposes, it is superior to a more traditional selection model because it accounts for unobserved factors that affect the commitment decision; it also "estimates the outcome equations for signatories and non-signatories separately... [and] does not assume that the independent variables affect the restriction behavior of the two groups in the same manner."[77]

The treatment model estimates *three* equations—an equation predicting the treatment assignment of HRT obligation, an equation predicting government repression or mobilized dissent in signatory states, and an equation predicting government repression or mobilized dissent in nonsignatory states.[78] We can then use the parameters estimated in these equations (which include the selection process) to compare the predicted probabilities of repression and dissent for the observed subsamples to counterfactuals that differ hypothetically in their treaty status. In this way, we can differentially estimate two treatment effects for each of our dependent variables using observational data, accounting for the unobservable processes related to selection into the treaty.

We estimate the likelihood of selection into obligated and unobligated status for each country-year and then the likelihood of repression/dissent for each selected sample. The conditional variables—executive job security and the probability of domestic adjudication costs—are included in both (a) the selection equation that estimates the likelihood that a government would or would not be obligated to an HRT in a given year and (b) the respective outcome equation for the two selected samples. Furthermore, we

76. Simmons and Hopkins (2005) criticize the von Stein estimator on several grounds. First, selection models are notoriously sensitive to model specification (e.g., Sartori 2003; Signorino and Yilmaz 2003). Our results are highly robust to myriad model specifications, including alternative measures of each of our measures. Second, in cases where the independent variables in the selection and outcome equations are the same, the model is identified exclusively on distributional assumptions. Simmons and Hopkins (2005) argue that von Stein (2005) does not justify the independent variables in her selection equation, which we have done extensively in this chapter. Finally, von Stein (ibid.) includes in her selection equation a binary indicator coded "1" in all years following the year of the initial commitment. This indicator is argued to violate the nonquasi-complete separation assumption (e.g., Albert and Anderson 1984; Simmons and Hopkins 2005). We do not include this indicator in our models, though the main obligation variable functions similarly. This means that states do not drop out of our sample when they first commit to the HRT, as they would if we predicted the onset of commitment. However, we assume that states can move between samples at any time, and they do so as appropriate in the estimated models.

77. von Stein 2005, p. 617.

78. For information on the derivation of the likelihood function, see von Stein (ibid.).

include an interaction term that multiplies EXECUTIVE JOB SECURITY by the measures of adjudication costs in the outcome and selection equations.[79]

To meet the exclusion restriction of the selection stage of our model, we require a measure of a concept that is correlated with government obligation to HRTs but is not known to affect government repression or popular dissent.[80] Powell and Staton (2009) include in their empirical model of HRT commitment a measure of the number of international NGOs to which citizens are members within a given country-year. In part because this measure limits the temporal domain of our analyses and in part because we believe it to be related to the government's repression decision,[81] we follow Mansfield and Pevehouse (2006, p. 149), who argue that the number of intergovernmental organization (IO) memberships a state maintains can approximate its affinity for international interdependence. Commitments in one area of international relations (e.g., trade or conflict) capture a state's affinity for international interdependence; as the number of memberships increases, we expect that countries will be more likely to commit to other areas of international law, including human rights law. Importantly, however, we do not expect compliance in one of these areas to be connected to compliance in another. The incentive structures of alliances or trade agreements, for example, are generally not available to state parties of human rights agreements. Indeed, while allies comply with their obligations most of the time,[82] states are often noncompliant with their obligations to international human rights law.[83]

Our measure of the number of intergovernmental organization (IO) memberships a state maintains during a given year, NUMBER OF IO MEMBERSHIPS, comes from the Intergovernmental Organizations (IOs) Data.[84] NUMBER OF IO MEMBERSHIPS includes diplomatic and trade organizations that are *unrelated* to human rights policies. The measure

---

79. Models in which the dependent variable is dichotomous produce inefficient estimates if there is temporal dependence within the units (Beck, Katz, and Tucker 1998). Our results are robust to the inclusion of a third-order polynomial time counter, t, t^2, and t^3, where t counts the period that the observation represents in each series (Carter and Signorino 2010), to account for temporal dependence. The confidence intervals for our tests on the CAT and the ICCPR increase in size; the confidence intervals for the CEDAW do not increase in size. These results are reported in the Online Appendix.

80. Sartori 2003, p. 112.

81. Murdie 2009; Murdie and Bhasin 2011; Murdie and Davis 2012.

82. Leeds 2003.

83. Hathaway 2002.

84. Ulfelder 2011.

counts several kinds of different IOs, ranging from the North American Treaty Association (NATO) to the European Union (EU) to the World Trade Organization (WTO). After dropping all organizations explicitly intended to improve human rights outcomes (e.g., the NATO Partnership for Peace, the Geneva Conventions, and several of the HRTs that are the focus of this book), there are eighteen potential IOs in the data to which states can be party.[85] Because many of the IOs are regional, however, the maximum observed value in our data is ten.

The measure captures a country's general affinity for international obligations, but it is unlikely to be related to government repression or opposition dissent—except through its effect on commitment to international law.[86] Obligation to international law in other areas is unlikely to be related to government repression or mobilized dissent; obligation to a trade agreement should not alter dissidents' expectations of repression or a state's desire to repress.[87]

4.2.4 Estimating Simultaneous Conflict Behaviors

In the formal model, repression and dissent are decisions that are endogenous and simultaneous. The government's expectations of popular dissent

85. The IOs include the European Union (EU), the North Atlantic Treaty Organization (NATO), the Organization for Security and Co-operation in Europe (OCSE), the Organisation for Economic Co-operation and Development (OECD), the Council of Europe (COE), the Commonwealth of Nations (CON), the General Agreement on Tariffs and Trade (GATT) or World Trade Organization (WTO), the Asia-Pacific Economic Cooperation (APEC), the Association of Southeast Asian Nations (ASEAN), the Southeast Asian Treaty Organization (SEATO), the Organization of American States (OAS), the Southern Common Market (MERCOSUR), the Organization of Petroleum Exporting Countries (OPEC), the Arab League, the International Organization of the French-Speaking World (OIF), the Economic Community of West African States (ECOWAS), the Organization of the Islamic Conference (OIC), and the Organization for African Unity (OAU). Because of its nearly universal membership, we do not include the United Nations.

86. We ran a number of additional tests to examine the usefulness of this instrument for our purposes, all of which can be found in the Online Appendix. Importantly, there is a distinct difference in the frequency of ratification among states that are "encouraged" by an above-average number of IO memberships and the frequency of those with a below-average number of memberships. Furthermore, Wald F-tests exceed 10 for every estimated model presented in the book, often exceeding 10 by a substantial amount. Finally, the instrument is relevant, being statistically related to HRT ratification according to simple regression and demonstrating the difference of frequency mentioned here.

87. Simmons (2009) argues that procedural ratification difficulty is related to (lack of) obligation to international human rights law, but not correlated with government human rights practices. As shown in the Online Appendix, our results are robust to the addition of an indicator of ratification difficulty and common-law status from Simmons (ibid.).

affect its decisions; a group's expectations of government repression affect its own decisions at the same time. Both actors observe the constellation of institutions around them—the values of the independent variables like HRT treaty status, domestic judicial effectiveness, and expectations of leader job security—and form expectations about what their opponent is likely to do with regard to violence, knowing their opponent is making similar calculations about government repression or about mobilized dissent at the same time.

Ideally, we should structure our empirical models to reflect this simultaneous structure. Endogenous processes can be modeled with simultaneous regression equations, with each process embedded in the other and estimated together. Recall, though, that the theory posits two sets of these simultaneous conflict processes: one in a country without a treaty obligation and one in the same country with a treaty obligation. We could estimate two separate sets of simultaneous equations, but the treatment—HRT obligation—is a non-random selection process for which we also need to account in the estimations. To actually account for the endogeneity of government repression and mobilized dissent empirically, we would need to estimate *five* equations (one selection equation and two simultaneous processes of two equations each), all estimated simultaneously with correlated errors. This type of model is beyond our capacity to specify, and more importantly, to interpret carefully.

Nevertheless, the empirical approach we use in the following chapters does implicitly account for the simultaneity of the conflict process in both selected and unselected contexts. Our *theoretical* model endogenizes the behaviors, yielding precise expectations as to what the effect of treaty status should be on government repression given the expectation of endogenous opposition dissent, and vice versa. The derived empirical patterns should only emerge if repression and dissent come about in a process consistent with the one we have posited. Therefore, it is not necessary to model the simultaneous process explicitly to be able to assess whether the data-generating process aligns with our assumptions about the effects of HRT obligation on domestic conflict. Instead, we estimate the effects of international human rights treaty obligation: on government repression in Chapter 5 and on mobilized dissent in Chapter 6.

CHAPTER 5

༄

Substantive Empirical
Results: Government Repression

I n recognition of International Human Rights Day in 2015, United Nations (UN) High Commissioner for Human Rights, Zeid Ra'ad Al Hussein, pointed to the importance of international human rights treaties (HRTs) as tools to decrease state repression, indicating that HRTs "have played an important role in securing better respect and recognition [of rights] during the past five at-times turbulent decades."[1] Although research suggests that treaties are unlikely to protect rights—by extension, suggesting that international organizations (IOs) and nongovernmental organizations (NGOs) should not advance international law as a solution to violations—we hypothesize that HRTs can sometimes improve human rights outcomes.

More specifically, we argue that human rights treaties have a variable effect on government repression as a function of the leader's expected benefits from and likelihood of retaining political office. Leaders who are likely to lose office regardless of domestic conflict over policies repress at similar levels whether or not they are obligated to a treaty. Conversely, leaders who have a high expected value for remaining in power are more likely to repress; because treaty obligation can subject repressive leaders to heightened costs, we predict that leaders with higher job security repress *less* when their governments are committed to HRTs than we would expect the same governments to repress if they were not so obligated.[2]

---

1. VOA News 2015.

2. In our theory, the effect of HRTs on government repression is also conditional on the probability that leaders face litigation costs for repression. We include that

In this chapter, we use the treatment models described in Chapter 4 to estimate, first, the probability that a government is obligated to an international human rights treaty—the CAT, the ICCPR, and the CEDAW. Second, for countries that are obligated to the terms of a particular HRT, we estimate the effect of the treaty on government repression relative to the counterfactual of how that country would have repressed if it were not treaty-obligated. For countries that are not obligated to a given HRT in a given year, we estimate the effect of a counterfactual treaty commitment on government repression relative to repression that actually occurred absent the treaty obligation. By comparing each government's level of repression under its observed treaty commitment status to the level of repression that it would have experienced under a counterfactual treaty-obligation condition, we are able to estimate the effect of international human rights law on various government violations of human rights.

Tables of results presenting estimated coefficients, standard errors, and other statistical parameters are located in Appendix 2 to this book. Table A2.1 reports the main estimates for government obligation to the CAT, Table A2.2 the main estimates for obligation to the ICCPR, and Table A2.3 the main estimates for obligation to the CEDAW. We present the estimates of the selection stage predicting treaty obligation status in the bottom halves of these tables and the estimates for the effect of that status on government repression in the top halves. Odd-numbered columns provide results for HRT-obligated countries, and even-numbered columns report results for countries that have not ratified the treaty in question. The parameter ρ represents the extent to which unobservable factors not captured in the selection stage affect the likelihood of SYS-TEMIC REPRESSION in both obligated and unobligated countries. In each estimated model, likelihood ratio (LR) tests of ρ for obligated countries compared to unobligated countries enable us to reject the null hypothesis that their joint effect is zero ($p = 0.000$ in all cases), which indicates the presence of selection effects like the ones we describe in Chapter 4. The estimates in Tables A2.1, A2.2, and A2.3 are the foundation of the main figures and inferences that we present in additional detail in this chapter. Given the complicated error correlations, interaction terms, and unobservables in these estimates, we focus in the bulk of this

conditionality in the empirical models (i.e., the tables) referenced in this chapter, but present our substantive effects (i.e., the figures) holding the operationalization of that concept at its in-sample mean rather than at variable levels of judicial effectiveness. Figures showing the substantive effect of HRT obligation on government repression at different levels of the probability of litigation costs are available in the Online Appendix.

chapter on presenting the substantive results of our estimates in graphical form.[3]

5.1 PRESENTING RESULTS BASED ON COUNTERFACTUALS

The empirical model that we describe in Chapter 4 estimates the effects of the leader's expected value of retaining power and the probability that the government will face litigation costs on the outcome of government repression in HRT-obligated and nonobligated countries. But the basic empirical model does not allow us to easily interpret whether, how much, and under what conditions international human rights treaties affect repression (or popular dissent, which we discuss in Chapter 6) without doing a little additional legwork. To draw inferences about the causal effect of an HRT on government repression, we need to compare a country's actual repression to what the government would have done if it were in the opposite treaty status (i.e., the extent to which HRT-committed countries would have repressed had they not ratified a treaty and the extent to which uncommitted countries would have repressed had they ratified a treaty). Looking across all countries in this manner, the average difference between actual repression and counterfactual repression is the average treatment effect (ATE) of an international treaty obligation.

As we noted in Chapter 4, however, it is impossible to observe (1) the repression that would have occurred in unobligated countries had those same countries committed to an HRT, and (2) the repression that would have occurred in HRT-obligated countries had they remained outside the terms of a given treaty. Instead, we estimate the difference between what would have happened to a country in one status if it were subjected to the other, counterfactual status: if HRT-obligated countries *did not* ratify

---

3. To ensure that our reported empirical results do not occur simply because of the measures we selected to operationalize each of our concepts, we conduct a variety of robustness checks for each of the empirical tests that are described in detail in this chapter. For example, in their baseline model of government repression, Hill and Jones (2014) demonstrate that many typically used covariates have limited effects on the ability to predict repression. In addition to democracy and civil conflict, they show that domestic courts and youth bulges are good predictors of government repression. Our empirical results are generally robust to the inclusion of these covariates (and others) in our models. Moreover, we find that all of the international human rights treaties are estimated to have our predicted effects whether or not there is prior rights protection (which accounts for the fact that laws may or may not be supported in practice). We discuss a portion of those robustness checks over the course of the chapter; additional robustness checks are available in the Online Appendix.

and if nonobligated countries *did* ratify international human rights law. To make either claim, we need to estimate the difference between the actual repression employed by a government and the repression that the government would have used if it were subjected to a different treaty status—a counterfactual treaty status.

We use the parameters from our estimated empirical models to predict probabilities corresponding to the observed and counterfactual scenarios. In what follows, we present a variety of figures using estimated theoretical counterfactual behavior and estimated actual behavior to showcase the substantive effects of international human rights treaty commitment on government repression. Because HRTs are intended to promote respect for a wide variety of human rights, the figures depict the effects of different HRTs on many different types of government repression. The figures are similar in that they all present the difference between (1) the predicted probabilities of government repression for the observed values of the variables, and (2) the predicted probabilities that would have occurred were a country to be placed—with its same characteristics and inclinations—in the opposite treaty treatment group. Put differently, we make two sets of comparisons from actual, observed government behavior to two counterfactuals: one in which all countries that have *not* committed to a treaty—the "control" sample—are made to ratify (i.e., treated), and one in which all countries that ratified the treaty—the "treated" sample—were imagined not to have such an obligation.

The first counterfactual, the average treatment effect on the controls (ATC), shows the "average effect, at the population level, of moving an entire population from untreated to treated."[4] In our case, the ATC shows the treatment effect if countries that choose not to be HRT-obligated were instead treated with an HRT obligation. To create figures illustrating the average treatment effect on the controls, we need to use the estimated parameters (which estimate the causal influence of a variable on the outcome of repression) from the outcome equations and the variable values for the states that have opted out of the HRT in a given year. In other words, we take what the average uncommitted state actually looks like and then use the estimated parameters from both the uncommitted equation and the committed equation to identify the difference that a treaty would make in that state's repression. To be more precise, we use the subsample average observed values of the variables for unobligated countries and insert them into the estimated unobligated equation to predict the probability

4. Austin 2011, p. 401.

of the average government engaging in systemic human rights violations. We then insert the same variable values into the obligated equation to predict what the same average unobligated countries would have done with a different HRT treatment. We plot the difference between the predicted probabilities of repression for the average uncommitted country for the real and counterfactual scenarios across the observed range of EXECUTIVE JOB SECURITY.[5] By estimating the probability with which a government would engage in repression by varying one dimension—its commitment status to international human rights law—we illustrate the predicted effect that such an obligation would have had on a unobligated government.

Figures representing the second counterfactual, the average treatment effect on the treated (ATT), illustrate the effect of human rights treaties for states that opted into treaty obligations: "the average effect of treatment on those subjects who ultimately received the treatment."[6] To create figures of the average treatment on the treated, we calculated the predicted probability of government repression using the estimated parameters for *obligated* governments with the values of all independent variables set at the means of that subsample. After estimating the probability of government repression that would have occurred had the obligated countries *failed to commit* to an international human rights treaty, we plotted the difference in these values across the range of EXECUTIVE JOB SECURITY. In short, the ATT provides information about what would happen if we were able to force all countries that are obligated to an international human rights treaty to renege on that commitment—or were able to prevent them from

---

5. We followed the process given in Brambor, Clark, and Golder (2006) for plotting marginal effects of a conditional hypothesis. The treatment model yields estimates of parameters for the selection and two outcome equations. We used repeated draws from a normal distribution defined by these estimated terms to simulate one thousand values of the model's parameters. For the unobligated sample, we used the simulated parameters from the unobligated outcome equation to calculate the predicted probability of SYSTEMIC REPRESSION, with the independent variables in the model set at their subsample means, EXECUTIVE JOB SECURITY set at zero, and HRT OBLIGATION set at zero. Next, we calculated the predicted probability of SYSTEMIC REPRESSION. We used the same unobligated subsample values for the independent variables, but we used the estimated model parameters from the *obligated* equation and set HRT OBLIGATION to one. We subtracted the first calculated predicted probability from the second predicted probability, then repeated this process at each 0.01 interval of EXECUTIVE JOB SECURITY up to a value of 1.0 (its maximum possible value). We graphed the first difference across the observed range of EXECUTIVE JOB SECURITY.

6. Austin 2011, p. 401.

committing to international law in the first place, despite their preference to join.[7]

For ease of interpretation, we are consistent in the presentation of the ATC and ATT figures in this chapter. Solid lines plot the predicted effect of a country's obligation to an international HRT on the probability of government repression (i.e., the difference in predicted repression behavior across actual and counterfactual obligation statuses) for each level of EXECUTIVE JOB SECURITY across its observed range. The estimated effects of HRT OBLIGATION are statistically significant when the upper and lower bounds of the 95 percent confidence intervals, drawn with dashed lines, do not encompass the horizontal zero lines. The right y-axis of each figure describes the marginal effect of moving a country from its actual treaty status to a counterfactual treaty status on SYSTEMIC TORTURE across the range of a leader's expected value of remaining in office. The left y-axis describes the histogram overlaid on each figure, listing the percentage of observations at each value of EXECUTIVE JOB SECURITY.

Before turning to our substantive results, readers should recall from Chapter 3 that governments considering HRT obligations generally have some expectation about how treaty ratification will constrain their ability to engage in repression; these constraint expectations influence the government's decision to commit to international law. Countries that will likely be the most constrained by obligation (in other words, the countries with the greatest difference between the repression they would like to use and the repression that they expect to be able to use) will opt out of HRTs; countries that foresee fewer consequences will be more willing to obligate themselves under international law. As a result of this self-selection process—because the treated and untreated populations differ systematically—the ATCs and ATTs presented below often differ in magnitude, even within the same empirical test;[8] our theory predicts that the magnitude of the effect of the ATCs will generally be larger than the magnitude of the effect of the ATTs.[9]

---

7. All ATT figures were created using similar procedures to those described in note 5.

8. Austin 2011, p. 411.

9. Computational simulations presented in Chapter 3 show that the gap between constrained repression and unconstrained repression is larger for countries that opt out of HRT obligations than for countries that commit to international law. However, most countries commit to human rights treaties over time, and this process leaves fewer (and less representative) cases in the unobligated pool from which to draw inferences, resulting in larger confidence intervals.

5.2 EFFECT OF CAT OBLIGATION
ON GOVERNMENT REPRESSION

We begin by discussing the effect of obligation to the UN Convention Against Torture and Other Cruel, Inhuman or Degrading Treatment or Punishment (CAT) on the government's use of systemic torture. The CAT expressly prohibits government authorities from ordering, allowing, or engaging in torture for any purpose. Moreover, the CAT, like many other international human rights treaties, obligates government parties to ensure that all acts of torture are criminal offenses under domestic legislation. Ratification requires obligated governments to adopt domestic laws if they do not already exist, refine existing laws so that they align with the international obligation, and, in common-law systems, appropriate international precedents developed through court cases around the world.[10] That means that new laws are put into place or existing laws are tweaked and reinforced, putting into place more standards that a victim can point to in a case against a violating authority. For example, Article 4 of the CAT states,

> (1) Each State Party shall ensure that all acts of torture are offences under its criminal law. The same shall apply to an attempt to commit torture and to an act by any person which constitutes complicity or participation in torture. (2) Each State Party shall make these offences punishable by appropriate penalties which take into account their grave nature.[11]

Following its signing of the CAT, the U.S. Congress passed 18 U.S. Code § 2340, which enacted the universal jurisdiction penal regime established by the CAT,[12] and 28 U.S. Code § 1350, the Torture Victim Protection Act (TVPA),[13] which related to the provision in CAT's Article 14 for civil redress, allowing victims of torture to file suit against state perpetrators in civil court. For an international human rights treaty to serve as the basis for claims raised by victims in the United States, Congress has to pass implementing legislation such as the TVPA; it has never been definitively decided by the courts whether criminal defendants can cite HRTs in their defense without such legislation.[14] Although the TVPA was intended to

---

10. Simmons 2009.

11. *Convention against Torture and Other Cruel, Inhuman or Degrading Treatment or Punishment* 1984.

12. *18 U.S.C. 2340A–Torture* 2011.

13. *Torture Victim Protection Act of 1991.*

14. Personal email from Beth Van Schaack, former executive director of the Center for Justice and Accountability (CJA); November 21, 2016.

serve victims of torture by *foreign* governments, it has been cited in court cases against the U.S. government.[15] NGOs such as the Center for Justice and Accountability (CJA)—a human rights organization based in San Francisco, California[16]—use civil litigation to hold violators of human rights (especially torturers) individually accountable under the Alien Tort Statute (ATS) and the TVPA. A senior member of CJA's staff highlighted the importance of U.S. ratification of the CAT for both the origination of their organization and their current work:

> After the United States became a signatory to the Convention Against Torture, it began implementing domestic legislation like the Torture Victims Protection Act. Such legislation helps give rise to organizations like CJA and likely would not have occurred without [international commitment].[17]

After CAT ratification in each state, international NGOs begin working to support litigants in domestic courts. The Association for the Prevention of Torture (APT), a Geneva-based NGO, conducts regular training workshops for domestic judges and attorneys to educate them on the use of the CAT in domestic adjudication. In 2009, for example, after Thailand committed to the CAT, the APT initiated a three-year campaign there, aimed at building judicial capacity by training judges and human rights lawyers.[18] APT also works toward the implementation of the CAT's required National Preventive Measures (NPMs), which issue annual reports on the status of human rights in their countries and support victims in their attempts to bring allegations of human rights violations before domestic courts.[19]

These examples suggest that obligation to the Convention Against Torture increases the probability that governments will experience litigation costs—a key assumption of the theory—both by adding to the canon of domestic law and by creating new (or reinforcing existing) situations in which obligated governments can be brought before a domestic court for rights violations; the CAT appears to add some variable probability that authorities will incur consequences for engaging in repression. Given this anticipated increase in the litigation costs associated with government violations of human rights, we predict that obligation to the CAT will lead to

15. See, for example, Meshal v. Higgenbotham, Case Number 14-5194, DC Circuit App. (2015).

16. Additional information on CJA is available at https://cja.org/.

17. Phone interview, October 4, 2010.

18. Association for the Prevention of Torture 2009.

19. For more detail on NPMs, see https://www.apt.ch/en/national-preventive-mechanisms-npms/.

a reduction of repression for leaders who have a high expected value for the retention of political office—those who would otherwise repress the most in the absence of obligation to an international constraint.

The substantive effects of CAT obligation on the likelihood of systemic torture—the ATC and ATT described above—are depicted in Figure 5.1. For countries that strategically choose to remain out of the purview of the Convention Against Torture, what change in behavior would we see if someone could "treat" them with the obligation? Figure 5.1a illustrates this predicted change. To create the estimate of the ATC for obligation to the CAT, we use the measurable characteristics of the average country in the unobligated group and estimate the predicted probability of countries in that group using torture as a widespread practice. We then subtract the estimates of the same average unobligated country if it were to have been in the obligated treatment. See note 5 in this chapter for the technical

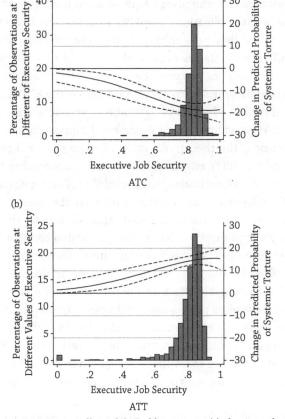

Figure 5.1 Average treatment effect of CAT obligation on (a) the controls (ATC) and (b) the treated (ATT) on the probability of SYSTEMIC TORTURE conditional on EXECUTIVE JOB SECURITY.

description of this process. Recall that we conceptualize the leader's expected value for retaining power as the combination of their value for the position and their probability of keeping it; we operationalize this concept using the latter, EXECUTIVE JOB SECURITY. Translating the measure back into the concept for interpretation, at the far left of Figure 5.1a is the effect of the CAT obligation for countries with leaders who value remaining in office the least. For the leaders with low job security, the effect of obligation to the Convention Against Torture is substantively very small and statistically indistinguishable from zero. Whatever level of repression these leaders use, it would not change if they were to become obligated to the Convention Against Torture. As we move to the right of Figure 5.1a and EXECUTIVE JOB SECURITY increases, the marginal effect of the CAT on the likelihood of systemic government repression becomes negative, crossing into traditional levels of statistical significance. Treaty obligation would decrease the probability that the modal unobligated country in our sample would engage in systemic government torture by nearly twenty points. Countries with leaders who place a high value on retaining office that have selected out of CAT obligation in real life would be less likely to engage in systemic torture if they were obligated under the international treaty.

Figure 5.1b represents the estimated effect that CAT obligation has on the behavior of countries that actually opted into the treaty relative to what they would have done absent treaty commitment—the ATT. As anticipated, estimating the effect of treaty obligation for those countries that actually do join the CAT provides additional empirical support for the hypotheses, and by extension, the theory. We calculated the marginal change in the probability of a country engaging in systemic torture using the opposite process of Figure 5.1a, estimating the probability of systemic torture for the average CAT-obligated country, estimating what the same country would do with only its treaty status changed, and subtracting the latter from the former. We hypothesized that a treaty-obligated country with a given level of repression would engage in comparatively *more* repression if it were not obligated under the CAT. Figure 5.1b supports this prediction. CAT obligation has a negligible effect on the probability of systemic torture in countries where leaders place a lower valuation on the retention of office. That effect increases in magnitude as leaders have a higher expectation of remaining in power. When EXECUTIVE JOB SECURITY is at its highest level, a country that was forced to revoke its obligation to the CAT would increase the probability of its engaging in systemic torture by approximately sixteen points.

As we predicted, the magnitude of the substantive effect shown in the ATC is larger than the one depicted by the ATT. This is consistent with our prediction that countries that would be the most constrained by a treaty tend to select out of the international commitment. This general trend continues with the presentation of the substantive effects of different treaties below.

5.2.1 Additional Test: Effect of OPCAT on Government Torture

When the CAT was adopted in 1984, a movement to create a protocol allowing for domestic inspection of prisons was not well received by the international community. Instead, the CAT came into existence with few mechanisms by which to directly hold noncompliant signatories accountable for their actions. The UN Committee Against Torture, which oversees the implementation of the CAT, was permitted to do little more than view self-reports from signatory countries about their own domestic human rights violations.[20] In an attempt to create an HRT that would further hold repressive governments accountable for torturing people, the UN Committee Against Torture created an Optional Protocol on the Convention Against Torture (OPCAT); the OPCAT opened to signatories in January 2003, but did not come into effect until June 2006 after it was ratified by a sufficient number of countries.

The OPCAT is unique among international human rights treaties and their optional protocols. It is the only international human rights document with a focus on the prevention of human rights violations, subjecting member states to increased international and domestic monitoring of human rights compliance.[21] The OPCAT calls for inspections of domestic places of detention: international inspections (via the UN Subcommittee for the Prevention of Torture, or SPT)[22] and national inspections (via state-established National Preventive Mechanisms, or NPMs). Countries

20. At the inception of the CAT, the committee also created special rapporteurs to investigate allegations of human rights violations, but these individuals are only permitted to conduct fact-finding missions at the invitation of a government.

21. All other HRTs are actionable only ex post. For example, the Optional Protocol to the International Covenant on Civil and Political Rights (ICCPR OP) allows only for individual citizens to bring a claim against their domestic governments ex post rather than mandating the implementation of preventative institutions ex ante. ICCPR OP does not have inspection capabilities or require its member states to make domestic changes; it merely allows a committee to hear complaints from victims when the state violates the treaty (Hafner-Burton and Tsutsui 2007).

22. In December 2006, states party to the OPCAT elected the ten members of the new International Subcommittee for the Prevention of Torture (SPT), enacted to monitor prisons and other holding places within the member states. Visits can be unannounced, and the members of the subcommittee have the right to interview prisoners without state representatives present.

that ratify the OPCAT are—in theory—committing to random SPT and NPM visits to places of detention to investigate human rights practices.

Ratifying the OPCAT deepens a state's commitment to the CAT; signatory states subject themselves to greater scrutiny and likely legal consequences if they allow or order torture. Therefore, OPCAT ratification is likely to increase the probability of litigation costs for leaders of obligated states more than ratification of the CAT on its own. We expect that, for leaders who have a high expected value for remaining in office, obligation to the OPCAT will decrease government repression more than CAT obligation. To test this idea, we collected data on ratification of the OPCAT beginning in December 2002,[23] coding OPCAT OBLIGATION as "1" in the year that a country ratifies the terms of the optional protocol, and in every year thereafter. To show the substantive effect of OPCAT OBLIGATION on government repression across the range of EXECUTIVE JOB SECURITY, we created the ATC and the ATT shown in Figure 5.2, using the same methods described above. The predicted effects shown in Figure 5.2a and 5.2b are consistent with the theory's implications across the range of EXECUTIVE JOB SECURITY.

When leaders do not place a very high value on remaining in power or are very likely to lose it, the effect of OPCAT obligation on government repression is not statistically distinguishable from zero. As leaders value office at higher levels, the ATC shows a decrease in the probability of SYSTEMIC TORTURE; the ATT shows an increase in the same. Consistent with our expectations regarding OPCAT obligation relative to CAT obligation, the point estimates when leaders value office the most are larger in magnitude for both the ATC and the ATT than those depicted in Figures 5.1a and 5.1b (e.g., an approximate decrease of forty points in the probability of SYSTEMIC TORTURE in the ATC and a similar increase in the probability of SYSTEMIC TORTURE in the ATT). Obligation to a deeper commitment has a larger effect on repression. Importantly, however, the confidence intervals in Figure 5.2 are much larger than the confidence intervals estimated for CAT OBLIGATION above. This is likely due to the shortened temporal domain of the empirical test, as well as the fact that far fewer countries have ratified the optional protocol than the CAT.

Although we have focused our argument primarily on the *obligation* to international human rights law on government repression, countries that *sign* international human rights treaties also send signals to potential dissidents—even if they fail to ratify their terms. Signing a human rights treaty can signal to potential dissidents a leader's intention to constrain himself with regard to repression, especially in countries where signing

---

23. The OPCAT opened for signatories in December 2002.

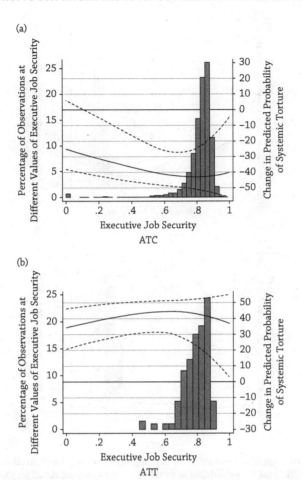

Figure 5.2 Average treatment effect of OPCAT obligation on (a) the controls (ATC) and (b) the treated (ATT) on the probability of SYSTEMIC TORTURE conditional on EXECUTIVE JOB SECURITY.

and ratification fall under the jurisdiction of different political actors and where ratification is subject to multiple potential veto points.[24] Because the OPCAT is arguably a more constraining HRT than the CAT, we suspect that signatory countries—not just ratifying countries—will engage in less torture when leaders place a high value on retaining office than they otherwise would, absent even such a token commitment to international human rights law.

Figures 5.3a and 5.3b show the ATC and the ATT for the effect of signing the OPCAT on the probability of systemic government torture.

24. See, e.g., Simmons 2009, Chapter 3.

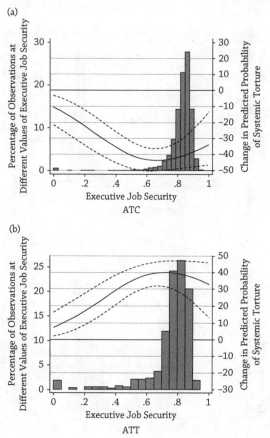

Figure 5.3 Average treatment effect of CAT signature on (a) the controls (ATC) and (b) the treated (ATT) on the probability of SYSTEMIC TORTURE conditional on EXECUTIVE JOB SECURITY.

The substantive effects of simply signing the Optional Protocol on the probability of government torture are consistent with our theoretical predictions—and quite large in magnitude compared to the size of the substantive effects of the other human rights treaties considered in this chapter. This suggests that the OPCAT is a much more constraining law than other international obligations *even in expectation*; just signing its terms leads to substantively large changes in the probability of government torture for leaders who highly value the retention of office. Note additionally that the confidence intervals surrounding these estimates are much smaller than those estimated in the context of OPCAT ratification above.

These results (as well as the robustness checks that we describe in the Online Appendix) suggest that the patterns of evidence are very consistent with the assumptions and predictions of our theory. When leaders are sufficiently motivated to torture (i.e., they have a high expected value for retaining office), obligation to the Convention Against Torture—and its associated Optional Protocol—reduces the probability of systemic torture as compared to the level of government torture that would have occurred absent such an obligation. Obligation to the CAT also would be very likely to reduce the probability of torture for similar leaders in countries that, in reality, decided not to ratify the terms in the treaty; it is the fear of such a constraint that keeps such leaders out of the purview of the international obligation in the first place.[25]

5.3 EFFECT OF ICCPR OBLIGATION ON GOVERNMENT REPRESSION

We find similar results when we estimate the effect of obligation to the International Covenant on Civil and Political Rights (ICCPR) on the likelihood of a country engaging in systemic torture. In addition to being illegal under the CAT, government torture is prohibited under the ICCPR's Article 7:

> No one shall be subjected to torture or to cruel, inhuman or degrading treatment or punishment. In particular, no one shall be subjected without his free consent to medical or scientific experimentation.[26]

To be clear, the ICCPR is a broad international human rights treaty, focusing not only on the elimination of torture, but on the protection of many different physical integrity and empowerment rights.[27] By analyzing the effect of both of these treaties—one specific to prohibiting torture

---

25. Additional empirical tests can be found in the Online Appendix. They suggest that our main results hold in both direction and statistical significance when we do the following: (1) operationalize adjudication costs using a measure of judicial effectiveness from Linzer and Staton (2015); (2) use as our dependent variable either a measure of latent protections for physical integrity violations from Fariss (2014) or a measure of government torture allegations from Conrad, Haglund, and Moore (2013); (3) control for temporal dependence using a third-order polynomial time-counter as advised by Carter and Signorino (2010); (4) include controls for dissent as measured by Banks (2010), latent protection for physical integrity right violations as measured by Fariss (2014), democracy as measured using Polity IV data (2009), media freedom as measured using data from Cingranelli, Richards, and Clay (2014), and youth bulges as discussed by Nordås and Davenport (2013); and (5) include as part of our instrument data a measure of the difficulty of a country's ratification procedures and a country's common-law status, as suggested and operationalized by Simmons (2009). Such detailed consistency implies the usefulness of the theory for understanding the effects of international human rights law on political conflict.

26. *International Covenant on Civil and Political Rights* 1966.

27. Some countries place reservations, understandings, or declarations (RUDs) on the extent to which they are committed under a given human rights treaty (e.g., Hill 2015; Neumayer 2007). The United States, for instance, ratified the ICCPR, but

and one much more general—on the likelihood of the same repressive activity, we can learn more about how different types of international human rights treaties affect state and leader behavior. The mechanism described in Chapter 2 of how treaty obligation changes the structure of the leader's decision is straightforward: it raises the probability that the leader will incur domestic legal consequences for repressing. We do not make theoretical claims as to how that marginal increase in litigation costs might differ by type or specificity of treaty. Since the argument rests on the concept of altered expectations, we might expect that a more general treaty would create more vague or varied assumptions among all actors, where the more narrow CAT sends a clear signal of which form of repression will be limited. However, this is conjecture on our part. Therefore, investigating the effect of the ICCPR on government torture does not only serve as an analysis of our theory; it also serves as an exploratory study of how specific versus general international laws differ in their likely effects on government repression.

Consider the average treatment effect of committing to the ICCPR on those countries that strategically avoided the obligation, depicted in Figure 5.4a. When EXECUTIVE JOB SECURITY is relatively low, the dashed lines of the estimated change in the probability of SYSTEMIC TORTURE resulting from commitment are substantively very close to zero, suggesting that ICCPR obligation has little meaningful effect on whatever torture decision government authorities make when they place little value on the retention of office or otherwise expect to lose it. This is not to suggest, of course, that these countries do not torture—only that their choice of torture does not differ systematically as a function of obligation to international human rights law. Moving from left to right in Figure 5.4a, leaders are more likely to value the retention of power; for leaders who highly value office (and the

placed sixteen reservations on its terms—six more than any other government that has ratified the covenant (Hill 2015). Reservations are qualifications that governments place on commitment to international law before they sign and/or ratify a particular treaty, usually exempting a state from commitment to a particular clause. They are intended "…to exclude or to modify the legal effect of certain provisions of the treaty in their application to that State" (*Vienna Convention on the Law of Treaties (1969)?*, Article 2.2). Although they exist in other areas of international law (see, e.g., Koremenos and Hong 2010; Koremenos, Lipson, and Snidal 2001), reservations are most commonly used in human rights law (Neumayer 2007), a fact that has been lamented by the UN Human Rights Committee (Redgwell 1997). Where an HRT might have altered laws, perceptions, or judicial practice, reservations remove the state's obligations to particular clauses. Although we do not conduct an empirical test of the effect of such treaty ratification because we do not consider strategic reservations in our theory, we suspect that—if reservations reduce the effect of HRT obligations on the probability of domestic adjudication—our proposed theoretical effects would lessen in magnitude as states place more reservations on their international obligations.

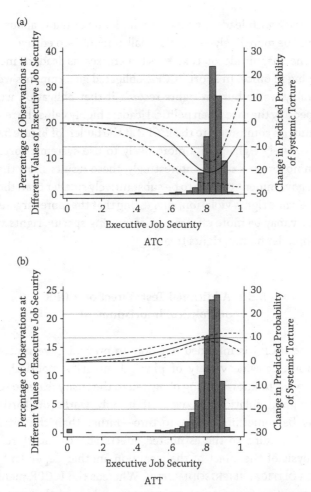

Figure 5.4 Average treatment effect of ICCPR obligation on (a) the controls (ATC) and (b) the treated (ATT) on the probability of SYSTEMIC TORTURE conditional on EXECUTIVE JOB SECURITY.

perks that come with it), obligation to the ICCPR would result in additional protections for human rights—if those leaders were to have ratified it. The solid line indicating predicted marginal effects shifts below the horizontal zero line, as do the confidence intervals indicating statistical significance. Government authorities that have so far selected out of obligation to the ICCPR would become significantly less likely to engage in systemic torture as a result of a counterfactual ICCPR commitment.

The ATT shown in Figure 5.4b provides even stronger evidence that ICCPR obligation can—under certain conditions—lead to decreases in government violations of human rights. When countries that are, in reality, obligated to the ICCPR are hypothetically relieved of that obligation, even countries with leaders who care a middling amount about retaining office would be more likely—albeit a small amount—to engage in systemic torture. The magnitude of that effect increases as leaders increasingly value staying in office. In short, ICCPR-obligated governments would have demonstrably worse human rights records if that obligation were lifted. This is especially the case when political leaders highly value the retention of office: countries committed to the ICCPR at the far left of Figure 5.4b would be approximately eight points more likely to use systemic torture if the obligation no longer existed. Interestingly, these results show the ICCPR's effects on government torture to be substantively smaller than those of the CAT on the same rights violation, suggesting that the more targeted human rights treaty may be more effective in decreasing specific rights violations than the broader human rights treaty.

5.3.1 Additional Test: Effect of ICCPR on Political Imprisonment

Because the ICCPR is intended not only to prevent government torture but to protect a wide variety of physical integrity, political, and civil rights, we want to know if being obligated to the treaty leads to reductions in other rights violations as well. If it only works on torture, then there may be something about torture—rather than the international law—that is leading to the estimated effects above. Therefore, we turn to an analysis of the effect of the treaty on another dependent variable: SYSTEMIC POLITICAL IMPRISONMENT.[28] Whereas the ICCPR mentions the right to protection from government torture only once, the treaty includes lengthier provisions covering individual rights related to detention and imprisonment: these rights are explained in Article 8 (on slavery, servitude, and compulsory labor), Article 9 (on arbitrary arrest and detention and the right to legal remedy), Article 11 (on rights while detained), and Article 11 (on imprisonment and contractual obligations).[29]

Figure 5.5 shows the effect of ICCPR obligation on the probability of a country engaging in the systemic imprisonment of individuals for political reasons across our two counterfactual conditions. The ATC in Figure 5.5a shows the estimated changes in the probability that the government will engage in systemic practices of political imprisonment if an unobligated government were to commit to the ICCPR. The results echo the effects

28. Table A2.2 in the Appendix reports these results.
29. *International Covenant on Civil and Political Rights* 1966.

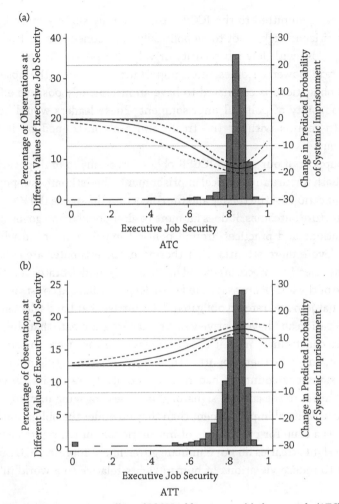

Figure 5.5 Average treatment effect of ICCPR obligation on (a) the controls (ATC) and (b) the treated (ATT) on the probability of SYSTEMIC POLITICAL IMPRISONMENT conditional on EXECUTIVE JOB SECURITY.

of the ICCPR on the likelihood of systemic government torture. The ICCPR has a substantively negligible effect on the probability of systemic imprisonment in countries whose governments are headed by leaders that place a relatively lower valuation on the retention of office. In countries headed by leaders who highly value remaining in power, however, ICCPR ratification can lead to over a fifteen-point decrease in the probability that a country systematically engages in widespread political imprisonment.

The ATT shown in Figure 5.5b tells a similar story about the normatively positive effect of the International Covenant on Civil and Political Rights on the extent of government repression. When obligated governments are.

no longer committed to the ICCPR, they are only slightly more likely to violate citizens' rights not to be politically imprisoned if their leaders are among those with low job security or value for power. As the retention of political power becomes more important to leaders, the absence of ICCPR obligations is estimated to have an increasingly positive effect on the probability of political imprisonment. These leaders would be more likely to repress without the treaty and are constrained by it in the status quo.

In support of our theory, ICCPR obligation seems to limit government use of both torture and political imprisonment. The estimates support both the implications of the theory and the conjecture that while the ICCPR does affect torture outcomes, it does far more to alter popular and governmental expectations and practices around political imprisonment, to which its terms devote more attention. Furthermore, the estimates are consistent with the selection effects predicted in the formal model. States that remain outside of the ICCPR are associated with deeper estimated constraints than those that join and remain obligated.[30] Countries that have selected out of the obligation and have relatively secure leaders anticipate that they would be more constrained in their use of repression if they were to commit. In contrast, and in further support of the theory, if the treaty did not exist—if actual signatory countries had no opportunity to ratify its terms—we would expect to see current signatory countries engaging in more torture and more political imprisonment than they do under the obligation.[31]

This is a coup for proponents of international human rights law: while human rights treaties do not eliminate government repression, treaties do appear to reduce violations of human rights relative to a world in which

---

30. We do not test for statistically identifiable differences between the size of the effect in the ATT and ATC. As this is an ancillary claim of the theory, we use the eyeball test on this one.

31. As above, additional empirical tests can be found in the Online Appendix. They suggest that our main results hold in both direction and statistical significance when we (1) operationalize adjudication costs using a measure of judicial effectiveness from Linzer and Staton (2015); (2) use as our dependent variable a measure of latent protections for physical integrity violations from Fariss (2014), a measure of government torture allegations from Conrad, Haglund, and Moore (2013), or a measure of LOW VIOLATIONS from Cingranelli, Richards, and Clay (2014) rather than SYSTEMIC VIOLATIONS; (3) control for temporal dependence using a third-order polynomial time-counter as advised by Carter and Signorino (2010); (4) include controls for dissent as measured by Banks (2010), latent protection for physical integrity right violations as measured by Fariss (2014), democracy as measured using Polity IV data (2009), media freedom as measured using data from Cingranelli, Richards, and Clay (2014), and youth bulges as discussed by Nordås and Davenport (2013); and (5) include as part of our instrument data a measure of the difficulty of a country's ratification procedures and a country's common-law status, as suggested and operationalized by Simmons (2009).

both general international treaties like the ICCPR and more specific ones like the CAT did not exist.

5.4 EFFECT OF CEDAW OBLIGATION ON GOVERNMENT REPRESSION

Finally, we turn to the results of estimating the effect of obligation to the Convention on the Elimination of Discrimination Against Women (CEDAW) on government repression. Whereas the ICCPR prohibits many different kinds of human rights violations for all persons living in obligated countries, and the CAT makes one specific activity illegal for all persons, the CEDAW focuses on protecting a wide variety of political, economic, and social rights for a particular subset of persons: women. The CEDAW was created to defend against government discrimination against women,[32] defined in Article 1 of the convention as

> any distinction, exclusion or restriction made on the basis of sex which has the effect or purpose of impairing or nullifying the recognition, enjoyment or exercise by women, irrespective of their marital status, on a basis of equality of men and women, of human rights and fundamental freedoms in the political, economic, social, cultural, civil or any other field.[33]

Article 2 of the CEDAW requires signatory countries to "embody the principle of the equality of men and women in their national constitutions or other appropriate legislation if not yet incorporated therein and to ensure, through law and other appropriate means, the practical realization of this principle."[34] For example, Japan and Colombia ratified the CEDAW and then "passed legislation or constitutional amendments that implemented its provisions or were compelled by their own courts to respect [the treaty's] provisions."[35] Although male dissidents are not specifically protected under the auspices of the CEDAW, men can anticipate that authorities are less likely to repress women who might participate in or support dissent activities; such anticipation works to the advantage of all dissidents, regardless of sex. Whether the effect of CEDAW obligation

32. Hill (2010) and Lupu (2013b) have shown that CEDAW ratification improves women's living conditions, even accounting for a state's strategic decision to join the treaty in the first place.

33. United Nations 1979.

34. Ibid.

35. Posner 2014, p. 70.

on government repression will be more muted than a treaty that provides rights protections for a wider subset of the population is not specified a priori by our theory.

As we have for the CAT and the ICCPR, we first assess the effect of CEDAW OBLIGATION on the probability that a state is accused of SYSTEMIC TORTURE. Unlike the other two treaties, the CEDAW does not explicitly call for the protection of women's right to not be tortured by the government.[36] In spite of the omission of a provision relating to torture, the treaty's Women's Committee does, in fact, consider allegations of torture in its jurisprudence, often adopting the definition of torture under the CAT. Edwards (2010, p. 256) reports that, in an inquiry into human rights allegations in the Ciudad Juarez area of Chihuahua, Mexico, the Women's Committee tied sexual crimes against women to government torture:

> As far as [the Committee] know[s], the method of these sexual crimes begins with the victims' abduction through deception or by force. [The women] are held captive and subjected to sexual abuse, including rape and, in some cases, torture, until they are murdered.[37]

Because the CEDAW has provisions that broadly relate to the protection of women's rights and because the committee considers allegations of torture directly, we predict that government commitment to the CEDAW will influence people's beliefs about repression and dissent according to our theory. In other words, dissidents (of all types, especially women) and government actors will believe that the treaty alters the government's consequences for torture, and their conflict decisions will reflect that differential expectation.

CEDAW OBLIGATION does indeed affect the government's use of systemic torture in a manner consistent with our argument. Figures 5.6a and 5.6b depict the effect of CEDAW OBLIGATION on SYSTEMIC TORTURE across the range of EXECUTIVE JOB SECURITY. Consider first the ATC depicted in Figure 5.6a. At low levels of EXECUTIVE JOB SECURITY, making an unobligated government commit itself to the CEDAW's terms does not have a substantively significant effect on the probability that the government engages in systemic torture. The repression decisions of leaders who place

36. Edwards (2010, p. 256) argues that the "omission" occurred because "the drafters of the CEDAW failed to recognise that women are victims of torture and in need of such protection."

37. In this passage, Edwards (2010 is discussing CEDAW's Report on Mexico.

a lower value on remaining in office do not depend on their CEDAW member status. As their expected value of retaining power increases, however, the effect of the CEDAW on the probability of SYSTEMIC TORTURE becomes negative and statistically and substantively significant, maxing out at an estimated eleven-point decrease at the highest levels of expected job security.

The ATT results shown in Figure 5.6b provide additional support for our claims. Obligated states made to renege on their CEDAW commitments would experience an estimated fourteen-point increase in the probability of

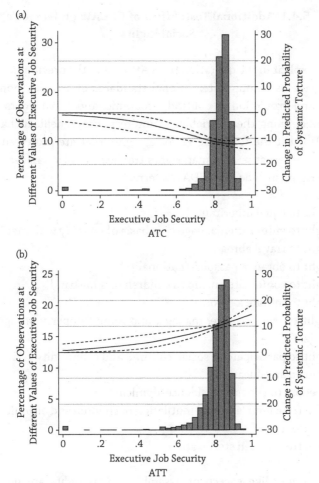

Figure 5.6 Average treatment effect of CEDAW OBLIGATION on (a) the controls (ATC) and (b) the treated (ATT) on the probability of SYSTEMIC TORTURE conditional on EXECUTIVE JOB SECURITY.

widespread torture without the obligation. For leaders with expected values for retaining office lower than those of other leaders, a change in treaty status would have no statistically meaningful effect on the probability of SYSTEMIC TORTURE. Those leaders are unlikely to consider the domestic political effects of the CEDAW as part of their decisions to torture. As leaders become more concerned with retaining office, however, lack of commitment to the CEDAW leads to a statistically and substantively significant increase in the likelihood of SYSTEMIC TORTURE as compared to the status quo of obligation to the CEDAW.

5.4.1 Additional Test: Effect of CEDAW on Women's Social Rights

As made explicit in the quotation from Article 1 in the previous subsection, CEDAW creates binding international standards of equality, nondiscrimination, and protection of political, economic, and social rights. In their codebook defining their variables of interest, Cingranelli, Richards, and Clay (2014) list the following as social rights that are protected under a number of international human rights treaties (we place an asterisk next to those rights included in CEDAW's terms):

- The right to equal inheritance*
- The right to enter into marriage on a basis of equality with men*
- The right to travel abroad
- The right to obtain a passport/nationality*
- The right to confer citizenship to children or a husband*
- The right to initiate a divorce*
- The right to own, acquire, manage, and retain property brought into a marriage*
- The right to participate in social, cultural, and community activities*
- The right to an education*
- The freedom to choose a residence/domicile*
- Freedom from female genital mutilation of children and of adults without their consent
- Freedom from forced sterilization

Unlike rights like speech or assembly, social rights are not directly connected to engagement in political life or to demands for change to the status quo. However, protecting these social rights allows women to participate more freely and equally in society. Education, participation in community life, and even the general perception of equality emboldens women to participate in dissent actions while the state is bound to curtail its violation of these rights.

We used the CIRI data to create a measure of SYSTEMIC VIOLATION OF WOMEN'S SOCIAL RIGHTS, coded "1" if a government is reported to have engaged in "a lot" of discrimination and violation of women's social empowerment rights in a given year and "0" otherwise.[38] The ATC depicted in Figure 5.7a follows the same general trend described for each of the treaties and rights violations discussed above.[39] At high levels of EXECUTIVE JOB SECURITY, when leaders have high expected values for retaining power, they are less likely to systemically violate the social rights of women if the government is party to the CEDAW. The treaty effect on rights violations decreases in magnitude as the probability that the leader retains power decreases. As leaders place lower value or confidence in holding political power, obligation to the CEDAW has little substantive effect on the probability that they violate women's social rights.

We can also look at the effect of obligation to the CEDAW on governments that have committed to the terms of the treaty. What would happen if they were instead unobligated? Again, the results are strongly consistent with our theoretical predictions. Figure 5.7b plots the estimated change in the probability of SYSTEMIC VIOLATION OF WOMEN'S SOCIAL RIGHTS for the average committed country if its CEDAW obligation were removed. States would be more likely to engage in violations of women's social rights if they were not committed to the CEDAW, even though they are the type of state to select into the obligation. As implied by the theory, the magnitude of this effect increases as leaders are more interested in the retention of power.

38. The CIRI codebook states, "A score of 0 indicates that there were no social rights for women in law and that systematic discrimination based on sex may have been built into law. A score of 1 indicates that women had some social rights under law, but these rights were not effectively enforced. A score of 2 indicates that women had some social rights under law, and the government effectively enforced these rights in practice while still allowing a low level of discrimination against women in social matters. Finally, a score of 3 indicates that all or nearly all of women's social rights were guaranteed by law and the government fully and vigorously enforced these laws in practice" (Cingranelli, Richards, and Clay 2014). We code our variable of systemic violation as 1 if the CIRI data is coded 0 or 1, and we code it as 0 otherwise.

39. These figures are based on the results reported in Table A2.3 in the Appendix to this book.

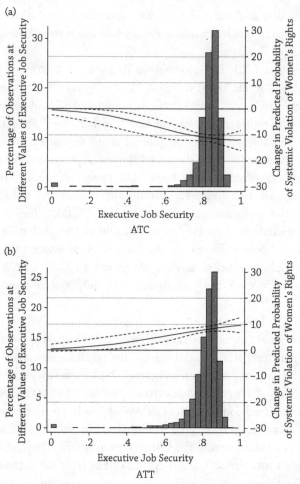

Figure 5.7 Average treatment effect of CEDAW OBLIGATION on (a) the controls (ATC) and (b) the treated (ATT) on the probability of SYSTEMIC VIOLATION OF WOMEN'S SOCIAL RIGHTS conditional on EXECUTIVE JOB SECURITY.

The empirical estimates focusing on the effect of CEDAW offer even stronger evidence that international treaty obligation reduces human rights violations as compared to what signatory countries would have done in the absence of those obligations. We might have thought that the CEDAW effects would be weaker in magnitude or even statistically insignificant, given that the treaty's prohibitions are limited to women—half of the population considering dissent. Nonetheless, the data offer strong evidentiary support, suggesting that the effects of the CEDAW on the likelihood of government repression are consistent with the effects of the CAT and the ICCPR. The treaty obligation has the predicted conditional effects on violations of human rights that are less directly categorizable as related to dissent, such as women's social rights. These results are weaker (and are a much looser match to the concept of repression under study in this book), but they still support the general trend: obligation to the CEDAW, like obligation to other human rights treaties, leads to improved rights practices in states whose leaders highly value remaining in a position of power. The estimated effects for both types of rights may be a result of women changing their assumptions about government constraint on the basis of treaty status, and therefore perhaps changing their decisions to participate in dissent. We find evidence of treaty effects on women's protest in the next chapter. However, these estimated results may also be a function of both women and men anticipating general government restraint in response to the state's commitment.[40]

5.5 SUMMARY OF FINDINGS: GOVERNMENT REPRESSION

In this chapter, we presented empirical evidence in support of the implications of our theory, testing operational hypotheses regarding the effect of state obligation to international human rights treaties on the likelihood that the state engages in systemic repression. The evidence includes support across three HRTs—the CAT, the ICCPR, and the CEDAW—and three types of human rights violations—government torture, political imprisonment, and women's social empowerment rights violations.[41] In addition to showing statistical support for the implications of our argument, we provided *substantive* support for the theory: Each of the counterfactuals above suggests that HRTs have large substantive effects on government

40. As above, additional empirical tests found in the Online Appendix suggest that our main results hold in both direction and statistical significance when we (1) operationalize adjudication costs using a measure of judicial effectiveness from Linzer and Staton (2015); (2) use as our dependent variable a measure of latent protections for physical integrity violations from Fariss (2014); (3) control for temporal dependence using a third-order polynomial time-counter as advised by Carter and Signorino (2010); (4) include controls for dissent as measured by Banks (2010), latent protection for physical integrity right violations as measured by Fariss (2014), media freedom as measured using data from Cingranelli, Richards, and Clay (2014), and youth bulges as discussed by Nordås and Davenport (2013); and (5) include as part of our instrument data a measure of a country's common-law status as suggested and operationalized by Simmons (2009).

41. The findings are also consistent with a large number of alternative specifications and measures, as we list in the Appendix for this chapter and present in the Online Appendix.

repression via their effects on domestic politics. They do not yield perfect government respect for human rights, but HRTs do markedly improve rights protection in many obligated states, and they would do so if those that remain outside of the treaty's domain were to change their status.

Although the dominant trend of scholarship on international human rights law takes a position of no effect, we find empirical support for the hypothesis that HRTs have a positive effect on rights protections when leaders who value remaining in office are at the helm. Scholars have found that domestic institutions decrease repression, but there has been very little support for the notion that international institutions do so; many scholars have found that treaties have no effect on rights practices or even lead to increases in violations. In contrast, we find that if international law has even a small effect on domestic politics and general assumptions of constraint, those effects can yield a substantively meaningful reduction in rights violations. Importantly, HRTs often influence domestic politics. In the United States, for example, obligation to international human rights law is often cited as a reason not to deport individuals who are likely to face repression upon deportation. In 2017, U.S. Army veteran Nahidh Shaou was exploring legal options, including his rights under the CAT, to avoid deportation to Iraq.[42] Similarly, in 2015, attorneys for Ibrahim Parlak sought to prove that his deportation would be in violation of the United States' obligations under the Convention Against Torture because he was "more likely than not to be tortured upon...return."[43] These examples and many others like them suggest that a treaty need not be enforced in policy for people to presume that it matters: people bring claims to court and reference treaty terms expecting the court and the government to respond to the obligation.

The empirical results presented in this chapter also contribute to the scholarly understanding of the role of political survival—a notion similar to our conceptualization of the value the leader places on retaining office—on domestic political processes. Tenure considerations affect both the government's willingness to repress[44] and its tactics.[45] However, scholars are only beginning to examine how leaders' value for and outlook regarding political survival mediate the effect of domestic and international institutions on government action. Our theory implies that a leader's expected value for political power has a mitigating effect on the ability of institutions to

---

42. Jackson 2017.
43. Johnson 2015.
44. Ritter 2014; Young 2009
45. Ritter 2014.

constrain authorities; the evidence presented in this chapter supports that claim. Leaders are able and willing to repress more when they more highly value the retention of political office,[46] and this makes them more subject to institutional constraints like international treaties.

In addition to their effects on government repression, HRTs—international institutions intended to constrain repression—also have a structural effect on mobilized dissent, altering the incentive structure in which potential dissidents make decisions. By increasing institutional costs for repression, HRTs create openings for citizens to challenge the government. International treaties designed to curb rights violations can encourage citizens to engage in mobilized dissent against the government by opening opportunities for action that is less likely to incur repressive consequences—which perversely creates new incentives for the government to further violate human rights. We discuss these dynamics in detail, and conduct empirical analyses of the effect of international human rights treaties on mobilized dissent, in the following chapter.

46. Ibid.

5.6 APPENDIX 2: EMPIRICAL RESULTS FOR GOVERNMENT REPRESSION

Table A2.1 EFFECT OF HRT (CAT) OBLIGATION ON GOVERNMENT REPRESSION

	CAT		OPCAT (Ratification)		OPCAT (Signature)	
	Obligated	Unobligated	Obligated	Unobligated	Obligated	Unobligated
Outcome DV: Systemic Torture						
Domestic Judicial Rights Protection	0.996	0.601	-0.700	2.000*	4.990	1.144
	(0.925)	(1.868)	(4.763)	(0.846)	(2.806)	(0.887)
Executive Job Security	0.416	-1.400*	1.643	0.544*	0.655	-1.000*
	(0.308)	(0.674)	(1.874)	(0.278)	(0.918)	(0.377)
Judicial Rights Protection x Executive Job Security	-0.442	-0.231	2.267	-1.676	-4.086	-0.847
	(1.121)	(2.231)	(6.058)	(1.026)	(3.529)	(1.073)
Constant	-0.798*	1.850*	-2.870	-0.377	-1.770*	0.985*
	(0.252)	(0.591)	(1.499)	(0.229)	(0.638)	(0.312)
Selection DV: CAT/OPCAT Obligation						
Domestic Judicial Rights Protection	-2.115		-0.050		0.401	
	(1.111)		(0.944)		(0.917)	
Executive Job Security	-2.229*		-1.296*		-3.166*	
	(0.390)		(0.360)		(0.352)	
Judicial Rights Protection x Executive Job Security	3.124*		1.385		0.203	
	(1.337)		(1.182)		(1.137)	
Number of IO Memberships	0.184*		0.157*		0.194*	
	(0.012)		(0.020)		(0.014)	
Constant	1.484*		-1.265*		0.522	
	(0.331)		(0.314)		(0.299)	
ρ	0.948*		0.566		0.597*	
Log-pseudo likelihood	-3,734.125		-2,654.659		-2,986.005	
N	2,982		2,990		2,990	

Notes: * Significant within 95% confidence interval; two-tailed test. Likelihood ratio test. Likelihood ratio test of the null hypothesis that the coefficients on the constants in the obligated and unobligated samples are equal (i.e., that the treaty has no influence independent of selection): $\chi^2 = 18.44$ (p < 0.000) (Model 1); $\chi^2 = 2.75$ (p < 0.097) (Model 2); $\chi^2 = 15.39$ (p < 0.000) (Model 3). Likelihood ratio test of the null hypothesis that ρ^S and ρ^N jointly equal zero (i.e., that there are selection effects): $\chi^2 = 134.59$ (p < 0.000) (Model 1); $\chi^2 = 40.05$ (p < 0.000) (Model 2); $\chi^2 = 76.60$ (p < 0.000).

Table A2.2 EFFECT OF HRT (ICCPR) OBLIGATION ON GOVERNMENT REPRESSION

	DV: Systemic Torture		DV: Systemic Imprisonment	
	Obligated	Unobligated	Obligated	Unobligated
Outcome DV: Systemic Torture/Imprisonment				
Domestic Judicial Rights Protection	1.367	0.006	0.469	-1.766
	(0.896)	(2.179)	(0.993)	(2.000)
Executive Job Security	0.519	-3.604*	1.613*	-4.057*
	(0.299)	(0.761)	(0.370)	(0.727)
Domestic Judicial Rights Protection x Executive Job Security	-0.819	0.940	-0.437	2.074
	(1.082)	(2.593)	(1.198)	(2.388)
Constant	-0.774*	3.860*	-2.106*	4.280*
	(0.246)	(0.675)	(0.306)	(0.635)
Selection DV: ICCPR Obligation				
Domestic Judicial Rights Protection	-2.245		-1.636	
	(1.120)		(1.281)	
Executive Job Security	-2.768*		-2.806*	
	(0.428)		(0.438)	
Domestic Judicial Rights Protection x Executive Job Security	3.704*		2.966*	
	(1.431)		(1.526)	
Number of IO Memberships	0.151*		0.164*	
	(0.011)		(0.012)	
Constant	2.426*		2.408*	
	(0.365)		(0.374)	
ρ	0.909*	0.790*	0.883*	0.800*
Log-pseudo likelihood	-4,4047		-3,788.546	
N	3,482		3,479	

Notes: * Significant within 95% confidence interval; two-tailed test. Likelihood ratio test of the null hypothesis that the coefficients on the constants in the obligated and unobligated samples are equal (i.e., that the treaty has no influence independent of selection): $\chi^2 = 44.08$ (p < 0.000) (Model 1); $\chi^2 = 86.52$ (p < 0.097) (Model 2). Likelihood ratio test of the null hypothesis that ρ^S and ρ^N jointly equal zero (i.e., that there are selection effects): $\chi^2 = 107.78$ (p < 0.000) (Model 1); $\chi^2 = 116.85$ (p < 0.000) (Model 2).

Table A2.3 EFFECT OF HRT (CEDAW) OBLIGATION ON GOVERNMENT REPRESSION

	DV: Systemic Torture		DV: Systemic Women's Social Rights Violations	
	Obligated	Unobligated	Obligated	Unobligated
Outcome DV: Systemic Torture/Women's Social Rights Violations				
Domestic Judicial Rights Protection	1.431	-0.632	5.925*	2.109
	(0.886)	(1.824)	(1.419)	(2.785)
Executive Job Security	0.730*	-3.036*	1.685*	2.478*
	(0.296)	(0.590)	(0.457)	(0.812)
Domestic Judicial Rights Protection x Executive Job Security	-0.750	1.156	-6.145*	-2.602
	(1.068)	(2.163)	(1.700)	(3.332)
Constant	-0.892	3.747*	-1.266*	-0.308
	(0.244)	(0.494)	(0.361)	(0.670)
Selection DV: CEDAW Obligation				
Domestic Judicial Rights Protection	-1.680		-1.334	
	(1.248)		(1.510)	
Executive Job Security	-1.923*		-1.646*	
	(0.436)		(0.514)	
Domestic Judicial Rights Protection x Executive Job Security	2.812		2.353	
	(1.488)		(1.794)	
Number of IO Memberships	0.099*		0.107*	
	(0.010)		(0.012)	
Constant	2.214*		1.730*	
	(0.370)		(0.435)	
ρ	0.913*	0.986*	0.856*	0.999*
Log-pseudo likelihood	-3,849.926		-2,698.315	
N	3,482		2,554	

Notes: * Significant within 95% confidence interval; two-tailed test. Likelihood ratio test of the null hypothesis that the coefficients on the constants in the obligated and unobligated samples are equal (i.e., that the treaty has no influence independent of selection): $\chi^2 = 79.64$ (p < 0.000) (Model 1); $\chi^2 = 1.82$ (p < 0.177) (Model 2). Likelihood ratio test of the null hypothesis that ρ^S and ρ^N jointly equal zero (i.e., that there are selection effects): $\chi^2 = 110.48$ (p < 0.000) (Model 1); $\chi^2 = 77.07$ (p < 0.000) (Model 2).

CHAPTER 6

ᴏⅴᴐ

Substantive Empirical
Results: Mobilized Dissent

In addition to potentially constraining government repression, we argue that obligation to an international human rights treaty (HRT) increases the potential for mobilized dissent. Dissent and repression frequently correlate, with increased protests sometimes leading to abuses or crackdowns. In Turkey, President Recep Tayyip Erdoğan responded to a July 2016 coup attempt, which he explicitly connected with a widespread popular opposition movement, by firing more than fifty thousand people, including members of the security forces, police, intelligence agents, teachers, judges, attorneys, and university employees,[1] and declaring a nationwide state of emergency.[2] This sort of government response to mobilized dissent is not atypical; scholars often refer to the strong probability that governments will respond to dissent with repression as the Law of Coercive Responsiveness or Threat-Response Theory.[3]

We contend that state obligations to human rights treaties encourage dissidents to take more or wider action against the government, because they anticipate that it will be relatively constrained from attacking them. Indeed, Turkey is party to four of the six core UN HRTs, which may have been part of the fuel for the popular movement against the government. In a more explicit example, Czech dissidents formed a group called Charter

1. Sariyuce and Dewan 2016.
2. Kirisci 2016.
3. Carey 2010; Davenport 2007a; Ritter and Conrad 2016a.

77, so named after a document signed by Czechs and Slovaks demanding respect for their human rights. In particular, the group was emboldened to take public action after the Soviet Bloc countries signed the Helsinki Accords in 1975, agreeing to protect basic civil liberties. Their founding document explicitly called on the Czech and Soviet governments to adhere to their international obligations for rights protection.[4] More importantly for our argument, groups such as Charter 77 developed all throughout the Soviet Bloc, emboldened to act by the protection nominally provided under the new Helsinki Accords.[5]

Because government repression emerges via conflict with discontented populations, our theory yields new and important implications about the effect of treaty obligations on mobilized dissent against the government. Although numerous studies point to the social causes and societal consequences of mobilization, we are among the first to systematically investigate the effect of international human rights law on popular dissent.[6] Previous scholarship that examines international institutions and dissident behavior focuses on how human rights treaties and other such organizations affect popular mobilization, but not dissent.[7] Yet institutions like HRTs that affect authorities' decisions to violate human rights influence not only the government's strategic repression of dissidents but also dissent itself.

Hypothesis 2 lays out the empirical implications as to how a government's obligation to international rights law affects the probability of mobilized dissent actions, according to our theory. Mobilized groups act under the assumption that the treaty obligation will (under the conditions that we test here and in Chapter 5) bind the ability of the leader to repress; this leads groups to dissent more than they would have absent such an international legal obligation. Both of the operational hypotheses we stated in Chapter 4 specify that treaty effects should be stronger as EXECUTIVE JOB SECURITY increases, and they note that this effect is further mitigated by the likelihood that a repressive leader will face domestic legal consequences for repressing. For purposes of clarity, we presented substantive effects of treaties on repression while job security varied, but we held DOMESTIC JUDICIAL RIGHTS PROTECTION at its subsample means.

---

4. For more information on Charter 77, see "In Charter 77, Czech Dissidents Charted New Territory," https://foreignpolicy.com/2017/02/03/in-charter-77-czech-dissidents-charted-new-territory//.

5. Morgan 2018.

6. For a more detailed discussion of the distinction between mobilization and dissent, please refer to Section 1.3.2 of this volume.

7. Bell, et al. 2014; Dai 2005; Keck and Sikkink 1998; Risse, Ropp, and Sikkink 1999; Simmons 2009.

To probe the conditionality of baseline expectations of domestic rights protections, in this chapter we examine how treaty effects differ at various ranges of this domestic baseline. When the latent variable of DOMESTIC JUDICIAL RIGHTS PROTECTION is low, we predict HRT obligation to have a positive effect on mobilized dissent when leaders sufficiently value the retention of power; when the probability of domestic legal protection is relatively high or when leaders do not place a high enough value on political office, we expect international treaty obligations to have a negligible effect on the probability of mobilized dissent actions against the government.

To test these implications, we use the treatment model described in Chapter 4 to estimate first the probability that a government will (or will not) be obligated to an international human rights treaty, placing that government into one of two selected sample groups, and then estimating the effect of treaty status on dissent activity in each subsample. Tables presenting the estimated coefficients, standard errors, and other statistical parameters are located in Appendix A3 of this volume.[8] The estimates in these tables are the foundation of the figures and inferences we present in this chapter. Like those for government repression presented in Chapter 5, the models have complicated error correlations, interaction terms, and unobservables, making interpretation of the statistical estimates on their own quite unintuitive. Therefore, we focus on presenting the substantive results of these estimates in a series of figures.

Figures illustrating the estimated average treatment effects on the controls (ATC) and the treated (ATT) were created using the same processes described in Chapters 4 and 5. Unlike the substantive empirical results that we present for government repression, the figures in this chapter show the substantive effect of HRT obligation on mobilized dissent at different levels of the probability that a repressive government will incur domestic litigation costs.[9] For each treaty—the Convention Against Torture (CAT),

8. We present the estimates of the selection stage predicting treaty obligation status in the bottom halves of these tables and the estimates for the effect of that status on the likelihood a country experiences mobilized dissent in the top halves. As in the Appendix associated with Chapter 5, odd-numbered columns provide results for HRT-obligated countries and even-numbered columns report results for countries that have not committed to the human rights treaty in question. In each estimated model, likelihood ratio (LR) tests of ρ for obligated countries compared to unobligated countries allow us to reject the null hypothesis that their joint effect is zero ($p = 0.000$ in all cases), which indicates the presence of selection effects like the ones we describe in Chapter 4.

9. As suggested by the theory and the operational hypotheses, the predicted treaty effects on repression are also conditional on both the leader's expected value for power and the probability of incurring domestic legal consequences. We control for the interaction to capture this conditionality in the empirical estimates in Chapter 5, but we do not present the substantive predictions as conditional on the domestic legal

the International Covenant on Civil and Political Rights (ICCPR), and the Convention for the Elimination of Discrimination Against Women (CEDAW)—we show both the ATC and the ATT for countries with low and high values on the measures that approximate the likelihood that the government will incur litigation costs for repression. The solid lines plot the predicted effect of HRT obligation on the probability of mobilized dissent activities for states with leaders across the observed range of the valuation of office. The estimated effects are statistically significant when the upper and lower bounds of the 95 percent confidence intervals (shown with dashed lines) do not encompass the horizontal lines indicating zero effect.

In what follows, we first discuss the results of hypothesis tests of the effect of international human rights treaty obligation on mobilized dissent at the country-year unit of observation. To state it plainly, the results of empirical tests at this level of observation are not supportive of Hypothesis 2. We discuss several reasons why we believe we encounter such lack of support and then turn to testing the implications about the effect of HRTs on mobilized dissent activity at a more temporally disaggregated unit of observation—the country-month rather than the country-year.

6.1 LEVELS OF ANALYSIS & THE STUDY OF MOBILIZED DISSENT

To begin an empirical examination of treaty effects on the likelihood of domestic dissent, we took a similar approach to the analyses presented in Chapter 5. Since most studies of human rights outcomes estimate the likelihood of government repression in a given country-year and many of our main predictor variables are typically measured at that unit of observation, we start with country-year observations to analyze the effect of HRT obligation on mobilized dissent. Table A3.1 in Appendix 3 reports these analyses. The left two columns of the table report the estimates for government obligation to the CAT, and the right two columns report the estimates for obligation to the ICCPR. We do not present results of the effect of the CEDAW on mobilized dissent at the country-year unit of observation; our statistical models failed to converge when conducting those analyses, likely for the reasons we discuss in additional detail below.

environment. In this chapter, we include that conditionality in the empirical models (the tables) and the substantive interpretations (the figures).

The results presented in Table A3.1 are echoed in Figures A3.1, A3.2, A3.3, A3.4, which are also included in Appendix 3; they do not provide support for Hypothesis 2. The point estimates of the treaty effects presented in the ATC figures are generally upward-sloping, and the estimates presented in the ATT figures are generally downward-sloping. We predicted effects in these directions. But none of the figures provide support for the conditional hypotheses; neither the extent to which the leader values the retention of office nor the probability of litigation costs conditions the relationship between HRT obligation and mobilized dissent. Each of the 95 percent confidence intervals—the dotted lines surrounding each solid line—are very wide, which indicates that we can only be confident that each treaty's effect on the likelihood of mobilized dissent is somewhere in this very wide range. Even if HRTs do have effects that are conditional on our covariates, we cannot be certain; we could easily draw a straight, an upward-sloping, or a downward-sloping line within each of the confidence intervals. These empirical results are not inconsistent with our hypotheses, but they certainly do not suggest support for our theory.

Why such inconsistent, weak results? We believe these weak findings are a consequence of overaggregating the data to the country-year. Scholars have shown that aggregating domestic conflict events, especially government repression and mobilized dissent, either spatially or temporally, can bias empirical findings.[10] A binary indicator that equals one if there is a mobilized dissent event occurring at any point over an entire year has the same value if there is one event or one thousand events. Qualitatively, these can be very different outcomes. Moreover, our measure of mobilized dissent captures so many types of events that nearly all of the countries under study at the country-year level of observation experience at least one dissent event in each year; as such, in the country-year data, there is very little variation on the dependent variable that allows us to capture more nuanced effects.

This sort of data aggregation matters less for government repression as we have conceptualized and measured it in this book. Scholars often think of repression as an environmental or systemic characteristic: the measure we use captures whether governments engage in repression regularly or not at all. Although almost all governments engage in at least one repressive event in a year,[11] there is quite a bit of variation across countries and years as to whether they engage in *systemic* repression. Based on our theory, we have good reasons to think that obligation to an international human

10. See, e.g., Shellman 2004a, 2004b.
11. This is especially the case for government torture. See, for example, Conrad and Moore 2010 and Conrad, Haglund, and Moore 2013, 2014.

rights treaty will constrain not just a particular repressive event but also the overall severity or frequency of repression, writ large.

Our theory is not one that posits a collection of dissenting groups choosing the severity of an entire dissent environment. We do not predict widespread dissent. Instead, we predict individual group choices to engage in mobilized dissent, which we operationalize as the presence or absence of individual events. Importantly, we cannot observe distinct choices about whether to dissent if we aggregate all events to the country-year level of analysis. A more accurate accounting of popular dissent choices (particularly, accounting for the absence of such events) requires a more disaggregated look at the available data on mobilized dissent. Therefore, we focus the empirical analyses in this chapter on estimates of the effect of international human rights treaty obligations on the likelihood of mobilized dissent as observed at the more temporally disaggregated country-month level of analysis.

To do this, we require monthly measures of the same concepts described in Chapter 4: international human rights treaty obligation, the probability of domestic adjudication costs, the value that the leader places on remaining in a position of power, and the level of mobilized dissent. We operationalize our concepts using the same measures discussed in Chapter 4, but adapted for observation at the monthly level of aggregation. The monthly DISSENT measure is drawn from IDEA using the same coding process as that described for the measures at the annual level, but the indicator is now coded "1" if a particular country-month sees any dissent event. CAT OBLIGATION, ICCPR OBLIGATION, and CEDAW OBLIGATION are binary measures coded "1" in the country-month in which a country ratifies a given treaty and every country-month thereafter that the country remains committed.

We reestimated the probability that a leader retains office—the EXEC-UTIVE JOB SECURITY—using the same process as discussed in Chapter 4, using monthly indicators of the constituent predictors whenever possible. The likelihood of a leader losing power in a given country-month is low (even lower than the likelihood of a leader losing power in a given country-year), so the measure is highly skewed toward one. Unless noted otherwise, we measure the probability that a leader faces litigation for repression—DOMESTIC JUDICIAL RIGHTS PROTECTION—using data from Hill (2015), which is described in detail in Chapter 1. Note that this measure is estimated for the country-year level of analysis; using a country-year measure in models where the unit of observation is the country-month means that we assume that the general assumptions over domestic legal consequences for repression do not change much over the course of a year. Because institutions are "sticky,"[12] and domestic court effectiveness is unlikely to change rapidly,[13] we do not think this is an unreasonable assumption.

Tables A3.2, A3.3, and A3.4 in Appendix 3 report the main results of the analyses of the effect of obligation to the Convention Against Torture (CAT), the International Covenant on Civil and Political Rights (ICCPR), and the Convention on the Elimination of Discrimination Against Women (CEDAW) on mobilized dissent actions at the country-month unit of observation. The figures presented throughout this chapter are based on the estimates shown in these tables, except where noted otherwise.

6.2 EFFECT OF CAT OBLIGATION ON MOBILIZED DISSENT

When dissidents engage in direct protest or other dissent actions against a government, they do so in the hopes they will not be beaten, arrested, killed, or experience other forms of retribution for their actions. Some dissidents will protest even when they anticipate repression, of course, but others use cues, such as laws, court actions, other group activities, and international obligations, to assess the probability the government will attack them if they join a dissent activity.

The Venezuelan government is no leader in rights protection. The Political Terror Scales data project codes the country as experiencing extensive political imprisonment, killings, and brutality every year since 2002, based on Amnesty International annual reports; using the U.S. State Department reports as the data source, the violence is frequently coded as widespread.[14] Yet in 2014, widespread protests developed in Caracas, demanding a resolution to inflation, release of those demonstrators being held without charge, and eventually the removal of President Nicolas Maduro.[15] These protests continued all the way through the time of this writing, shifting in waves of intensity around political events. Some of the protests in 2016 and 2017 swelled to over a million participants.[16] The majority of protests have been nonviolent, with only occasional violence or property destruction by small groups. Although the demonstrators do not necessarily cite international law or concepts of human rights in their demands, they

12. Grief and Laitin 2004; Page 2006.
13. Carrubba 2009; Staton 2006.
14. Gibney et al. 2016. We used the PTS-App (Haschke n.d.) to examine these patterns.
15. BBC News 2014.
16. Martín 2016.

have chosen to take dissent actions under a particular environment of obligations. Venezuela is party to all six core UN human rights treaties, including the CAT.[17] The pattern of state terror suggests that authorities have acted with little domestic repercussion, but the UN Committee Against Torture[18] and a variety of international and domestic NGOs[19] have vociferously denounced the political imprisonment and torture of thousands of demonstrators and provided public evidence of use of these repressive measures. In other words, the Venezuelan people are protesting under an environment of international obligation, which has created public international consequences for the government that would repress its citizens. Even if the effect of these public consequences is small, it creates a popular expectation that the government will be somewhat constrained in its repression, opening space for wider participation in protest.

In what follows, we first examine the effect of obligation to the CAT on the probability that a government will experience mobilized dissent actions. Recall that we expect obligation to international human rights treaties to influence groups to be more likely to dissent than they would be if their country were not part of the treaty—but only when leaders highly value the retention of political office and consequently are the most likely to engage in repression. Furthermore, our theory suggests that dissidents—whatever their demanded policy change—will be more likely to engage in mobilized dissent under HRTs because they believe that the international obligation will make government authorities less willing to torture them than they would be absent such a commitment to international law.

As in Chapter 5, ATC figures—depicted in the leftmost subfigure of each set of figures below—illustrate the estimates of the probability of mobilized dissent that we would expect to see if all countries that opt out of the CAT were forced to obligate themselves to its terms. The ATT figures—shown in the right-hand subfigure of each set of figures below—depict the expected difference in mobilized dissent behavior if the countries that are in reality obligated to the CAT were removed from that obligation. Reading from left to right on each subfigure shows the change in predicted probability of MOBILIZED DISSENT ACTION across the observed range of EXECUTIVE JOB SECURITY, measured at the country-month. To fully analyze the theoretical implications for mobilized dissent, we assess a pair of ATC and ATT figures for countries with a high probability of domestic legal consequences (where

17. *Ratification of International Human Rights Treaties—Venezuela* n.d.

18. *Concluding Observations on the Combined Third and Fourth Periodic Reports of the Bolivarian Republic of Venezuela* 2014.

19. International Rehabilitation Council for Torture Victims 2014.

we expect international HRT obligation to have no meaningful effect on mobilized dissent) and a pair of ATC and ATT figures for countries with ineffective courts or legal structures for human rights (where we expect HRT obligation to lead to an increase in mobilized dissent as leaders increasingly value the retention of political office).

Figure 6.1 shows (a) the ATC and (b) the ATT for CAT obligation in countries where the probability that a repressive government would experience litigation costs is high. We predicted that HRT obligation would have no meaningful substantive effect on mobilized dissent in countries where the probability of domestic adjudication costs is high as compared to

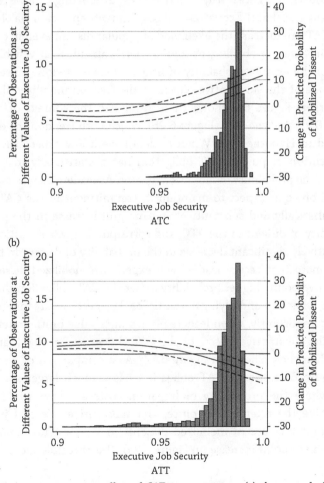

Figure 6.1 Average treatment effect of CAT OBLIGATION on (a) the controls (ATC) and (b) the treated (ATT) on the probability of MOBILIZED DISSENT ACTION conditional on EXECUTIVE JOB SECURITY in countries where DOMESTIC JUDICIAL RIGHTS PROTECTION is at its subsample maximum.

countries where the probability of facing costs associated with litigation is relatively low; when the baseline is little constraint, the treaty obligation creates different assumptions about constraint. Figure 6.1a shows that, as EXECUTIVE JOB SECURITY increases, dissidents are increasingly likely to take action against the government as a result of obligation to the CAT. The ATT, which shows the opposite counterfactual in Figure 6.1b, provides information about what would happen if all CAT-committed countries were absolved of their obligations. In countries where the probability of litigation-associated costs is high, renouncing the CAT obligation leads to a lower probability of mobilized dissent activity as executives place more value on the retention of office. We expected to see these results for *ineffective* courts, not necessarily effective ones. Interestingly, however, these results suggest that the constraint of government repression via obligation to the CAT can increase the likelihood of popular dissent even in countries where the extant probability of adjudication is already relatively high.

When the ex ante probability of litigation costs are low, however, the magnitude of the substantive effects of the CAT on mobilized dissent is even larger. Figure 6.2 shows these results in the context of the ATC (Figure 6.2a) and the ATT (Figure 6.2b), which both trend in the direction specified in Hypothesis 2. When leaders have a low expected value for the retention of power, CAT obligation has a statistically insignificant effect on the probability of mobilized dissent. As leaders increasingly value political office or expect to maintain it, commitment to the CAT results in a statistically and substantively meaningful increase in the predicted probability of dissent in the ATC, and correspondingly, a statistically and substantively significant decrease in the probability of dissent in the ATT. We estimate that secure leaders will experience mobilized dissent with twenty-five points higher probability under the CAT obligation than in its absence, when the underlying domestic legal protections are minimal.

Most importantly, when leaders place a high value on the retention of office, the substantive effects of the CAT shown in Figure 6.2 are much larger than those shown in Figure 6.1.[20] As a comparison of Figure 6.1a and Figure 6.2a shows, CAT obligation has a much larger substantive effect where the probability of litigation costs are low: when leaders most value the retention of office, the substantive effect of just over a ten-point increase in mobilized dissent (in Figure 6.1a) jumps to an almost thirty-point increase (in Figure 6.2a). This threefold increase in the

---

20. As implied by the theory, the difference in the substantive effects across levels of DOMESTIC JUDICIAL RIGHTS PROTECTION narrows as we run the simulations at the 25th and 75th percentiles, though the results remain consistent with our expectations. These results are available in the Online Appendix.

estimated substantive effect of CAT obligation is echoed in comparisons of the ATTs shown in Figures 6.1b and 6.2b. In addition, although the confidence intervals shown across Figure 6.2 are larger than those depicted in Figure 6.1, even the lower bounds of the confidence intervals for the ATC and the ATT depicted in Figure 6.2 are substantively larger than the point estimates shown in Figure 6.1. Thus, even when we account for the uncertainty of our estimates, the estimated substantive effect of CAT obligation on the probability of mobilized dissent is much greater in countries where leaders are unlikely to face high costs of litigation absent HRT commitment.

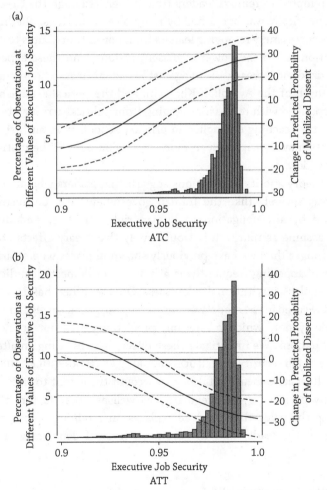

Figure 6.2 Average treatment effect of CAT OBLIGATION on (a) the controls (ATC) and (b) the treated (ATT) on the probability of MOBILIZED DISSENT ACTION conditional on EXECUTIVE JOB SECURITY in countries where DOMESTIC JUDICIAL RIGHTS PROTECTION is at its subsample minimum.

6.2.1 Additional Test: Alternative Measure of Leader Security

A leader's expected value for retaining power is a concept capturing their stakes in a conflict over policy with dissidents. So far, we have used a measure that is ostensibly exogenous to the conflict itself. The estimates we created for EXECUTIVE JOB SECURITY derive from a statistical model including personal and institutional characteristics related to turnover separate from domestic conflict. However, in many cases, turnover is the direct result of popular protest, violence, or both. Iran, for instance, has a history of leaders losing power as a result of popular unrest and rebellion, and widespread protests such as the Green Revolution in 2009 have attempted to remove leaders from power, although the Green Revolution specifically was squelched by repressive authorities. The history of protests successfully removing leaders from power contributes to common expectations as to the power of dissent actions, and these expectations incentivized widespread dissent against President Hassan Rouhani, despite the strength of the Ayatollah Khameini and the clerical establishment.[21] Iran responded with repression ranging from political arrests[22] to general bans on the teaching of English in primary schools.[23] In such situations, dissidents may anticipate even more repression but still be motivated to dissent widely.[24]

Our theory and its implications suggest that leaders who are expected to repress severely (like the Iranian government) will be meaningfully restricted by any obligation to human rights treaties, and dissidents should assume as much. This would imply that treaty effects should be even stronger than we have previously shown in places where turnover is *irregular*, happening frequently as a function of domestic conflict rather than "regular" institutional processes. On the other hand, while the concept we used in the model was necessarily exogenous, irregular turnover is decidedly not, which means our predictions may not apply well to these situations. We investigate these effects here by using an alternative measure of job security we call JOB SECURITY WITH IRREGULAR HISTORY.

The alternative measure takes into account the extent to which leaders are likely to lose power irregularly, as well as other factors that may influence the value that the leader places on retaining office, including the age of the leader and the country's level of democracy. To create

---

21. Reuters News Service 2018b.
22. Reuters News Service 2018a.
23. Perper 2018.
24. This would indeed be implied by the contest function we specified in the theoretical model.

our original operationalization, we used parametric survival models to estimate a measure of the leader's expected value of retaining office based on time in office to date, previous trends in leadership change, and annual economic growth.[25] To create an alternative measure accounting for irregular turnover, we again use a parametric survival model to create an estimate, but we base that estimate on different covariates, including previous trends in irregular leadership change (i.e., leadership change that occurs outside of planned institutional turnover), the age of the leader, and the country's level of democracy. As with the previous measure, converting the hazard estimates to a probability of leadership turnover yields a range from zero (the lowest probability of leadership turnover) to one (the highest probability of leadership turnover). We reverse the scale to create a measure of the JOB SECURITY WITH IRREGULAR HISTORY that takes into consideration trends in irregular turnover and the country's level of democracy.

We use this alternative measure to produce the empirical estimates shown in Table A3.2 in Appendix 3. Using those estimates, we create Figures 6.3 and 6.4, which provide information on the average treatment effects on the controls of CAT obligation in countries where the probability of litigation costs is high and where it is low, respectively. The ATC—the effect of forcing an uncommitted country to obligate itself under the Convention Against Torture—is shown in Figures 6.3a and 6.4a. In each of these figures, the effect of CAT obligation on the probability of mobilized dissent is nearly indistinguishable from zero when our alternative measure of the JOB SECURITY WITH IRREGULAR HISTORY is low. As the expectation of retaining power increases, the effect of CAT obligation on mobilized dissent becomes positive in countries with either a high or a low value of DOMESTIC JUDICIAL RIGHTS PROTECTION.

Importantly, however, the *magnitude* of the effect of the CAT on the probability of mobilized dissent is significantly higher in countries where leaders face a relatively low probability of paying litigation costs for engaging in repression. Compare, for example, the approximately 7 percent (and statistically negligible) increase in countries where leaders value the retention of office (and face a high probability of domestic adjudication), shown in Figure 6.3a, against the approximately 13 percent increase in the probability of mobilized dissent in countries with executives who similarly value the retention of office but face a high probability of litigation costs, shown in Figure 6.4a. These results are consistent with our expectation that obligations to international human rights law should have the greatest

---

25. Additional information on the creation of this measure is available in Chapter 4.

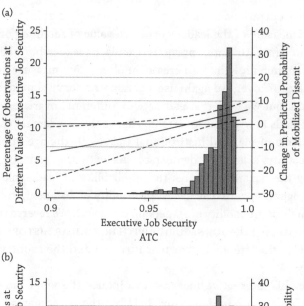

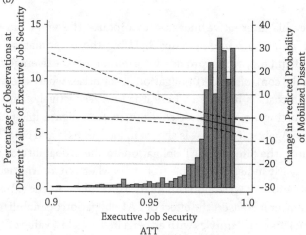

Figure 6.3 Average treatment effect of CAT OBLIGATION on (a) the controls (ATC) and (b) the treated (ATT) on the probability of MOBILIZED DISSENT ACTION conditional on JOB SECURITY WITH IRREGULAR HISTORY in countries where DOMESTIC JUDICIAL RIGHTS PROTECTION is at its subsample maximum.

effect on mobilized dissent in countries where the extant likelihood that authorities will experience consequences for violating human rights is low.

These hypothesis-supporting results are echoed by the ATT—the effect of removing a committed country from its CAT obligation—shown in both Figure 6.3b and Figure 6.4b. When executives are less likely to retain power, and especially when a country has a history of irregular turnover, removing a country from its obligation to the CAT would have very little substantive effect on the probability of mobilized dissent, regardless of the extant level of domestic rights protection. In countries with executives who value

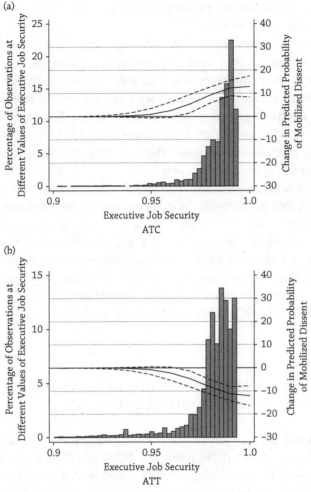

Figure 6.4 Average treatment effect of CAT OBLIGATION on (a) the controls (ATC) and (b) the treated (ATT) on the probability of MOBILIZED DISSENT ACTION conditional on JOB SECURITY WITH IRREGULAR HISTORY in countries where DOMESTIC JUDICIAL RIGHTS PROTECTION is at its subsample minimum.

political office, on the other hand, making countries renege on their CAT obligations has a statistically significant negative effect on the probability of mobilized dissent. The magnitude of that negative effect is larger (i.e., more negative) in countries where leaders are unlikely to face domestic litigation costs. These results support our theory: HRT obligation is most associated with increases in mobilized dissent in countries where leaders value their positions of power and where there are fewer ex ante litigation costs associated with repression. It is in those countries where HRT obligations most severely constrain governments from violating human rights, and consequently, provide incentives for people to mobilize and take action against the government.

Notably, the substantive results using this alternative (irregular) specification of leader security are lesser in magnitude than the ones reported using our preferred measure. This may indicate that the theory is useful, yet insufficient to explain institutional constraints on repression and dissent in states with irregular turnover histories. Leaders may be less prone to consider international obligations in such turbulent systems, and dissidents may assume as much. These circumstances may benefit from more exploration in future research.

To summarize, the estimated empirical models focusing on obligation to the CAT and its effect on the occurrence of mobilized dissent provide strong support for our theory.[26] When leaders sufficiently value the retention of office, commitment to the CAT increases the probability that leaders will face mobilized dissent. Although this effect seems to hold regardless of the extent to which leaders expect to incur domestic litigation costs for repression, CAT obligation has a substantively larger effect when the extant probability of litigation in a court of law is low.

6.3 EFFECT OF ICCPR OBLIGATION ON MOBILIZED DISSENT

International Human Rights Day, a commemoration of the UN General Assembly's (UNGA) December 10, 1948, adoption of the Universal Declaration of Human Rights (UDHR), often incites worldwide protests aimed at pressuring abusive governments to decrease state repression. In 2015, the United Nations specifically intended the date to increase awareness of two international human rights treaties—the International Covenant on Civil and Political Rights (ICCPR) and the International Covenant on Economic, Social and Cultural Rights (ICESCR). To celebrate their countries' commitments to the international human rights treaties—and to draw attention to the disjuncture between commitment

---

26. Additional empirical tests can be found in the Online Appendix. They suggest that our main results hold in both direction and statistical significance when we (1) use an alternative measure of EXECUTIVE JOB SECURITY; (2) control for temporal dependence using an annual third-order polynomial time-counter as advised by Carter and Signorino 2010; (3) include controls for media freedom as measured using data from Cingranelli, Richards, and Clay 2014; and (4) include as part of our instrument data various measures of the difficulty of a country's ratification procedures and a country's common law status as suggested and operationalized by Simmons 2009.

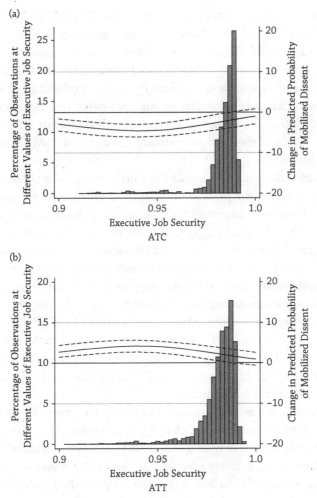

Figure 6.5 Average treatment effect of ICCPR obligation on (a) the controls (ATC) and (b) the treated (ATT) on the probability of MOBILIZED DISSENT ACTION conditional on EXECUTIVE JOB SECURITY in countries where JUDICIAL EFFECTIVENESS is at its subsample maximum.

to and compliance with their terms—advocacy groups in Cuba and the Philippines took to the streets.[27] Does commitment to the ICCPR increase the probability of mobilized dissent actions against the government more generally?

Figure 6.5 shows the marginal effect of obligation to the ICCPR on change in the probability of MOBILIZED DISSENT ACTION in countries where the latent probability of litigation costs is relatively high (i.e., where courts are likely to be relatively effective). When we used a measure of

27. VOA News 2015.

DOMESTIC JUDICIAL RIGHTS PROTECTION from Hill (2015), as we did for the CAT and throughout Chapter 5, empirical models of the effect of ICCPR and CEDAW obligation on the likelihood of MOBILIZED DISSENT ACTION failed to converge on estimated parameters. In the remainder of this chapter, we instead measure the latent probability of domestic litigation and its costs using data on JUDICIAL EFFECTIVENESS from Linzer and Staton (2015).[28] The average treatment on the controls (ATC) is shown in Figure 6.5a, and the average treatment on the treated (ATT) is shown in Figure 6.5b.

We predicted that HRTs would have little effect on mobilized dissent in countries where the population already assumes that the government will be somewhat constrained by an effective judicial system, and that is indeed what the data suggest. In both the ATC and the ATT, the 95 percent confidence intervals surround the zero line in country-months for the majority of leaders, especially where leaders have a high expected value for retaining power. These estimates suggest that obligation to the ICCPR does have a statistically significant effect on the probability of mobilized dissent activity—a negative effect in the case of the ATC and a positive effect in the case of the ATT. These findings are counter to the implications of the theory. However, for this range of statistically significant effects, the size of the substantive effect of ICCPR obligation on the probability of mobilized dissent is quite small.

In contrast, the results presented in Figure 6.6 show (a) the ATC and (b) the ATT for the effect of ICCPR obligation in countries with courts that pose relatively little risk of litigation cost to repressive leaders. Potential dissidents in these countries would not expect the leader or authorities to be held accountable in domestic courts; this is the case in Venezuela, as previously described. According to our theory, these are the countries

---

28. This measure accounts for several concepts: (1) whether judges are permitted to rule without interference (Keith 2002b; Staton and Moore 2011), (2) whether judges' rulings are translated into policy (Cameron 2002; Staton and Moore 2011), and (3) whether the population believes the court is effective according to points (1) and (2) and is inclined to use the court for remedy from the government (Powell and Staton 2009). These concepts capture the likelihood that people will litigate, as well as how likely it is to be costly to the government. Linzer and Staton use a heteroskedastic graded response item response theory model to cull information from eight existing measures of judicial independence, power, activity, and overall popular confidence in the rule of law to capture the underlying latent concept of judicial effectiveness (LJI). LJI draws on data from Tate and Keith 2007, Howard and Carey 2004, Cingranelli, Richards, and Clay 2014, Marshall and Jaggers 2009, Clague et al. 1999, Feld and Voigt 2003, PRS Group 2009, and Gwartney and Lawson 2006, 2007. The information from these constituent measures means that the final continuous indicator of JUDICIAL EFFECTIVENESS (which ranges from 0 to 1, where higher values represent higher levels of effectiveness) captures both what the court does and what the population expects.

where obligation to an HRT will most strongly influence people to engage in dissent activity against the government (as compared to their dissent choices without HRT obligation)—but only when leaders have a high expected value for the retention of power and thus are the most likely to be constrained by a treaty obligation.

As above, the average treatment effect on the controls shows the counterfactual of forcing all uncommitted countries to obligate themselves to the ICCPR. Figure 6.6a shows that when EXECUTIVE JOB SECURITY is high, such that leaders have a high expected value for retaining political office, potential dissidents are significantly more likely to engage in mobilized

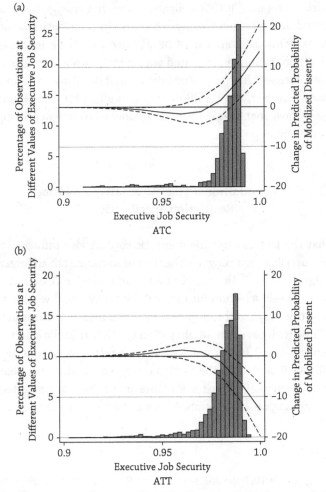

Figure 6.6 Average treatment effect of ICCPR obligation on (a) the controls (ATC) and (b) the treated (ATT) on the probability of MOBILIZED DISSENT ACTION conditional on EXECUTIVE JOB SECURITY in countries where JUDICIAL EFFECTIVENESS is at its subsample minimum.

dissent actions against the government as a result of commitment to the ICCPR. When leaders place comparatively less value on maintaining their positions of power, commitment to the ICCPR has a negligible substantive effect on decisions to dissent against the government, suggesting that potential dissidents do not expect the ICCPR to constrain authorities' choices to repress.

The average treatment effect on the treated , which shows the opposite counterfactual in Figure 6.6b, provides additional evidence in support of our main hypotheses by showing what would happen if we made all ICCPR-committed countries exit their obligations under international law. In countries where leaders face a low probability of litigation costs associated with repression, ICCPR obligation does not change the probability of mobilized dissent when leaders are secure in their positions of power; as the LEADER'S EXPECTED VALUE OF RETAINING POWER increases, however, ICCPR obligation is associated with a statistically and substantively significant decrease in the probability of mobilized dissent. In both of these cases, however, the ICCPR only has an effect for a small number of countries—those that have at the helm a leader who places a very high value on the retention of power.

6.3.1 Additional Test: Alternative Exclusion Restriction Specification

Recall that the factors affecting domestic conflict also influence the government's decision regarding whether or not to commit to an international human rights treaty.[29] In order to meet the exclusion restriction to deal with potential self-selection into TREATY OBLIGATION,[30] we must include in the selection stage of the empirical models a measure that is believed to be correlated with government obligation to HRTs (i.e., the selection-stage dependent variable) but is not known to affect government repression or mobilized dissent (i.e., the outcome-stage dependent variables).[31] To this point, we have included a measure of the number of intergovernmental organization (IO) memberships a state maintains during a given year.[32]

---

29. See, e.g., Hill 2010; Lupu 2013b; Powell and Staton 2009; von Stein 2016.
30. We discussed the requirements of the exclusion restriction in detail in Chapter 4.
31. Sartori 2003, p. 112.
32. For additional information on the justification for and operationalization of this concept, please refer to Chapter 4.

Simmons (2009) argues in favor of an additional instrument, suggesting that procedural ratification difficulty is (1) related to (lack of) obligation to international human rights law, but (2) not correlated with government human rights practices. To consider the robustness of the empirical results to our choice of an instrument, we include in the models below two exclusion restrictions: (1) IO MEMBERSHIP, a count variable from Ulfelder (2011) described in detail in Chapter 4, and (2) RATIFICATION DIFFICULTY, a five-category ordered measure from Simmons (2009), where higher numbers indicate more difficult domestic treaty ratification procedures.

The ATC and ATT depicted in Figure 6.7 are consistent with Hypothesis 2.[33] In fact, these results are more in line with the theoretical predictions than the estimates presented in Figure 6.5. When the domestic judicial system is considered effective, secure leaders should experience more dissent actions under obligation to the ICCPR. In each of the subfigures, the effect of the ICCPR on mobilized dissent is statistically indistinguishable from zero—and substantively small—when EXECUTIVE JOB SECURITY is low. As leaders increasingly value the retention of political office, the effect of ICCPR obligation begins to reach traditional values of statistical significance, becoming positive in the case of the ATC shown in Figure 6.7a and negative in the case of the ATT shown in Figure 6.7b. Importantly, however, the substantive effect of ICCPR obligation on the probability of mobilized dissent is relatively small when leaders already anticipate domestic litigation costs for repression.

When leaders are unlikely to face meaningful domestic litigation costs for repression, ICCPR commitment should have a much larger substantive effect on changes in the probability of mobilized dissent activity, as illustrated in Figure 6.8. If countries that opted out of ICCPR obligation were forced to commit (Figure 6.8a), those with the most secure leaders at the helm would face an increased probability of mobilized dissent of more than twenty points. Similarly, if countries that selected into the ICCPR were forced to renege on their commitments (Figure 6.8b)—if the ICCPR did not exist, for example—leaders who most highly value the retention of office would face a decrease in the probability of mobilized dissent of a similar magnitude. In both Figures 6.8a and 6.8b, ICCPR OBLIGATION leads to little change in the probability of mobilized dissent when EXECUTIVE JOB SECURITY is sufficiently low.

Although we relegate the bulk of our robustness checks to the Online Appendix that accompanies this book,[34] we think it particularly important

---

33. Table 8 in Appendix 3 reports the results on which these figures are based.

34. As above, additional empirical tests can be found in the Online Appendix. They suggest that the main results hold in both direction and statistical significance when

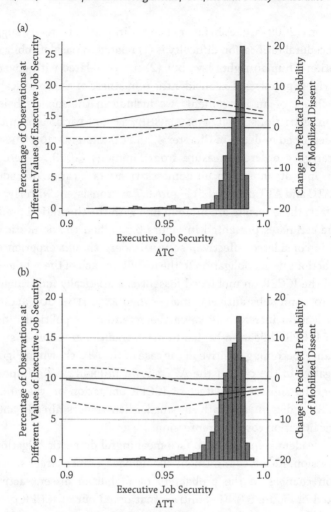

Figure 6.7 Average treatment effect of ICCPR OBLIGATION on (a) the controls (ATC) and (b) the treated (ATT) on the probability of MOBILIZED DISSENT ACTION conditional on EXECUTIVE JOB SECURITY in countries where JUDICIAL EFFECTIVENESS is at its subsample maximum, with the additional instrument variable RATIFICATION DIFFICULTY.

to show the robustness of our main empirical results to changes in our base-line empirical specification. In particular, the empirical analyses presented in this section show that our results do not seem to be strictly dependent on the measure used to represent domestic judicial consequences for

we (1) include controls for latent protection for physical integrity right violations as measured by Fariss 2014, democracy as measured using Polity IV data, and youth bulges as discussed by Nordås and Davenport 2013, and (2) include as part of our instrument data various measures of the difficulty of a country's ratification procedures and a country's common-law status as suggested and operationalized by Simmons 2009.

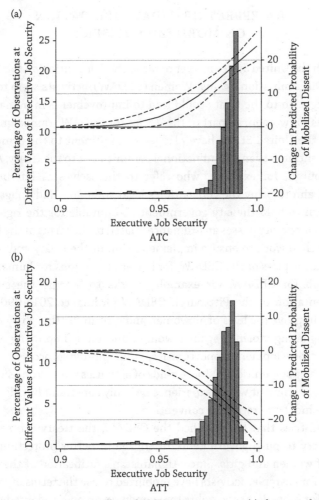

Figure 6.8 Average treatment effect of ICCPR OBLIGATION on (a) the controls (ATC) and (b) the treated (ATT) on the probability of MOBILIZED DISSENT ACTION conditional on EXECUTIVE JOB SECURITY in countries where JUDICIAL EFFECTIVENESS is at its subsample minimum, with the additional instrument variable RATIFICATION DIFFICULTY.

repression nor our choice of an exclusion restriction. Because selection models often face the criticism of being sensitive to minor changes in specification,[35] showing the robustness of the results to changes in the instruments we use is especially important.

---

35. See, e.g., Simmons and Hopkins 2005.

6.4 EFFECT OF CEDAW OBLIGATION
ON MOBILIZED DISSENT

Although the United States has yet to ratify the Convention on the Elimination of Discrimination Against Women (CEDAW), activists seem to believe that obligation to the treaty could lead to improvements in human rights outcomes for women. As part of the "Cities for CEDAW" campaign, several cities in the United States have pledged commitment to the principles of the convention—even absent national commitment to the treaty. Activists in Pittsburgh, for example, who refer to themselves as Pittsburgh for CEDAW, aim to bring the convention's legal standards and obligations to Pittsburgh to hold the city government accountable for the rights of all women. Once a city passes an ordinance related to the terms of the CEDAW, activists then work to ensure implementation of the treaty and mobilize, under the auspices of the CEDAW, for better protections for human rights. Pittsburgh for CEDAW, for example, works to "ensure the successful implementation of the Pittsburgh CEDAW Ordinance 2016-0905 which seeks to improve the lives of all women and girls in Pittsburgh by reducing and eliminating violence against women and girls, improving access to economic development opportunities, and improving access to quality education opportunities."[36] These kinds of activities are a strong signal that the U.S. government would experience not only constraint but also dissent if it were indeed to ratify the convention.

In countries that have ratified the CEDAW, the treaty can serve as a rallying cry to push governments to engage in better protections of the rights of women and girls. Since Afghanistan's ratification of the CEDAW in 2010, for example, activists have mobilized to use the terms of the treaty to push for more domestic rights for women. In an op-ed adapted from her testimony before a U.S. Senate Judiciary subcommittee hearing on CEDAW ratification, Afghani activist Wazhma Frogh spoke of the effect of CEDAW obligation in pushing forward the women's rights agenda in Afghanistan:

> CEDAW has been a banner, a torch we've held high, as we've made our journey towards basic rights. In 2004... we used its terms to lobby for Article 22, which states that Afghan women and men are equal before the law. Since the country had no significant history for such an argument to be accepted by the Grand Assembly of elders and conservative elements, CEDAW was our main basis for advocacy... A major success of our Afghan Women's Network was in using CEDAW terms to develop and lobby for the Elimination of Violence Against Women (EVAW) law... The law made rape a crime in Afghanistan for the first

36. Pittsburgh for CEDAW 2018.

time, and nullified forced marriages and early marriages without consent of the girl, punishing the perpetrators with imprisonment. Such an arrangement was taken from CEDAW Article 16, which makes the state responsible for eliminating discrimination around issues of marriage and family matters.[37]

These dissidents use activism to constrain the government into compliance, and the substance of the treaty itself fuels their participation in dissent actions.

Cross-nationally, the CEDAW offers the strongest evidence in support of the implications of our theory with regard to mobilized dissent. Countries where leaders expect to face a high probability of litigation costs for engaging in repression would see virtually no differences in mobilized dissent activity if they were moved from one treaty status to the other. Results supporting this conjecture are shown in Figure 6.9, which illustrates the (a) ATC and the (b) ATT for changes in CEDAW obligation status for countries where the probability of repressive leaders experiencing litigation costs is high. Substantively, the effect of CEDAW obligation on the probability of mobilized dissent in such countries is very small and does not meet the common standard of 95 percent statistical confidence. In essence, obligation to the CEDAW makes little difference to mobilized dissent outcomes when leaders are already concerned with the possibility of facing domestic litigation costs for violations of human rights.

In comparison to the substantive effects shown in Figure 6.9, Figure 6.10 graphs the estimated marginal effect of CEDAW obligation in countries where the probability of repressive leaders facing domestic litigation costs is relatively low. Although both the ATC and the ATT trend in the same direction as the results shown in Figure 6.9, the magnitudes of the effects are much larger, and the confidence intervals hug the point estimates much more closely, easily meeting the 95 percent confidence standard. In both subfigures, the effect of CEDAW obligation on mobilized dissent is substantively near zero when EXECUTIVE JOB SECURITY is relatively low. The ATC depicted in Figure 6.10a shows that as executives are more invested in the retention of political office, forcing unobligated countries to obligate themselves to the CEDAW increases the probability of mobilized dissent. In hypothetical countries with the most secure leaders, CEDAW obligation would increase the probability of dissent by nearly thirty points. Forcing CEDAW-obligated countries to drop their commitments would similarly decrease the probability of mobilized dissent action (in countries where executives most highly value the retention of political office) by approximately the same amount, as shown by the ATT in Figure 6.10b. These

37. Frogh 2010.

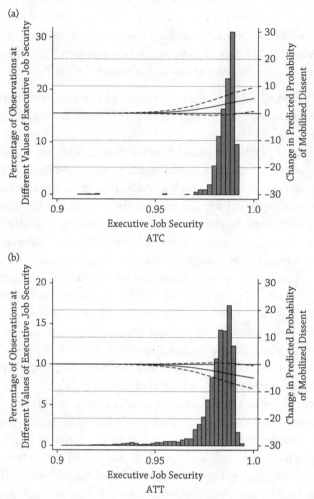

Figure 6.9 Average treatment effect of CEDAW OBLIGATION on (a) the controls (ATC) and (b) the treated (ATT) on the probability of MOBILIZED DISSENT ACTION conditional on EXECUTIVE JOB SECURITY in countries where JUDICIAL EFFECTIVENESS is at its subsample maximum.

results are consistent with our argument about the effect of obligation to international human rights law on popular dissent against the government, and they provide strong support for Hypothesis 2.

6.4.1 Additional Test: Alternative Measure of Mobilized Dissent

The scope of the theory presented in this book is not limited to the effect of HRTs on demands for the protection of particular rights or to demands by groups with particular demographics. Obligations to international human

(a)

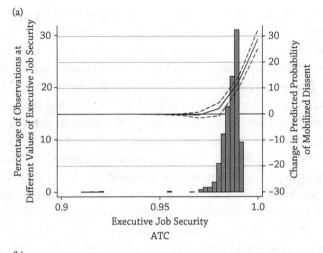

(b)

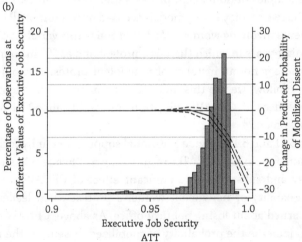

Figure 6.10 Average treatment effect of CEDAW OBLIGATION on (a) the controls (ATC) and (b) the treated (ATT) on the probability of MOBILIZED DISSENT ACTION conditional on EXECUTIVE JOB SECURITY in countries where JUDICIAL EFFECTIVENESS is at its subsample minimum.

rights treaties constrain the leader from repressing some groups in some ways, making the overall environment more favorable for any groups considering dissent. In other words, we expect obligation to the CEDAW to improve the conditions for any type of dissent, leading to an increase in the probability of dissent activities under the contexts we have laid out. Importantly, the effect of the CEDAW should *not* be limited to dissent activities carried out by predominantly female groups or to demands specifically related to women's issues.

Nevertheless, to better understand the effects of HRTs on mobilized dissent, we conduct an additional analysis investigating the effect of CEDAW obligation specifically on women's protest activities. We use replication data from Murdie and Peksen (2015) that counts the number of nonviolent protests carried out by women. In conjunction with Virtual Research Associates, Murdie and Peksen generated these data based on a new coding of the updated IDEA data (this dataset is described in detail in Chapter 4). In particular, the data include only nonviolent protest events in which the actor was "clearly stated to be a 'woman,' 'women,' or 'feminist' in the body or header of the event and a protest event is cited in this same body or header."[38] Events are considered to be nonviolent protest activities according to coding rules by Bhasin (2008); demonstrations, sit-ins, protest marches, strikes, formal written petition drives, and boycotts are some common examples of nonviolent protests under this framework. The final measure that we employ in our models is based on a count of all nonviolent protest events involving women. We dichotomize this variable, coding it as "1" in country-years in which there is a protest and as "0" in country-years in which there is not an instance of nonviolent protest by women. In the results that follow, we use this indicator as our main dependent variable, testing the effect of CEDAW obligation on the likelihood of nonviolent protest by women.[39]

Figures 6.11 and 6.12 provide additional support for our hypotheses and, by extension, for our theory.[40] The results shown in Figure 6.11 show a small statistically and substantively significant effect of CEDAW commitment on the probability of nonviolent women's protest when leaders are the most concerned about losing political office. As above, CEDAW obligation appears to increase the probability of mobilized dissent on the rightmost side of each figure even when leaders already expect to face high domestic litigation costs for repression. Importantly, however, these substantive effects grow when leaders are not constrained by the possibility of domestic litigation costs. The ATC and ATT shown in Figure 6.12 show that CEDAW obligation has the largest substantive effect on changing the probability of mobilized dissent in countries helmed by secure leaders who face few ex ante litigation costs for violating human rights. Under those conditions, both the ATC and the ATT suggest that commitment to the CEDAW can increase the probability of nonviolent women's protest by over 20 percent.

38. Murdie and Peksen 2015.

39. Data from Murdie and Peksen 2015 are coded at the country-year unit of observation. We include these data in country-month models, which means we likely overestimate the number of dissent events.

40. Table 9 in Appendix 3 reports the results on which these figures are based.

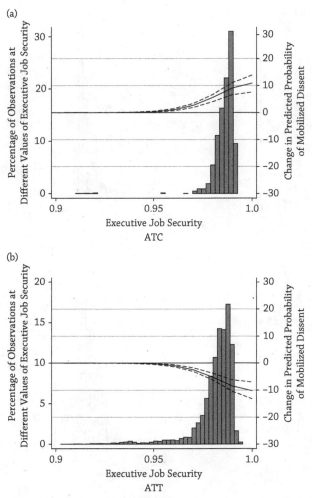

Figure 6.11 Average treatment effect of CEDAW OBLIGATION on (a) the controls (ATC) and (b) the treated (ATT) on the probability of NONVIOLENT WOMEN'S DISSENT ACTION conditional on EXECUTIVE JOB SECURITY in countries where JUDICIAL EFFECTIVENESS is at its subsample maximum.

The empirical estimates focusing on CEDAW pose the strongest evidence of the three treaties that international human rights treaty obligation leads to an increase in the predicted probability of mobilized dissent as compared to what countries would have experienced in the absence of such international obligations.[41] Countries where domestic judicial systems

41. As above, additional empirical tests can be found in the Online Appendix. They suggest that our main results hold in both direction and statistical significance when we (1) employ an alternative measure of EXECUTIVE JOB SECURITY; (2) include controls for latent protection for physical integrity right violations as measured by Fariss 2014, democracy as measured using Polity IV data, media freedom as measured using data

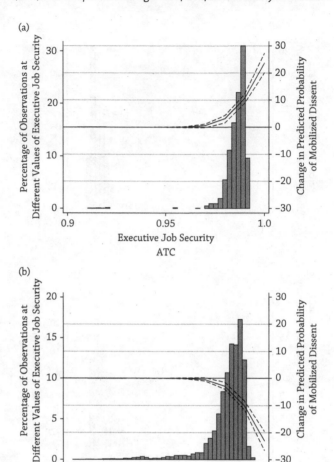

Figure 6.12 Average treatment effect of CEDAW OBLIGATION on (a) the controls (ATC) and (b) the treated (ATT) on the probability of NONVIOLENT WOMEN'S DISSENT ACTION conditional on EXECUTIVE JOB SECURITY in countries where JUDICIAL EFFECTIVENESS is at its subsample minimum.

are such that leaders are concerned about the possibility of litigation costs in the absence of CEDAW commitment see very small or negligible effects on mobilized dissent; countries where leaders are unconcerned about remaining in power see similarly small effects of HRT obligation on mobilized dissent activity. But in countries where the domestic

from Cingranelli, Richards, and Clay 2014, and youth bulges as discussed by Nordås and Davenport 2013; (3) control for temporal dependence using an annual third-order polynomial time-counter as advised by Carter and Signorino 2010; and (4) include as part of our instrument various measures of the difficulty of a country's ratification procedures and a country's common-law status as suggested and operationalized by Simmons 2009.

environment fails to place litigation costs on repressive leaders—and where leaders are most likely to repress because they highly value the retention of political office—obligation to the CEDAW leads dissidents to expect relative constraint, such that they are more likely to engage in dissent activities.

6.5 SUMMARY OF FINDINGS: MOBILIZED DISSENT

In this chapter, we presented empirical support for our theory, analyzing the extent to which state obligation to three international human rights treaties—the CAT, the ICCPR, and the CEDAW—influences the likelihood of dissent actions against the government. Our empirical analyses provide strong statistical and substantive support for the theory: Each of the counterfactuals presented above suggests that HRTs have very large substantive effects on the probability of dissent actions via their expected effects on government repression. The analyses show very consistent evidence that obligation to an HRT can lead to increases in the probability of mobilized dissent as compared to what a state would see without the obligation. International human rights treaties—intended primarily to constrain government repression—also have a structural effect on mobilized dissent, altering the incentive structure within which potential dissidents make decisions. Although it has previously been argued that international human rights treaties act as focal points to facilitate coordination,[42] we show that these international institutions also influence the actions of dissidents. By increasing expected institutional costs for repression, HRTs create openings for citizens to challenge the state.

Our theory and empirical analyses clearly describe the conditions under which international law adds value to the act of dissent, changing dissidents' expectations about the cost-benefit ratio of engaging in dissent actions, and the conditions under which it does little to alter conflict behavior. Potential dissidents' expectations about whether and when their rights will be violated by the state are based on how likely *domestic* institutions are to constrain authorities. When those institutions create high expectations that authorities will experience consequences, dissidents will expect a treaty not to change that environment, or to change it very little. Thus, international treaties designed to curb rights violations can encourage dissidents to dissent against the government by opening opportunities for action with less likely repressive consequences—and perversely, this increased dissent creates new incentives for the government to further violate human rights.

---

42. Finnemore and Sikkink 1998; Simmons 2009; Vreeland 2008a.

Studying how potential dissidents respond to these opportunities in anticipation of government repression allows us to learn a great deal about how HRTs affect popular decision-making. In particular, HRTs have the largest effect on changes in the probability of dissent actions when domestic litigation costs are unlikely to influence the leader's repressive behavior. Effective judiciaries—those that limit leader behavior with the potential for litigation costs—largely constrain leaders from violating rights with or without an obligation to an international standard of protection. Under these circumstances, government repression and mobilized dissent remain comparatively low, and obligation to international human rights law does little to shift these behaviors. Conversely, when the ex ante probability of litigation costs is low, we expect overall levels of repression to be much higher because leaders are relatively less constrained by domestic institutions. This low level of constraint differs significantly with the introduction of new legal standards and the attendant popular expectations associated with HRT commitment, such that we see the greatest magnitude of HRT effects on repression—and therefore dissent—when judiciaries are relatively poor at imposing litigation costs on repressive leaders.

HRTs thus have their strongest effect when states lack the domestic mechanisms to constrain leaders; in these cases, HRTs lead to increases in mobilized dissent against the government. This finding runs counter to existing scholarly arguments, which expect that courts need to be effective to enforce HRT obligations. Because HRTs influence both state repression and dissent, these obligations have potentially divergent effects: when they are most effective at constraining state violations of human rights, they provide incentives for citizens to dissent against the government. Consequently, even when treaties successfully constrain human rights violations, they may indirectly increase incentives to repress via their effects on popular dissent. Effective domestic courts potentially provide a solution. When states with secure leaders have ineffective courts, dissent increases with HRT obligation, providing indirect incentives to repress. But when these states have effective courts, groups are as likely to protest as they are in an opposite treaty status, leaving governments to face dissent while constrained by strong domestic laws and courts.

6.6 APPENDIX 3: EMPIRICAL RESULTS FOR MOBILIZED DISSENT

Table A3.1 EFFECT OF HRT (CAT) OBLIGATION ON MOBILIZED DISSENT (COUNTRY-YEAR)

	CAT		ICCPR	
	Obligated	Unobligated	Obligated	Unobligated
Outcome DV: Mobilized Dissent				
Domestic Judicial Rights Protection	-0.797*	0.250	-0.420*	-0.028
	(0.193)	(0.150)	(0.155)	(0.176)
Executive Job Security	-2.907*	-2.590*	-3.716*	-1.306
	(0.968)	(1.099)	(0.840)	(1.455)
Domestic Judicial Rights Protection x Executive Job Security	-0.011*	-0.703*	-0.275	-0.274
	(0.311)	(0.270)	(0.217)	(0.477)
Constant	3.865*	2.408*	4.512*	0.986
	(0.763)	(1.012)	(0.678)	(1.399)
Selection DV: CAT/ICCPR Obligation				
Domestic Judicial Rights Protection	0.155		0.232*	
	(0.105)		(0.112)	
Executive Job Security	-1.835*		-1.816*	
	(0.377)		(0.473)	
Domestic Judicial Rights Protection x Executive Job Security	1.214***		1.125*	
	(0.141)		(0.156)	
Number of IO Memberships	0.134*		0.100*	
	(0.017)		(0.018)	
Constant	0.716*		1.339*	
	(0.327)		(0.411)	
P	-0.290	-0.710*	-0.631	-0.673
Log-pseudo likelihood	-2,141.754		-1,985.715	
N	2,048		2,044	

Notes: * Significant within 95% confidence interval; two-tailed test. Likelihood ratio test of the null hypothesis that the coefficients on the constants in the obligated and unobligated samples are equal (i.e., that the treaty has no influence independent of selection): $\chi^2 = 1.34$ (p < 0.2478) (Model 1); $\chi^2 = 5.26$ (p < 0.022) (Model 2). Likelihood ratio test of the null hypothesis that ρ^S and ρ^N jointly equal zero (i.e., that there are selection effects): $\chi^2 = 9.28$ (p < 0.010) (Model 1); $\chi^2 = 6.07$ (p < 0.048) (Model 2).

Table A3.2 EFFECT OF HRT (CAT) OBLIGATION ON MOBILIZED DISSENT (COUNTRY-MONTH)

	CAT		CAT	
	Obligated	Unobligated	Obligated	Unobligated
Outcome DV: Mobilized Dissent				
Domestic Judicial Rights Protection	-0.049	0.365*	-34.433*	31.281*
	(0.036)	(0.051)	(3.326)	(8.033)
Executive Job Security	-6.432*	26.118*	-	-
	(0.779)	(2.407)		
Irregular Executive Job Security	-	-	-9.432*	-19.672*
			(0.882)	(1.817)
Domestic Judicial Rights Protection x (Irregular) Executive Job Security	0.221*	0.274*	34.958*	32.081*
	(0.077)	(0.104)	(3.382)	(8.146)
Constant	6.265*	24.952*	9.296*	19.015*
	(0.749)	(2.401)	(0.846)	(1.822)
Selection DV: CAT Obligation				
Domestic Judicial Rights Protection	-0.108*		-23.193*	
	(0.030)		(3.495)	
Executive Job Security	-8.673*		-	
	(1.117)			
Irregular Executive Job Security	-		-14.366*	
			(0.848)	
Domestic Judicial Rights Protection x (Irregular) Executive Job Security	0.998*		23.635*	
	(0.039)		(3.548)	
Number of IO Memberships	0.117*		0.152*	
	(0.005)		(0.005)	
Constant	7.890*		13.769*	
	(1.104)		(0.836)	
ρ	-0.468	-0.186	-0.363*	0.072
Log-pseudo likelihood	-26,591.821		-29,315.558	
N	21,074		22,730	

Notes: * Significant within 95% confidence interval; two-tailed test. Likelihood ratio test of the null hypothesis that the coefficients on the constants in the obligated and unobligated samples are equal (i.e., that the treaty has no influence independent of selection): $\chi^2 = 55.57$ (p < 0.000) (Model 1); $\chi^2 = 23.29$ (p < 0.000) (Model 2). Likelihood ratio test of the null hypothesis that ρ^S and ρ^N jointly equal zero (i.e., that there are selection effects): $\chi^2 = 124.08$ (p < 0.000) (Model 1); $\chi^2 = 85.08$ (p < 0.000) (Model 2).

Table A3.3 EFFECT OF HRT (ICCPR) OBLIGATION ON MOBILIZED DISSENT (COUNTRY-MONTH)

	ICCPR		ICCPR	
	Obligated	Unobligated	Obligated	Unobligated
Outcome DV: Mobilized Dissent				
Domestic Judicial Rights Protection	5.576	−7.099	9.998*	9.058
	(4.336)	(9.380)	(4.123)	(9.286)
Executive Job Security	−11.952*	−36.072*	−8.199*	−19.340*
	(3.303)	(6.487)	(3.061)	(7.228)
Domestic Judicial Rights Protection x Executive Job Security	−5.728	7.810	−10.312*	−9.035
	(4.430)	(9.559)	(4.205)	(9.453)
Constant	11.808*	35.325*	8.196*	17.960*
	(3.227)	(6.431)	(3.001)	(7.163)
Selection DV: ICCPR Obligation				
Domestic Judicial Rights Protection	−47.744*		−39.789*	
	(4.138)		(4.114)	
Executive Job Security	−38.270*		−31.249*	
	(3.013)		(3.026)	
Domestic Judicial Rights Protection x Executive Job Security	49.476*		41.343*	
	(4.207)		(4.183)	
Number of IO Memberships	0.101*		0.081*	
	(0.005)		(0.005)	
Ratification Difficulty	—		0.235*	
			(0.014)	
Constant	37.482*		30.261*	
	(2.968)		(2.983)	
ρ	−0.717*	0.453*	−0.815*	0.330*
Log-pseudo likelihood	−28,997.714		−28,370.225	
N	24,578		24,254	

Notes: * Significant within 95% confidence interval; two-tailed test. Likelihood ratio test of the null hypothesis that the coefficients on the constants in the obligated and unobligated samples are equal (i.e., that the treaty has no influence independent of selection): $\chi^2 = 10.08$ (p < 0.002) (Model 1); $\chi^2 = 1.65$ (p < 0.199) (Model 2). Likelihood ratio test of the null hypothesis that ρ^S and ρ^N jointly equal zero (i.e., that there are selection effects): $\chi^2 = 83.76$ (p < 0.000) (Model 1); $\chi^2 = 167.05$ (p < 0.000) (Model 2).

Table A3.4 EFFECT OF HRT (CEDAW) OBLIGATION ON MOBILIZED DISSENT (COUNTRY-MONTH)

	DV: Mobilized Dissent		DV: Nonviolent Women's Protest	
	Obligated	Unobligated	Obligated	Unobligated
Outcome DV: Mobilized Dissent/Nonviolent Women's Protest				
Domestic Judicial Rights Protection	29.153*	-57.065*	27.491*	-36.102*
	(4.070)	(11.983)	(4.219)	(10.607)
Executive Job Security	9.985*	-68.330*	13.476*	-13.489
	(2.962)	(17.979)	(3.122)	(15.788)
Domestic Judicial Rights Protection x Executive Job Security	-29.492*	58.418*	-27.501*	36.768*
	(4.142)	(12.206)	(4.297)	(10.801)
Constant	-9.960*	66.280*	-13.507*	12.069
	(2.913)	(17.943)	(3.067)	(15.719)
Selection DV: CEDAW Obligation				
Domestic Judicial Rights Protection	-26.364*		-20.367*	
	(5.735)		(5.787)	
Executive Job Security	70.334*		-68.773*	
	(3.751)		(3.733)	
Domestic Judicial Rights Protection x Executive Job Security	26.915*		20.807*	
	(5.828)		(5.881)	
Number of IO Memberships	0.059*		0.052*	
	(0.005)		(0.005)	
Constant	69.893*		68.389*	
	(3.695)		(3.678)	
ρ	-0.923*	-0.323	-0.889*	-0.632*
Log-pseudo likelihood	-26,037.013		-26,254.718	
N	24,578		24,578	

Notes: * Significant within 95% confidence interval; two-tailed test. Likelihood ratio test of the null hypothesis that the coefficients on the constants in the obligated and unobligated samples are equal (i.e., that the treaty has no influence independent of selection): $\chi^2 = 17.66$ (p < 0.000) (Model 1); $\chi^2 = 2.58$ (p < 0.108) (Model 2). Likelihood ratio test of the null hypothesis that ρ^S and ρ^N jointly equal zero (i.e., that there are selection effects): $\chi^2 = 165.64$ (p < 0.000) (Model 1); $\chi^2 = 135.35$ (p < 0.000) (Model 2).

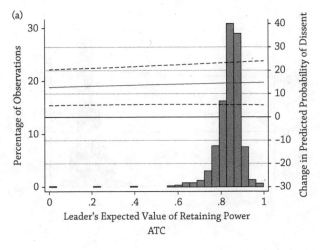

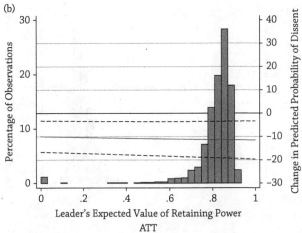

Figure A3.1 Average treatment effect of CAT OBLIGATION on (a) the controls (ATC) and (b) the treated (ATT) on the annual probability of MOBILIZED DISSENT ACTION conditional on EXECUTIVE JOB SECURITY in countries where DOMESTIC JUDICIAL RIGHTS PROTECTION is at its sub-sample maximum.

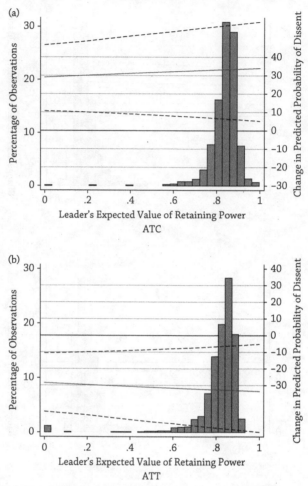

Figure A3.2 Average treatment effect of CAT OBLIGATION on (a) the controls (ATC) and (b) the treated (ATT) on the annual probability of MOBILIZED DISSENT ACTION conditional on EXECUTIVE JOB SECURITY in countries where DOMESTIC JUDICIAL RIGHTS PROTECTION is at its subsample minimum.

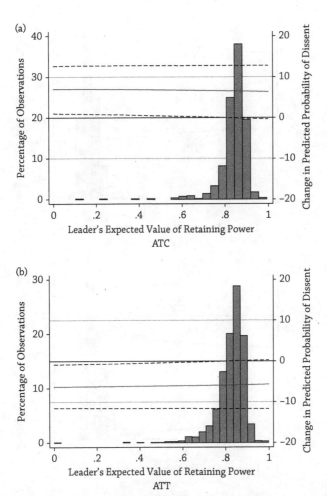

Figure A3.3 Average treatment effect of ICCPR obligation on (a) the controls (ATC) and (b) the treated (ATT) on the annual probability of MOBILIZED DISSENT ACTION conditional on EXECUTIVE JOB SECURITY in countries where JUDICIAL EFFECTIVENESS is at its subsample maximum.

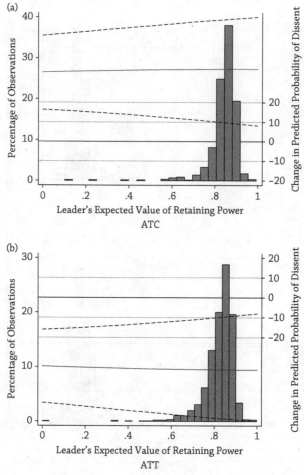

Figure A3.4 Average treatment effect of ICCPR obligation on (a) the controls (ATC) and (b) the treated (ATT) on the annual probability of MOBILIZED DISSENT ACTION conditional on EXECUTIVE JOB SECURITY in countries where JUDICIAL EFFECTIVENESS is at its subsample minimum.

PART III

Conclusion

CHAPTER 7

༄

Conclusion: Human Rights Treaties (Sometimes) Protect Rights

I n a *New York Times* debate with Eric Posner about the effectiveness of international human rights law,[1] Kenneth Roth, the executive director of Human Rights Watch (HRW), listed several instances when obligation to a human rights treaty seems to have improved human rights outcomes:

> The use of antipersonnel landmines and cluster munitions plummeted after treaties were adopted banning these indiscriminate weapons. Chile and Argentina cited human rights treaties to strike down military self-amnesties for mass atrocities and then convicted hundreds of people. Brazil followed treaty requirements to enhance punishment for domestic violence and permit regular prison visits against torture... Kenya cited the women's rights treaty [CEDAW] to grant women equal access to inheritances. Europe's human rights treaty led Britain to end corporal punishment in schools, Ireland to decriminalize homosexual acts, and France to grant detained people access to lawyers. A new labor treaty spurred an increased minimum wage, social security protections, and days off for domestic workers in parts of Asia and Africa. The South African Constitutional Court ruled that the right to health requires that people with

---

1. In addition to engaging in this debate with Mr. Roth, Mr. Posner makes a lengthy case against the effectiveness of international human rights law in his book (Posner 2014).

HIV be granted access to anti-retroviral drugs, saving hundreds of thousands of lives.[2]

In this book, we present a theory and empirical evidence consistent with Mr. Roth's observations. Human rights treaties decrease government repression. Not all the time. Not in every country in the world. But obligation to international law can constrain leaders from violating human rights and encourage potential dissidents to rise up against their governments. Our argument that HRTs "work" is contrary to the explanations of a wide variety of scholars who maintain that the international human rights regime has been an abject failure. Although scholars have found evidence that domestic institutions can constrain repression, there has been little support for the argument that international institutions do so. Many scholars have found treaties either to have no effect on rights practices or to lead to an increase in violations.[3] In contrast, we find that if international law creates even the smallest shift in assumptions over domestic institutional consequences for repressive authorities, these effects can yield a substantively meaningful reduction in rights violations when leaders have significant stakes in domestic conflicts over policy.

Our scholarship diverges from the existing orthodoxy about HRTs for several reasons. Much of the previous research on the effectiveness of international human rights law compares countries that have ratified treaties to their preratification selves or to similar states that have not ratified the treaty,[4] and these studies tend to find that countries with the worst rights records do not improve their practices with treaty ratification. Making before-and-after comparisons and comparisons with similar cases requires researchers to make heroic assumptions to claim differences in effect; it is impossible to determine how authorities would act under identical circumstances with a single difference in (nonrandom) treaty treatment status.[5]

Although we face the same observability problems, we depend on theory to predict how outcomes would differ as a function of treatment and then conduct empirical analyses, adhering as closely as possible to the data-generating process assumed by the theory. More specifically, we determine the extent to which treaties reduce human rights violations

2. Posner and Roth 2014.

3. See, e.g., Hafner-Burton and Tsutsui 2007; Hathaway 2002; Hill 2010; Vreeland 2008a.

4. See, e.g., Hafner-Burton and Tsutsui 2007; Hathaway 2002; Lupu 2013b; Neumayer 2005; Vreeland 2008a.

5. Holland 1986.

by engaging in a theoretical and empirical analysis of the counterfactual: for any given country, we ask, does commitment to a human rights treaty improve government respect for human rights relative to the level of abuse that would have occurred absent such an obligation? The formal model yields many implications as to the conditionality of treaty effects, suggesting they depend on a leader's expected value for holding power, the baseline propensity for repressive authorities to incur legal consequences, and underlying tendencies to select into or out of international treaty obligations. These complex interactions with precisely derived predictions yield many points of attack, and we work to falsify the theory with observable patterns of evidence, using a statistical estimator that allows us to examine these many predictions about both observable and counterfactual behavior at many points of entry. Yet our predicted patterns emerge from the empirical estimates under a variety of treaties and data.

Importantly, the theory's many conditional implications hold up to scrutiny for both government repression and mobilized dissent activity, lending support to the argument that repression cannot be considered without its connection to dissent. In another departure from dominant scholarship on institutional constraints on repression, we demonstrate that government repression is one outcome of a strategic interaction between a government and group of people who are dissatisfied with that government's status quo policies and practices. The creation of an international human rights treaty—an institution intended to constrain leaders from repression—alters a game in which the government is but one player. Because repression is part of a conflict, tying the hands of a leader via an international human rights treaty does not always decrease repression, and the expectation of constraint also creates opportunities for dissent. Thus, scholars who are interested in the effect of institutions on government behavior must equally concern themselves with the effect of the same institutions on dissident behavior.

This approach to the study of international human rights law yields new information about the conditions under which HRTs might actually improve human rights. More specifically, we argue that (1) governments repress to control mobilized dissent and dissidents expect repression when deciding to dissent, (2) authorities and dissidents consider the extent to which the government will face domestic consequences for violating human rights, and (3) human rights treaties have a small but meaningful effect on increasing the probability of consequences. Authorities balance these conflicting incentives depending on the extent to which they value the retention of political office: leaders who expect to lose office regardless of conflict outcomes have little incentive to repress and so do not condition decisions about repression on the likelihood of facing litigation costs. In contrast, leaders sitting securely in power (i.e., those who highly value political office) repress less under treaty obligations so as to minimize potential litigation costs. At the same time, dissidents are also more likely to take mobilized action against the state under these conditions—when they expect the leader to be relatively more constrained by the additional costs associated with commitment to international law.

In this chapter, we step back to look at our theory and empirical findings from a wider perspective. First, we review the project presented in this book, summarizing the theory and findings to highlight its main contributions. Next, we discuss how the claims and findings we have made here work to advance social science scholarship in the broader areas of international institutions and domestic conflict. How does our approach alter the way scholars and practitioners should think about government repression and mobilized dissent? We also think beyond the boundaries of this particular study to consider its implications for future research in other areas. Finally, we turn to the policy implications of our research: What should policymakers take away from the argument and empirical findings presented in this book? Can the lessons presented here actually help to improve government respect for human rights?

7.1 A (MORE) COMPLETE PICTURE OF DOMESTIC CONFLICT

In this book, we present a theory of conflict between government authorities and potential dissidents. The incentives faced by the leader and the dissidents are purposely generalizable; both actors in the theory share the core incentives of a wide variety of countries and dissidents around the world. Chapters 2 and 3 present the theory and its empirical implications in detail. The subsequent chapters expound on these ideas, providing arguments and evidence supporting the theory. In Chapters 5 and 6, we find evidence of the following patterns using observational data:

- Human rights treaties have *no effect* on government repression or mobilized dissent when a leader has low expected value for retaining political office. (By "no effect" here and below, we mean that the effect is not statistically and/or substantively distinguishable from zero.)
- Human rights treaties have *no effect* on government repression and mobilized dissent when the domestic environment of institutional

constraint—the probability that a repressive leader faces litigation costs—is high apart from treaty commitment.

- Human rights treaties have a *negative effect* on government repression when a leader places a high value on the retention of political office and so is more likely to violate human rights, especially when the probability that a repressive leader faces domestic legal consequences is low.
- Human rights treaties have a *positive effect* on mobilized dissent when a leader places a high value on the retention of political office, especially when the probability that a repressive leader faces domestic legal consequences is low.

7.1.1 Human Rights Treaties and Conflict

We argue that treaties work not by enforcing their rules, but by altering the structure of the strategic conflict between political authorities and potential dissidents, significantly decreasing government repression and increasing the likelihood of mobilized dissent. Governments do not decide in a vacuum to comply (or to fail to comply) with international human rights obligations; they decide whether to repress as part of a conflict with potential dissidents over policy outcomes. As we note in Chapter 1, *compliance* with international human rights law is a function of *contention*. We do not find these effects of international human rights treaties because we have discovered new information about treaties themselves, but because we proposed a new way of thinking about compliance with those treaties. The government's decision to repress is not a simple choice: it is part of a strategic game with potential dissidents.

We uniquely consider the consequences of HRT obligation within a theory of domestic *conflict*, and our results regarding the effect of HRTs on mobilized dissent offer another unique contribution. By affecting a leader's ability to repress, HRTs open space for mobilized dissent. In studying how people respond to these opportunities in the expectation of a repressive government response, we learn a great deal about how HRTs affect popular decision-making in light of structural changes like commitment to international law.

Our findings suggest that commitment to international human rights treaties does not only affect dissent by creating a focal point for overcoming collective action problems, as previous scholarship has suggested; HRTs also structure the interaction between potential dissidents and the government. Written obligations provide important information to actors considering dissent, helping to identify common ideas of state transgression and increasing expectations of cooperation within dissident groups.[6] Although this current understanding of treaty effects on coordinating dissent is very likely true, it is insufficient to explain when a group willing to incur the costs of dissent actually undertakes this costly activity. Deriving implications from a theory that includes a strategic interaction with a repressive government, we find that treaty obligation can affect the likelihood of mobilized *action* by creating a constraint on the government's ability to respond repressively.

Because HRTs influence both government repression and mobilized dissent, an additional implication of our theory is that human rights treaties have potentially divergent effects: when they are most effective at constraining government violations of human rights (i.e., when leaders have a high value for retaining political office and when the probability of litigation costs is low), HRTs potentially provide incentives for people to dissent against the regime. Consequently, even when international human rights treaties successfully constrain human rights violations, they may indirectly increase leader incentives to repress via their effects on popular dissent. Effective domestic courts that credibly threaten repressive leaders with legal consequences provide a potential solution. When countries with leaders who highly value the retention of power do not have to worry about litigation costs, mobilized dissent increases with HRT obligation, providing indirect incentives for leaders to repress. But when the leaders of those countries face domestic legal rights protection, HRT obligation does not increase the likelihood of dissent. In this situation, the HRT obligation leaves government authorities more constrained from repressing, but no more vulnerable to threatening challenges.

In short, our approach shows that human rights treaty obligation not only influences repression but also modifies the incentive structure of government-society interactions writ large. Under the conditions that make HRTs most effective at constraining governments from repressing, people face increased incentives to take dissent actions to push for political change. HRT obligation creates structural conditions that constrain government repression, allowing openings for dissident groups to challenge the government in order to change status quo policies in their interest.

6. Dai 2005; Simmons 2009; Weingast 1997.

7.1.2 Treaty Constraint Despite Selection

In addition to the hypotheses we analyze against evidence in Chapters 5 and 6, the theory yields an additional implication we did not test:

Implication 4 *A government is less likely to commit to an HRT as a leader's expected value for retaining power increases and more likely to commit as the probability of domestic adjudication costs increases.*

The conditions under which we expect international human rights treaty obligation to have the largest effects on conflict behavior are the very conditions under which we expect governments to select out of the obligation. These implications should not be surprising, given our previous discussions of selection; we include the government's choice to commit to an HRT in the formal model presented in Chapter 2, and we motivate the use of a treatment model with a selection stage in Chapters 4, 5, and 6. The theory suggests that the effect of HRT obligation would have been largest in countries that decided *not* to obligate themselves under international law. Importantly, this means that previous empirical studies investigating how HRTs influence government repression were likely to be biased against finding effects, as many admit and address with statistical fixes.

Some governments under conditions that would make them most likely to experience conflict do ratify and remain obligated to treaties. In some cases, leaders join treaties that are likely to constrain them to gain other benefits besides those that we have explicitly theorized here. Consider Côte d'Ivoire, which ratified the Convention Against Torture and subsequently continued to torture people. Côte d'Ivoire ratified the CAT in 1995 under Henri Konan Bédié, who was relatively secure in office and thus should have highly valued its retention; according to our estimates, EXECUTIVE JOB SECURITY in Côte d'Ivoire equalled 0.989 in 1995. The country reported widespread, systematic levels of torture (as coded by CIRI (2014)) in 1995, but the level fell in the two years following CAT commitment, increasing again only in the year before Bedie lost power via a military coup. This example suggests that Bédié was willing to reduce torture under the CAT while he placed a high value on the retention of power, even though the country had a fairly ineffective judiciary that likely threatened low litigation costs for repression.[7] In other words, a leader with a high expected value for

---

7. Côte d'Ivoire averages a low 0.270 using the Linzer and Staton (2010) measure of judicial effectiveness.

power and few domestic consequences for repression reduced torture levels under the CAT.

By comparison, Bolivia ratified the CAT in 1999 under Hugo Bánzer Suárez, a comparatively insecure leader with a lower expected value for power then Bédié.[8] Middling levels of torture in 1999 increased slightly in 2000, leveling out to pre-2000 levels in the following years.[9] Commitment to the CAT seemed to do little to alter torture decisions in Bolivia. Although this is not a systematic case study, the comparison between commitment and compliance in Côte d'Ivoire and Bolivia supports our theory: secure leaders who believe the retention of political office to be relatively more valuable torture less under obligations to the CAT; insecure leaders who place relatively less value on the retention of political office do not respond to treaty constraint.[10] Moreover, for whatever reason, both types of leader ratified the treaty despite the fact that Bédié should have expected more conflict and constraint than Suárez.

For a broader illustration, consider the maps in Figures 7.1 and 7.2. Figure 7.1 is an attempt to identify which countries are the most likely to have their behaviors affected by an international human rights treaty in a given year—here, 1995. Light-gray countries are those with values of EXECUTIVE JOB SECURITY below the 1995 sample median. Repressive authorities in these countries should be unaffected by international treaty obligations; the probability of mobilized dissent will be similarly unchanged because potential dissidents will see no additional opening for pushing forward their policy preferences.

Medium-gray states have leaders with values of job security above the sample median; these are the countries where we would expect more severe or frequent repression. Medium-gray countries also have domestic courts that we believe to generate relatively high litigation costs for repressive leaders, with Linzer and Staton (2015) judicial effectiveness scores above the 25th percentile for the 1995 sample. Treaty obligation should have little effect on the probability of mobilized dissent in these states as well. While

8. Our measure of EXECUTIVE JOB SECURITY is coded 0.949 for Bolivia in 1999, which is meaningfully less secure than Bédié in our right-skewed data.

9. As above, these values are based on data from CIRI (2014).

10. Although Bolivia (coded 0.652 on the Linzer and Staton measure of judicial effectiveness) has more effective domestic courts than Côte d'Ivoire (which averages a low 0.289 on the Linzer and Staton measure), there is little change in judicial effectiveness over time in either state. Thus, the cross-national difference in the leaders' valuation of political office suggests that the treaty may be responsible for these differences in human rights.

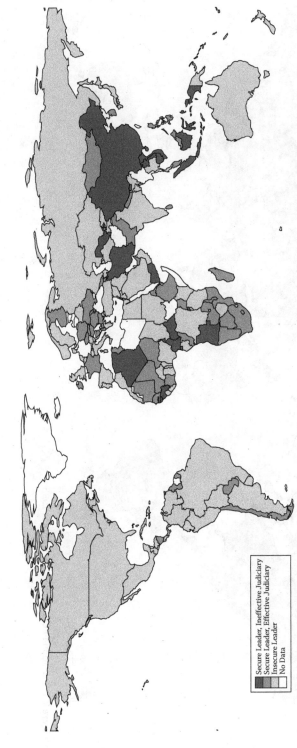

Figure 7.1 Map displaying combinations of EXECUTIVE JOB SECURITY and JUDICIAL EFFECTIVENESS in 1995

Secure Leader, Ineffective Judiciary
Secure Leader, Effective Judiciary
Insecure Leader
No Data

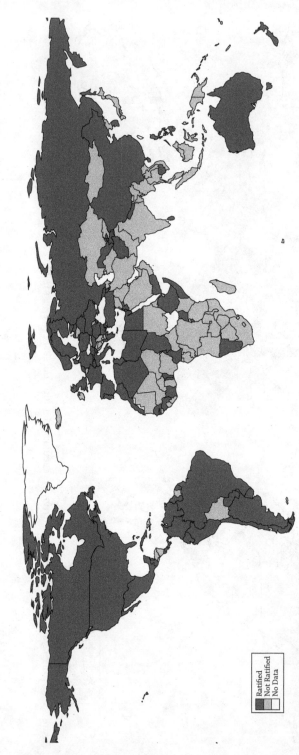

Figure 7.2 Variation in CAT ratification status in 1995

these leaders are motivated to repress, domestic institutions keep them in check before international human rights treaties do.

The dark-gray countries in Figure 7.1 have secure leaders (above the median) that highly value the retention of political office, as well as relatively ineffective courts (below the 25th percentile) that are unlikely to threaten legal costs for repressive authorities. These are the countries where we would expect that obligation to an international human rights treaty does (or would, if they selected out of the obligation in the first place) have a large, distinguishable negative effect on government repression and a positive effect on the probability of mobilized dissent.

Figure 7.2 shows that some of these countries are obligated to international human rights law—specifically, the CAT in 1995—while others have selected out of that obligation. For instance, Angola, Iran, and Indonesia are shaded in dark gray in Figure 7.1; because these countries had relatively secure leaders and ineffective courts in 1995, their leaders should expect commitment to international human rights law to have a significant constraining effect on their abilities to employ repression. Figure 7.2 shows that these countries did indeed opt out of the Convention Against Torture as of 1995, perhaps in anticipation of the constraining effect we describe in this book. In contrast, Figure 7.2 shows that China, Algeria, and Yemen—also countries where we would expect HRT constraint based on the values depicted in Figure 7.1—are obligated to the CAT in 1995. These countries have not selected out of commitment to international human rights law, and they are precisely the sorts of countries in which our theory predicts treaties to be the most constraining.

Nevertheless, many strategic government actors will avoid HRT ratification when such an obligation would lead to constraint and even more conflict in the form of mobilized dissent. Importantly, however, most international human rights treaties are lingering obligations. A country may ratify an HRT under a leader who does not expect to be affected but its terms, then later find itself constrained under a different leader. Leaders who ratify international human rights law at time t are not always the ones who are subject to its constraint at time $t + 1$.[11]

In 1999, for example, the British government, under the direction of Prime Minister Tony Blair, passed legislation for the Human Rights Act,

---

11. Even leaders who commit to international human rights law themselves may not be able to anticipate the behavior of other domestic actors with regard to human rights; Lupu (2015) finds that the effect of HRTs on government respect for human rights is conditional on the extent to which the preferences of legislative veto players differ from those of the executive. Accordingly, domestic constraints—emboldened by HRT commitment—can limit human rights violations even for leaders who wish to repress.

which implemented the European Convention on Human Rights (ECHR) into domestic law. This was prior to the 2001 shift in priorities regarding terrorism. In 2016, Conservative Theresa May went on record as wanting to quit the ECHR should she become prime minister, arguing that the treaty "can bind the hands of Parliament, adds nothing to our prosperity, makes us less secure by preventing the deportation of dangerous foreign nationals, and does nothing to change the attitudes of governments like Russia's when it comes to human rights."[12] In other words, the treaty binds the government when she would rather it did not. According to the Conservative Party's manifesto, however, Britain will continue to be party to the ECHR for the duration of the party's first term—regardless of Prime Minister May's disillusion with the terms of the agreement.[13]

These examples, illustrations, and the data presented in Chapter 5 all suggest that the selection "problem" does not eliminate all or even most cases of constraint. Over time, the vast majority of countries join individual and multiple human rights treaties, meaning that countries with a wide variety of expected values for power and domestic constraints are in the sample of obligated states. This is where treaty effects reveal themselves in the data. However, the process of selection can also imply that treaties are effective. Scholars frequently frame the question of treaty effectiveness in terms of screening or constraining:[14] are the treaties "working" to bind states into doing what they otherwise would not (constraining), or are they no more than parchment institutions, only attracting those states that would comply with their terms in their absence (screening)? We have argued throughout this book that countries that select out of treaty obligations do so because they expect the treaty to be effective: in other words, selecting out of a treaty obligation still implies effectiveness. We focus on counterfactuals in both the theory and analyses, contending that understanding and measuring the expected effects of the treaty for those that do not join it is an important element of identifying treaty influence. It is because treaties constrain repression and motivate dissent that states want to avoid them. Selecting out is not about symbolism, expressions, or independence from world trade. The patterns we have found in data are consistent with the idea that it is precisely those states that would have the incentive to repress without domestic constraint that would expect the largest treaty effects, and who remain out of the obligated sample. In other

12. BBC News 2017.
13. Hope 2017.
14. See, inter alia, Cole 2005; Downs and Jones 2002; Hathaway 2002, 2007; Hill 2010; Lupu 2013b; Simmons 2009; Simmons and Hopkins 2005; von Stein 2005, 2016.

words, "screening" is a behavior entirely consistent with our predictions for an effective treaty. Screening implies constraining.

7.2 THE EFFECT OF TREATY STATUS ON POPULAR EXPECTATIONS

We argue that international human rights treaty obligations affect dissident behavior because they alter popular expectations about the likelihood that a government will be constrained from violating human rights. For the data-generating process to resemble the theoretical process presented here, individuals, lawyers, NGOs, and so forth need to expect that treaties constrain the government from repressing at least in part and condition their behavior accordingly. People do seem to pay attention to changes in domestic laws affecting government respect for human rights. In December 2015 and again in March 2018, tens of thousands of Polish citizens took to the streets to oppose the conservative government's plans to make abortion illegal—an act that would be a violation of the Convention on the Elimination of Discrimination Against Women.[15]

To explain this sort of behavior, scholars often argue that international treaty obligations coordinate disorganized actors, enabling and encouraging people to mobilize for the purpose of dissent. Formal obligations like HRTs serve as focal points, creating common goals around which individuals can rally.[16] Furthermore, NGOs often refer to international obligations when mobilizing collective demands, drawing on the law to convince actors of the importance of an issue and the government's obligation to respond.[17] These scholars see treaties as a coordination device: dissidents see the content of the treaty as relevant to their concerns and will be more likely to take direct action in an area connected to treaty substance.

Our argument differs from the idea of a treaty as a focal point in a number of ways. The most fundamental divergence is that we assume away the dissidents' coordination problem: we assume that dissidents have already formed a group of some size when deciding how much to dissent against the government. In our theory, the conflict the dissidents face is not with each other (a mobilization problem) but with government authorities (a bargaining problem). If the problem of concern is one of

---

15. *The Guardian* 2015.
16. Carey 2000; Dai 2005; Keck and Sikkink 1998; Weingast 1997.
17. Hafner-Burton and Tsutsui 2005; Keck and Sikkink 1998; Risse, Ropp, and Sikkink 1999; Simmons 2009.

bargaining, the treaty interacts with the problem differently. Instead of acting as a focal point, the treaty acts as an external cue about the leader's decision-making structure. Potential dissidents can expect that secure leaders will repress less under the treaty obligation than without it and condition their behavior accordingly. Importantly, potential dissidents not only dissent in the substantive area of the treaty; they dissent more on *any* topic they disagree with because they expect the treaty will protect their right to dissent without government reprisal.

It is important, then, to think hard about the conditions under which potential dissidents would expect a treaty to constrain a leader from repressing them. To consider the plausibility of our assumption, we administered a convenience-sample survey using Amazon's Mechanical Turk (MTurk) polling mechanism. Two hundred persons with a variety of gender, age, and educational characteristics responded to a survey on the anticipated effects of international law.[18] All respondents were from the United States, which we considered sufficient to demonstrate the plausibility of our assumption. In the survey instrument, we proposed a hypothetical scenario in which a police officer engages in illegal uses of violence in the course of duty. This setup invokes respondents to think about government-sanctioned authorities using inappropriate violence against individuals in their jurisdiction, which is considered by many to be a violation of human rights. Respondents were asked to assess the likelihood that the officer would be brought to trial for the illegal behavior.

In a follow-up question, we suggested that an international organization has proposed the creation of an international treaty intended to reduce the use of violence by police officers in the course of duty. This is a hypothetical international treaty, so respondents could have no prior knowledge of a state's ratification status or compliance status. Respondents were then again asked to assess the likelihood that the officer would be brought to trial for the illegal behavior, taking into consideration the creation of the international human rights instrument. This process allows us to see whether individuals tend to believe that an obligation to an HRT will increase the probability that a government authority will be brought to trial (and thus experience court-related costs) for repression.

---

18. MTurk participants are argued to behave similarly to individuals recruited to participate in surveys through other venues (Berinsky, Huber, and Lenz 2012), and they tend to be more heterogeneous than convenience samples solicited in other ways (Huff and Tingley 2015). For concerns about MTurk as a survey platform, please see Krupnikov and Levine 2014 and Paolacci and Chandler 2014.

To capture their baseline expectations, respondents were first asked to report their expectation of the probability that a police officer would be brought to trial for engaging in illegal uses of violence in the course of official duties. Persons chose the quartile encompassing the percentage of likelihood that they believed this would occur, e.g., 0 to 24 percent, 25 to 49 percent, and so on. Then respondents read about a proposed international treaty intended to reduce police violence, and read that their country had chosen *not* to join this treaty. Again they were asked, "What do you think is the percent chance that this officer will be brought to trial over this incident," adding the clause, "given that your state is not part of the international treaty?" Thirty percent of respondents reported that the probability that the officer would go to court was lower in a state of the world where their country had opted out of international legal protections than when the question was asked without mention of the treaty. These lowered expectations may reflect beliefs that refusing to join an international rights treaty suggests a government-level disrespect for rights.

The real question of interest in this survey is how treaty obligations alter everyday expectations that authorities will experience costs for repressive actions. Sixty-five percent of respondents chose a quartile of probability that an officer would go to trial for repression that was higher than their original belief once they were told that their state had decided to ratify the proposed international treaty. Sixty-four percent reported that they "think that a government commitment to an international treaty to reduce police violence will lead to AN INCREASE [emphasis added to highlight the elected phrase] in the likelihood that police officers will be brought to trial for engaging in illegal violence in the course of duty." In other words, survey takers not only chose probabilities that suggested an updated increase in the likelihood that authorities will experience court costs for violating rights, but they also explicitly categorized this shifting belief as an increase. These findings, depicted in Figure 7.3, serve as preliminary evidence supporting the specific assumption that we make as to how international human rights treaties affect popular expectations: that HRTs can affect the popular expectation of the likelihood that government authorities can experience trials for repression.

Finally, we tried to assess people's broader beliefs about the effect of treaties on government behavior. If treaties affect the probability that officials will experience consequences for repression, rational actors should reason that authorities will repress less to avoid those consequences. In the survey instrument, we asked, "Do you think that a government commitment to an international treaty to reduce police violence will lead a reduction in police violence?" Figure 7.4 shows that 64 percent of

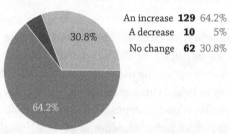

An increase **129** 64.2%
A decrease **10**   5%
No change **62** 30.8%

Figure 7.3 Individual responses to "I think that a government commitment to an international treaty to reduce police violence will lead to [an increase/a decrease/no change] in the likelihood that police officers will be brought to trial for engaging in illegal violence in the course of duty."

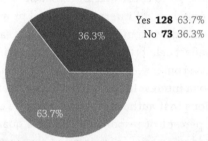

Yes **128** 63.7%
No **73** 36.3%

Figure 7.4 Individual responses to "Do you think that a government commitment to an international treaty to reduce police violence will lead a reduction in police violence?"

survey takers responded yes to this statement. Although our respondents were all from the United States, these results suggest the plausibility of the assumption that observers have expectations that a treaty will lead to an increase in institutional consequences and a decrease in repression.[19]

Of course, not all people in a country know about the existence of particular treaties or their country's ratification status. But they need not have this information for the treaty obligation to alter their behavior. What actually affects the government's and population's conflict behavior is a heightened expectation of constraint. If more people believe that authorities will experience consequences under obligation than would believe it without that obligation, then people's conflict behavior will be consistent with that predicted in the theory. There might be more cases being brought

19. These results are intended to simply to suggest the plausibility of our assumption and are not intended to be causal claims. We sought to examine the likelihood of within-subject differences in expectations associated with treaty ratification. The results we report here may be partially the result of priming; an alternative test could compare treatment and control groups across subject.

against government authorities—an effect that individuals can observe without realizing the increase is related to a new treaty status. Or there might be more public discourse that uses the language of rights protections without explicitly mentioning the treaty. If these things—or things like them—heighten people's expectation of consequences for repression, the theory is a relevant model of government-dissident interactions.

7.2.1 The Conditioning Effect of Political Survival

This research also contributes to the scholarly understanding of the effect that leaders and their preferences have on domestic political processes. Leader tenure considerations, which we conceptualize as a leader's expected value for retaining political office, have a mitigating effect on the ability of domestic institutions to constrain authorities. Interestingly, authorities who sit securely in power and highly value the retention of political office are more likely to respond to the prospect of institutional constraint than more vulnerable leaders. Since government repression and mobilized dissent affect the leader's ability to retain power, the extent to which they value power (ex ante to a policy challenge) is a key condition for understanding (a) how much the government will repress and (b) how susceptible they are to consequences for that decision.

Surprisingly, and quite differently from most scholarship on the effects of international human rights law, we find that treaties have the greatest effect on reducing rights violations in countries where we would expect high levels of domestic political conflict. If treaties create costs that leaders want to avoid, they should be most likely to alter the repressive behavior of leaders who would otherwise repress the most—in our theory, leaders who place the highest value on the retention of political office. There is no reason to avoid costs if authorities do not face conditions that would make repression the optimal choice. Thus, the leaders who should be most constrained by HRT obligation are those who otherwise highly value the retention of power.

The implications for dissent activities also represent important contributions to our understanding of the effects of HRTs on domestic politics—as mitigated by leader considerations of political survival. We build upon work by Simmons (2009), which claims that international human rights treaties lead populations to expect that dissent is more likely to be successful. We explicitly theorize this claim: we argue that people are more likely to take costly action against the government because they expect the treaty to constrain leaders from repressing them, and we identify the conditions under which they will take such action. Simmons (ibid.) argues that this expectation of success varies by regime type, such that treaties have different effects on repression according to type. Instead, we focus on the leader's sensitivity to removal from office—a more precise and variable signal of potential dissidents' ability to threaten governments and alter the status quo.

As previous work on human rights outcomes has shown, tenure considerations broadly affect a government's willingness to repress,[20] as well as its tactics. However, to our knowledge, scholars are only beginning to examine how job (in)security and leaders' benefits from retaining office mediate the effect of institutions on state action. Most human rights treaty scholarship to date focuses on the conditioning effects of political regime type (e.g., democracy versus nondemocracy) rather than leader-specific incentives.[21] Regime type can be quite slow-moving or static, yielding little more than cross-sectional variation with which to test hypotheses; leader-particular stability and incentives vary considerably more over time and across countries,[22] providing scholars with a unique opportunity to generate more precise theories and conduct better causal tests of the implications of those theories.

Nevertheless, regime type comprises the domestic political institutions that determine the process of leader replacement, and so it shapes and influences all of the moving parts of our theory. The benefits and likelihood of retaining power differ in a democracy and a nondemocracy. Although democracies tend to have more effective judicial systems than nondemocracies, many do not have effective courts—and many nondemocracies do have effective judiciaries. Most importantly, however, it is very likely that government authorities and potential dissidents would both perceive the incentives and constraints on repression differently across these systems.

While the concept of democracy is vague and often too inclusive to be useful in identifying causal mechanisms,[23] we can learn more about the process of international human rights treaty effects and domestic conflict by considering how frames like democracy and nondemocracy either institutionally or by perception condition or alter the process we have posited here. Is the process we have modeled one that only applies in

20. Ritter 2014; Young 2009.

21. See, e.g., Goodliffe and Hawkins 2006; Hathaway 2002; Simmons 2009; von Stein 2016; Vreeland 2008a.

22. Chiozza and Goemans 2011; Goemans, Gleditsch, and Chiozza 2009; Licht 2010; Wolford 2007.

23. See, e.g., Gandhi 2008; Przeworski, Alvarez, and Cheibub 2000; Vreeland 2008b.

countries where leaders are more constrained in general, as in democracies? Or is it better suited to describe how expectations can diverge from the domestic baseline in dictatorships?

In this book, we have not clearly defined the concept of regime type, nor carefully considered how it might alter or fit into the many moving parts and concepts of our theory, nor estimated empirical models derived from a careful theory of regime type. In other words, in no way can we make what we would consider a logical or causal claim as to how regime type might alter the story presented in Chapter 2. To further investigate possible scope conditions of our theory, however, we reestimated the empirical models presented in Chapter 5 on a split sample of democracies and nondemocracies.[24] Does one regime type or the other drive our empirical findings?

For this simple analysis, we define a DEMOCRACY as a country with a Polity democracy score of seven or higher.[25] Consider Figure 7.5, which shows the substantive results of our treatment model estimating the effect of the Convention Against Torture (CAT) on the probability of SYSTEMIC TORTURE across the range of EXECUTIVE JOB SECURITY. The top two graphs show the ATC (left) and the ATT (right) for democracies; the bottom two show the ATC (left) and the ATT (right) for nondemocracies. For ease of comparison, we reprint the main findings from Chapter 5 (labeled here as Figure 7.6) regarding the effect of CAT obligation on the probability of SYSTEMIC TORTURE in the pooled sample.

The substantive results presented in Figure 7.5 suggest that democratic countries are the main drivers of the CAT's effect on systemic government torture in the pooled estimates. The estimated effect of making unobligated states commit (ATC) or obligated states renege (ATT) has the same pattern, direction, and magnitude in the democratic sample as the pooled sample in Figure 7.6. On the contrary, state obligation to the Convention Against Torture has no statistically identifiable effect on the likelihood that a given nondemocratic state uses systemic patterns of torture.

The split-sample results for the CAT would suggest that international human rights treaties only work in the manner we have theorized in states that reach a certain threshold of democratic institutions and practice.[26]

---

24. Tables of estimated parameters underlying the substantive results presented here can be found in the Online Appendix.

25. Marshall and Jaggers 2009.

26. For more discussion of democratic thresholds and human rights practices, see Bueno de Mesquita, et al. 2005 and Davenport and Armstrong 2004.

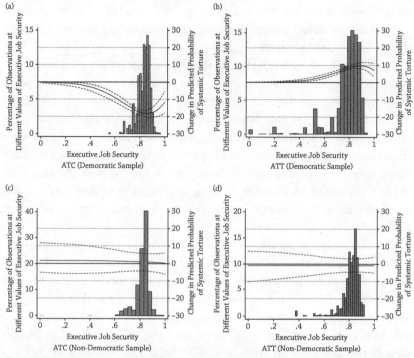

Figure 7.5 Average treatment effect of CAT obligation on (a) the democratic unobligated sample (ATC), (b) the democratic obligated sample (ATT), (c) the nondemocratic unobligated sample (ATC), and (d) the nondemocratic obligated sample on the probability of SYSTEMIC TORTURE conditional on EXECUTIVE JOB SECURITY.

If so, our theory would also logically imply that it is only this subsample of countries where the CAT would affect mobilized dissent. Importantly, however, these results are also consistent with a selection story. A close look at the scale of the histograms on these figures (the left y-axis) reveals that while democracies tend to select in and out of the CAT at similar rates and patterns, far more nondemocracies remain out of its jurisdiction than join it. Furthermore, the split-sample results for the International Covenant for the Protection of Civil and Political Rights (ICCPR) tell a different story about the effects of regime type.

Consider Figure 7.7, which shows the substantive results of our treatment model estimating the effect of the ICCPR on the probability of SYSTEMIC TORTURE across the range of EXECUTIVE JOB SECURITY. As above, the top two graphs show the ATC (left) and the ATT (right) for democracies; the bottom two show the ATC (left) and the ATT (right) for nondemocracies. For ease of comparison, we again reprint Figure 7.8, which we originally presented and discussed in Chapter 5.

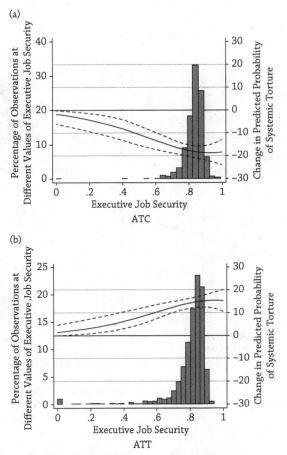

Figure 7.6 Average treatment effect of CAT obligation on (a) the controls (ATC) and (b) the treated (ATT) on the probability of SYSTEMIC TORTURE conditional on EXECUTIVE JOB SECURITY.

Estimated effects of ICCPR obligation for both regime types trend in the predicted direction: leaders with low expected values for power are mostly unaffected by ICCPR obligations, whereas leaders who are more secure in office will be constrained from torture if forced to join (ATCs) or more likely to be associated with torture if made to renege (ATTs). These grouped patterns are both consistent with the patterns originally estimated with the pooled sample. Although each effect appears weaker in statistical strength (especially democracies)—probably because we have subdivided the sample twice—both regime types follow the theoretical story we have proposed.

This quick exercise suggests that there is more to the story than we have captured in our necessarily simplified model. Institutions and norms condition common expectations and thus behavior. This is what we have argued in a general sense, but there are many institutions and norms about

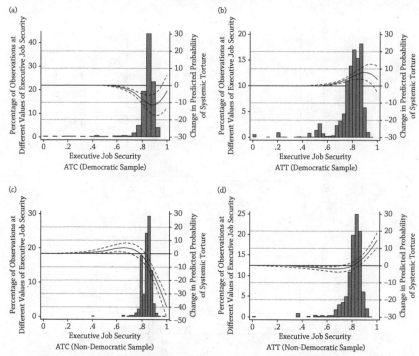

Figure 7.7 Average treatment effect of ICCPR obligation on (a) the democratic unobligated sample (ATC), (b) the democratic obligated sample (ATT), (c) the nondemocratic unobligated sample (ATC), and (d) the nondemocratic obligated sample on the probability of SYSTEMIC TORTURE conditional on EXECUTIVE JOB SECURITY.

which we have not explicitly theorized. The look at split samples across regime type suggests that some element(s) of democracy combine with some element(s) of particular treaty obligations to condition popular and state expectations. Further investigation of this possibility requires far more careful and rigorous study. Regardless of regime type, the patterns presented here remain consistent with our main claims: international human rights treaties constrain leaders with high values for power more than those likely to leave office soon.

7.3 EXTENDING THE THEORY

Throughout the book, we have defended the plausibility and generality of a number of assumptions that help us understand the scope and limits of the theory. If, for instance, states that would expect constraint do not join human rights treaties, then we cannot expect to see constrained conflict behavior in observed data. If instead leader security *increases* with the loss

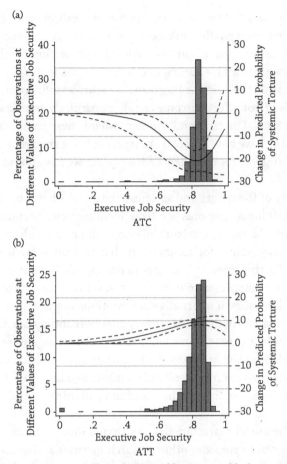

Figure 7.8 Average treatment effect of ICCPR obligation on (a) the controls (ATC) and (b) the treated (ATT) on the probability of SYSTEMIC TORTURE conditional on EXECUTIVE JOB SECURITY.

of policy ground to dissidents, then we should expect different effects of treaties on conflict behavior. Similarly, if dissidents do not believe that international law can affect state behavior, then we should not expect to see treaties affecting dissent (and thus repression) as we have suggested here.

We can imagine other scenarios where the theory would not predict decision-making that looks like this model. If a leader would prefer to lose power rather than keep it—having a cushy resource fund and a villa to retire in another country, perhaps—then we cannot assume that leader would act according to the theory. Leaders may set policies to weaken the court, diminish individual standing, threaten (potential) litigants, or otherwise reduce individuals' propensity to bring suit against repressive authorities. Leader intervention in the court's power undermines the assumption that the domestic consequences for repression are exogenously given. Such actions would weaken the link between treaties and consequences for repression, biasing any empirical analyses against finding that treaties reduce repression and encourage dissent. If leaders do not concern themselves with the costs of litigation, or even benefit from them, then treaties should not affect outcomes at all, particularly as a function of job security. In spatial or temporal contexts where these things (rather than the assumptions we have posited) are true, evidence should bias against us finding any support for our nuanced theory. Yet we have found support, in spades.

The clarity of the theory and assumptions on which it is based offer two kinds of usefulness. For one, we have identified clear conditions under which we should expect our conclusions to be observable in the world, providing many points for falsification that instead showed evidence of our theory. Furthermore, the theory—a description of logical connections from a set of assumptions to derived conclusions—helps us to know how things should change if alternative assumptions are the case. Clearly, we have not solved a formal model for every possible contingency, but the logic of the model helps us to know what to expect if things were to change, slightly modifying the premises. More importantly, it helps us to predict outcomes when values on several independent variables vary in a complex theory, allowing us to simplify the world and still think carefully about how it works.

One of the useful characteristics of a simple theoretical model is that it can be extended to consider other research questions. One method to do this is by relaxing some of the assumptions. As one example, we assume that all commitments to HRTs are similar in the way they affect observers' expectations and thus behaviors, but there is unique variance in the extent to which we might expect them to constrain rights violations. As another example, we assume that obligation to international human rights law does not influence the effectiveness of the domestic judiciary. What are the implications of the theory if that assumption is relaxed? Additionally, although we focus on the probability that a repressive leader will experience domestic legal consequences, other aspects of a country's domestic environment might condition leaders' and groups' conflict choices. Similarly, while we are interested in the effect of international human rights treaties on domestic conflict, future scholars and practitioners may wish to focus on the effects of other constraints on government repression—institutions like international courts and international advocacy. How might we think about other domestic and international institutions in the context of the theory presented in this book?

7.3.1 Variance in Treaty Effectiveness

Our arguments about the effect of international human rights law on domestic conflict focus on general obligation to HRTs. Although we contend that even treaties without enforcement mechanisms can constrain repression, we expect the effects to be even more pronounced when treaties have more bite. The empirical tests of the effect of the Optional Protocol on the Convention on Torture (OPCAT) presented in Chapter 5 provide suggestive evidence on this point. In addition, Smith-Cannoy (2012) focuses on the effect of HRTs that allow petitioners the right of individual complaint before the United Nations, arguing that these more enforceable provisions can constrain government repression. We agree: in cases where countries commit to international human rights treaties as well as the terms allowing individual complaint before the United Nations, we expect to see heightened treaty effects on repression and dissent.

In theory, each of the treaties we discuss in this book allows for individual complaint before the United Nations. In practice, however, many of the countries that ratify the CAT, the ICCPR, and the CEDAW place reservations on the specific articles allowing for such petition.[27] Countries often place reservations on other treaty articles as well; for example, the Convention Against Torture's universal jurisdiction clause, discussed in detail below, is an article on which reservations are commonly placed when states ratify the CAT. We do not make use of this variance in either our theory or our empirical tests, but we generally expect reservations to international human rights law to dilute the increase in the probability of litigation costs faced by leaders in domestic courts.[28]

The ICCPR is particularly subject to this concern; the United States, for instance, ratified the treaty with sixteen reservations—six more than any other government that has ratified the covenant.[29] Despite domestic laws that retain the primacy of domestic law over international law,[30] the U.S. government typically enters multiple reservations, understandings, and/or declarations (RUDs) when ratifying international human rights treaties.

---

27. See Smith-Cannoy 2012 and Hill 2015 for additional information on HRT reservation rates.

28. In addition to reservations to HRTs, Mulesky and Sandholtz 2018 argue that the extent to which treaty obligations are "demanding" influences the likelihood that they are ratified.

29. Hill 2015.

30. Sloss 2009.

It often goes so far as to declare treaties "non–self executing," meaning treaty terms do not apply in domestic courts without additional legislation. RUDs effectively limit the effect of HRTs through domestic courts. For example, when a Nevada court sentenced a seventeen-year-old to death, he challenged the punishment with reference to the terms of the ICCPR.[31] The Nevada Supreme Court upheld the sentence, arguing that the Unined States' reservation to that particular article meant the treaty had no bearing on the case.[32]

7.3.2 Other Domestic Institutional Constraints

We assert that international human rights treaties constrain government repression through domestic courts, increasing (even if only marginally) the extent to which leaders expect to face litigation costs for violating human rights. We assume that the domestic probability of litigation costs—often a function of domestic judicial effectiveness—increases a small amount when countries obligate themselves to international human rights law. But we do not consider the possibility that (1) leaders can manipulate the judiciary, or (2) HRT commitment could have a more direct influence on the judicial process.[33] If membership in an international human rights treaty actually serves to constrain leaders as we claim, such constraint should affect not only opportunities for dissidents to mobilize against the government but also opportunities for the court to rule without interference. Increases in this sort of judicial independence should allow the court to endogenously build public support for its own legitimacy,[34] making it more difficult for leaders to manipulate the judiciary as they wish.

Future work in this area could focus on predicting the behavior of three actors instead of two: the judiciary, the leader, and potential dissidents. How does a newly emboldened judiciary choose cases in light of changes that come with treaty obligation? How do leaders' decisions to violate human rights change if the judiciary can or cannot be manipulated by the executive[35] or legislature?[36] How does the behavior of potential dissidents change as judicial independence strengthens? Do dissidents move away

31. Article 6, paragraph 2 of the ICCPR prohibits the execution of persons younger than eighteen.
32. Bradley 2000; Hill 2015.
33. See, e.g., Epp 1998.
34. Carrubba 2009; Staton 2010.
35. Hilbink 2007; Ríos-Figueroa and Staton 2014; Staton and Moore 2011.
36. Clark 2009

from protesting in the streets and instead take their grievances before the court?

In addition to the extensions that directly involve adjudication and the domestic court, other domestic institutions and processes exist through which HRTs may affect repression and dissent.[37] Domestic legislatures may use international law to shift the policy agenda toward rights protection, which would be another way of keeping authorities from repressing as much as they would otherwise prefer.[38] Lupu (2015), for example, finds that veto players or blocking points in the legislature keep government leaders from deviating from the rules set by international law.

Nongovernmental organizations and the media can also draw attention to and create costs for leaders who violate international treaty terms.[39] In April 2017, at the behest of nongovernmental organizations, Tunisia's report to the Committee Against Torture was shown live in a movie theatre "to an audience that included government officials, activists, media and victims."[40] Such publicity can complement more traditional "naming and shaming" campaigns, in which NGOs and other domestic and international actors call out violating governments for their bad behavior in an attempt to increase the costs of government repression.[41]

Because of the clear connection between international law and domestic law, we interpreted the consequential effect of treaty obligation in the theoretical model to be one of legal consequence. However, the mathematical theory itself is indifferent to its interpretation by researchers. In other words, while our read of these parameters stands up to empirical scrutiny, the core directional effects on behavior could be interpreted instead as any shift by which a treaty would marginally increase negative consequences for a repressive leader. Future analysts could explore this dynamic, considering whether and how different kinds of consequences may or may not conceptually apply in the type of mechanisms and process we have explored here.

---

37. Simmons 2009.

38. Ibid., Chapter 4.

39. Hafner-Burton 2008; Whitten-Woodring 2009; Whitten-Woodring and James 2012.

40. Al Hussein 2017.

41. The effects of naming and shaming on government violations of human rights are mixed; see, e.g., Ausderan 2014, DeMeritt 2012, Franklin 2008, Hafner-Burton 2008, Hendrix and Wong 2013, Krain 2012, and Murdie and Davis 2012.

7.3.3 Other International Institutional Constraints

Although we focus on the effects of international human rights law on conflict, scholars should also think about other international institutions that function similarly to HRTs. Consider international courts, which are mechanisms by which to impose legal costs—like the domestic ones we described above—without relying on domestic enforcement. The International Criminal Court (ICC), a permanent international human rights tribunal, can prosecute specific human rights violations including genocide, war crimes, and crimes against humanity. Two types of governments have ratified the Rome Statute associated with the International Criminal Court: democracies not at civil war, which pay few costs for ratification because they are de facto compliant,[42] and autocratic governments that have recently been involved in a civil war, to make a credible commitment to the end of violence.[43] Our expectation is that these states differ enormously in the extent to which their leaders value the retention of office and wish to remain in power; as such, testing the extent to which ICC obligation operates similarly to HRTs strikes us as an important area for future inquiry.

The ICC can also prosecute individuals who are *not* from signatory countries if they commit crimes in a signatory country or are referred to the court by the United Nations Security Council (UNSC). More importantly, permanent courts with the jurisdiction to prosecute crimes of human rights violations represent potential consequences that political authorities must consider when deciding whether to repress. If such an action would invoke an international trial, whether at the ICC, the International Court of Justice (ICJ), or some other permanent or ad hoc tribunal, leaders may be deterred from engaging in major human rights crimes against civilians regardless of the consequences they expect to face domestically.[44] Our theory would suggest that the international court would alter governments' use of atrocities when the court represents a constraint that is otherwise missing from the domestic environment.[45] Furthermore, we expect that the courts will only alter behavior when the conflict would be severe and otherwise unconstrained at home, incentivizing leaders to consider the weight of the costs from the international court.

42. Simmons and Danner 2010.
43. See also Chapman and Chaudoin 2013.
44. Gilligan 2006; Ritter and Wolford 2012. For an alternative position, see Goldsmith 2003 and Goldsmith and Krasner 2003.
45. See also Simmons and Danner 2010.

Africa, Europe, and the Americas have also created special regional human rights courts to prosecute government authorities who violate human rights. If effective international courts begin to systematically try violators of international human rights law, executives may be dissuaded to violate rights even if their domestic courts are relatively ineffective. Under the Convention Against Torture's universal jurisdiction clause, for example, executives considering repression may also need to consider potential domestic court costs in states other than their own. In February 2011, former U.S. president George W. Bush cancelled a trip to Switzerland, an action that may have occurred over concerns about being held accountable in Geneva for alleged torture in Guantanamo Bay.[46] If leaders anticipate the international costs of violations resulting from their obligations to protect rights—some of which they may bear even after their removal from office—they should be less likely to repress severely.

In 2012, the International Court of Justice ordered the country of Senegal to prosecute Hissene Habre, who spent more than twenty years in exile in Senegal following his ouster as the president of Chad amid allegations of severe violations of human rights.[47] Senegal did not relent until 2013, when the ICJ ruled that Senegal's unwillingness to arrest and prosecute such a violator of human rights was in violation of its obligations under the Convention Against Torture. Senegal arrested Mr. Habre soon after the ICJ ruling.[48] This example suggests an interaction between an international court and an international treaty commitment—one that strikes us as an interesting avenue for future research on the effect of institutions on repression and dissent.

7.4 A FINAL NOTE ON POLICY PRESCRIPTIONS

This book contributes not only to the scholarly debate about how international human rights treaties affect government repression and mobilized dissent; it also yields important implications for actors who are interested in improving government rights practices on the ground. Perhaps the most important is for policymakers to consider the effect of institutions—not just treaties—on *conflict*. Investigating the effect of institutions like HRTs

---

46. Reuters News Service 2011.
47. Simons 2012.
48. Nossiter 2013.

on government behavior produces an incomplete picture, because institutional constraints also change the behavior of the general population.

For example, our findings suggest that "propping up" vulnerable leaders to make them more secure in power—to make them value political power *more*—may lead them to be more responsive to international human rights obligations. Importantly, however, propping up otherwise weak leaders also leads the government to repress more severely or frequently; leaders' high value for power is the reason that international human rights treaties affect human rights outcomes in the first place. In addition, secure leaders who are relatively constrained by HRT obligation will be more likely to face mobilized dissent, providing them with indirect reasons to violate human rights. Policymakers will want to consider these tradeoffs carefully when making decisions about how to best minimize government violence.

International human rights treaties are not a panacea for the protection of human rights, and this is not only due to their complicated policy tradeoffs. We investigate the effect of treaty obligation on government repression and mobilized dissent, comparing the probability of conflict in (1) an HRT-committed country to the conflict that country would have experienced absent such an obligation, and (2) a non-HRT-committed country to the conflict that that country would have experienced if it had made such an obligation. Although these are useful comparisons, this book does not consider several aspects of the international human rights treaty regime that are potentially interesting to policymakers.

In this book, we consider the effects of the CAT, the ICCPR, and the CEDAW in isolation from one another. But nearly all countries have ratified more than one of these treaties. How does a portfolio of treaties—or different combinations of treaties—influence conflict outcomes? How does the effect of HRT obligation change in a given country as the number of obligations increases over time? We have posited that treaties affect repression and dissent because they change government and population expectations about the constraint environment, but we have also explicitly argued that this effect is largest when the treaty-produced constraint environment is dramatically different from the domestic judicial status quo. Such logic would suggest that the first treaty obligation may have a much larger effect on outcomes than later ones. However, there may be different treaty terms or combinations of treaties that have larger effects than others. Are later treaties less influential in improving human rights outcomes than earlier treaties, or are more recent treaties more effective in decreasing conflict? Although the answers to these questions would be of great interest to policymakers, to our knowledge, no one has yet undertaken a study to shed light on these questions.

Relative to HRTs, domestic institutions are likely to be more effective in constraining rights violations because they can impose higher costs (or impose costs that have a greater probability of being carried out) than international ones. We expect that human rights practices will overall be much better in countries with effective domestic judiciaries than in countries with ineffective courts. International human rights treaties are "necessary" in these countries. Building domestic judicial institutions is consequently the surest—although not necessarily the quickest—way to improve protections for human rights.

Nevertheless, as a method of last resort, commitment to an international human rights treaty can constrain repression. HRTs have their greatest effects when domestic courts cannot limit rights violations via litigation costs and when the leader represses so much that the treaty's boost to litigation is likely to have a meaningful influence on the leader's decision. It is when things look bleakest for rights protection—when governments are most likely to repress—that an international human rights treaty can make the biggest difference for the protection of human rights.

PART IV

Appendix

APPENDIX 4

Appendix to Chapters 4, 5, 6: Summary of Robustness Checks

W e reference a number of robustness checks over the course of the book, especially as related to the research design presented in Chapter 4 and the empirical results presented in Chapters 5 and 6. In what follows, we provide a list of each of the robustness tests previously referenced in the book; full results—and a color-coded summary of those results—across the Convention Against Torture (CAT), the International Covenant on Civil and Political Rights (ICCPR), and the Convention for the Elimination of Discrimination Against Women (CEDAW) are available in the Online Appendix.

A4.1 GOVERNMENT REPRESSION

Chapter 5 reports the main empirical results investigating the effect of HRT obligation on government repression. Additional empirical models testing the robustness of those reported results include models that...

- Measure the *probability of domestic litigation costs* using DOMESTIC JUDICIAL RIGHTS PROTECTION from Linzer and Staton (2015) rather DOMESTIC JUDICIAL RIGHTS PROTECTION from Hill (2015).
- Measure *government repression* using (dichotomized) LATENT PHYSICAL INTEGRITY RIGHTS from Fariss (2014) rather than SYSTEMIC REPRESSION from Cingranelli, Richards, and Clay (2014).

- Measure *government repression* using ANY REPRESSION from Cingranelli, Richards, and Clay (2014) rather than SYSTEMIC REPRESSION from Cingranelli, Richards, and Clay (2014).
- Measure *government torture* using (dichotomized) SYSTEMIC TORTURE ALLEGATIONS from Conrad, Haglund, and Moore (2013) rather than SYSTEMIC TORTURE from Cingranelli, Richards, and Clay (2014).
- Measure *expected value of leader retention* using IRREGULAR EXECUTIVE JOB SECURITY rather than EXECUTIVE JOB SECURITY, as described in Chapter 5.
- Control for temporal dependence using an annual third-order polynomial time counter, as discussed by Carter and Signorino (2010).
- Control for *mobilized dissent* using (dichotomized) MOBILIZED DISSENT from the Integrated Data for Events Analysis (IDEA) Project by Bond et al. (2003), as compiled by Ritter (2014) and described in Chapter 6.
- Control for additional *government repression* using LATENT PHYSICAL INTEGRITY RIGHTS from Fariss (2014).
- Control for *political regime type* using DEMOCRACY from Polity (2009).
- Control for *media freedom* using FREEDOM OF SPEECH from Cingranelli, Richards, and Clay (2014).
- Control for *youth bulges* using data from Nordås and Davenport (2013).
- Plot substantive results at different values of DOMESTIC JUDICIAL RIGHTS PROTECTION from Linzer and Staton (2015) and DOMESTIC JUDICIAL RIGHTS PROTECTION from Hill (2015).
- Test the strength of the IO instrument from Ulfelder (2011).
- Substitute the IO instrument from Ulfelder (2011) for an (ordered) measure of RATIFICATION DIFFICULTY from Simmons (2009).
- Add to the IO instrument from Ulfelder (2011) an additional (ordered) measure of RATIFICATION DIFFICULTY from Simmons (2009).
- Substitute the IO instrument from Ulfelder (2011) for a (binary) measure of COMMON LAW LEGAL SYSTEM from Simmons (2009).
- Add to the IO instrument from Ulfelder (2011) an additional (binary) measure of COMMON LAW LEGAL SYSTEM from Simmons (2009).
- Split the sample by *political regime type* using the (dichotomized) POLITY IV SCALE from Polity (2009).
- Split the sample by *political regime type* using DEMOCRACY from Cheibub, Gandhi, and Vreeland (2010).

A4.2 MOBILIZED DISSENT

Chapter 6 reports the main empirical results investigating the effect of HRT obligation on mobilized dissent. Additional empirical models testing the robustness of those reported results include models that...

- Use the country-year as the unit of observation.
- Measure the *probability of domestic litigation costs* using both DOMESTIC JUDICIAL RIGHTS PROTECTION from Linzer and Staton (2015) and DOMESTIC JUDICIAL RIGHTS PROTECTION from Hill (2015).
- Measure *expected value of leader retention* using IRREGULAR EXECUTIVE JOB SECURITY rather than EXECUTIVE JOB SECURITY, as described in Chapter 5.
- Control for temporal dependence using a monthly and an annual third-order polynomial time counter, as discussed by Carter and Signorino (2010).
- Control for *government repression* using LATENT PHYSICAL INTEGRITY RIGHTS from Fariss (2014).
- Control for *political regime type* using DEMOCRACY from Polity (2009).
- Control for *media freedom* using FREEDOM OF SPEECH from Cingranelli, Richards, and Clay (2014).
- Control for *youth bulges* using data from Nordås and Davenport (2013).
- Plot substantive results at different levels of DOMESTIC JUDICIAL RIGHTS PROTECTION from Linzer and Staton (2015) and DOMESTIC JUDICIAL RIGHTS PROTECTION from Hill (2015).
- Test the strength of the IO instrument from Ulfelder (2011).
- Substitute the IO instrument from Ulfelder (2011) for an (ordered) measure of RATIFICATION DIFFICULTY from Simmons (2009).
- Add to the IO instrument from Ulfelder (2011) an additional (ordered) measure of RATIFICATION DIFFICULTY from Simmons (2009).
- Substitute the IO instrument from Ulfelder (2011) for a (binary) measure of COMMON LAW LEGAL SYSTEM from Simmons (2009).
- Add to the IO instrument from Ulfelder (2011) an additional (binary) measure of COMMON LAW LEGAL SYSTEM from Simmons (2009).

BIBLIOGRAPHY

Abbott, Kenneth W. and Duncan Snidal (1998). "Why States Act through Formal
    International Organizations". In: *Journal of Conflict Resolution* 42.1, pp. 3–32.

Acemoglu, Daron and James A. Robinson (2006). *Economic Origins of Democracy and
    Dictatorship*. New York: Cambridge University Press.

Al Hussein, Zeid Ra'ad (2017). *Naming and Shaming Human Rights Violators*. Address
    to the 35th Session of the UN Human Rights Council in Geneva. Accessed
    December 11, 2017. URL: http://www.ipsnews.net/2017/06/naming-and-
    shaming-human-rightsviolators/.

Albert, A. and J. A. Anderson (1984). "On the Existence of Maximum Likelihood
    Estimates in Logistic Regression Models". In: *Biometrick* 71.1, pp. 1–10.

Amnesty International (2012). *Amnesty International Report 2012: The State of the
    World's Human Rights*. Technical Representative. London, UK: Amnesty
    International.

Amnesty International (2013). *Amnesty International Report 2013: The State of the
    World's Human Rights*. Technical Representative. London, UK: Amnesty
    International.

Association for the Prevention of Torture (2009). *Thailand: Implementing the UN
    Convention Against Torture*. Accessed January 19, 2011. URL: http://www.apt.
    ch/index.php?option=comk2&view=item&id=874:thailand-implementing-
    the-un-conventionagainst-torture&lang=en.

Asthana, Anushka and Rowena Mason (2016). "UK Must Leave European Convention
    on Human Rights, says Theresa May". In: *The Guardian*. Accessed September 19,
    2017. URL: https://www.theguardian.com/politics/2016/apr/25/uk-must-
    leave-european-convention-on-human-rights-theresa-may-eu-referendum.

Ausderan, Jacob (2014). "How Naming and Shaming Affects Human Rights
    Perceptions in the Shamed Country". In: *Journal of Peace Research* 51.1, pp.
    81–95.

Austin, Peter C. (2011). "An Introduction to Propensity Score Methods for Reducing
    the Effects of Confounding in Observational Studies". In: *Multivariate
    Behavioral Research* 46.3, pp. 399–424.

Axelrod, Robert (1984). *The Evolution of Cooperation*. New York: Basic Books.

Babones, Salvatore (2018). "China's Constitutional Amendments Are All about the
    Party, Not the President". In: *Forbes*. Accessed March 11, 2018. URL: https://
    www.forbes.com/sites/salvatorebabones/ 2018/03/11/chinas-constitutional-
    amendments-are-all-about-the-party-not-thepresident/% 5C#479995a31615.

Banks, Arthur S. (2010). *Cross-National Time-Series Data Archive*. URL: http://
    www.databanksinternational.com. Jerusalem: Databanks International.

BBC News (2014). "What Lies behind the Protests in Venezuela?" In: *BBC News*. Accessed April 13, 2018. URL: http://www.bbc.com/news/world-latin-america-26335287.

BBC News (2017). "Theresa May: Human Rights Laws Could Change for Terror Fight". In: *BBC News*. Accessed January 28, 2018. URL: http://www.bbc.com/news/election- 2017-40181444.

Beck, Nathaniel, Jonathan N. Katz, and Richard Tucker (1998). "Taking Time Seriously: Time-Series-Cross-Section Analysis with a Binary Dependent Variable". In: *American Journal of Political Science* 42.4, pp. 1260–1288.

Bell, Sam R., Tavishi Bhasin, et al. (2014). "Taking the Fight to Them: Neighborhood Human Rights Organizations and Domestic Protest". In: *British Journal of Political Science* 44.04, pp. 853–875.

Bell, Sam R., K. Chad Clay, and Amanda Murdie (2012). "Neighborhood Watch: Spatial Effects of Human Rights INGOs". In: *The Journal of Politics* 74.02, pp. 354–368.

Berinsky, Adam J., Gregory A. Huber, and Gabriel S. Lenz (2012). "Evaluating Online Labor Markets for Experimental Research: Amazon.com's Mechanical Turk". In: *Political Analysis* 20.3, pp. 351–368.

Berlatsky, Noah (2014). "At the United Nations, Chicago Activists Protest Police Brutality". In: *The Atlantic*. URL: https://www.theatlantic.com/national/archive/2014/11/ we-charge-genocide-movement-chicago-un/382843.

Bhasin, Tavishi (2008). "Democracy and Dissent: Explaining Protest and State Response". PhD thesis. Atlanta: Emory University.

Bhasin, Tavishi and Jennifer Gandhi (2013). "Timing and Targeting of State Repression in Authoritarian Elections". In: *Electoral Studies* 32.4, pp. 620–631.

Blanton, Shannon Lindsey and Robert G. Blanton (2007). "What Attracts Foreign Investors? An Examination of Human Rights and Foreign Direct Investment". In: *Journal of Politics* 69.1, pp. 143–155.

Blattman, Christopher and Edward Miguel (2010). "Civil War". In: *Journal of Economic Literature* 48.1, pp. 3–57.

Bond, Doug et al. (2003). "Integrated Data for Events Analysis (IDEA): An Event Typology for Automated Events Data Development". In: *Journal of Peace Research* 40.6, pp. 733–745.

Boockmann, Bernhard (2001). "The Ratification of ILO Conventions: A Hazard Rate Analysis". In: *Economics & Politics* 13.3, pp. 281–309.

Bozorgmehr, Najmeh (2018). "Iranian General Claims Anti-Regime Protests Have Ended in Failure". In: *Financial Times*. URL: https://www.ft.com/content/ea1e3adc-f08d- 11e7-b220-857e26d1aca4/.

Bradley, Curtis A. (2000). "Chevron Deference and Foreign Affairs". In: *Virginia Law Review*, 86.4, pp. 649–726.

Brambor, Thomas, William Roberts Clark, and Matt Golder (2006). "Understanding Interaction Models: Improving Empirical Analyses". In: *Political Analysis* 14.1, pp. 63–82.

Bueno de Mesquita, Bruce, George W. Downs, et al. (2005). "Thinking Inside the Box: A Closer Look at Democracy and Human Rights". In: *International Studies Quarterly* 49.3, pp. 439–457.

Bueno de Mesquita, Bruce, Alastair Smith, et al. (2003). *The Logic of Political Survival*. Cambridge, MA: MIT Press.

Butler, Christopher K., Tali Gluch, and Neil J. Mitchell (2007). "Security Forces and Sexual Violence: A Cross-National Analysis of a Principalâ£"Agent Argument". In: *Journal of Peace Research* 44.6, pp. 669–687.

Calvert, Randall L. (1995). "The Rational Choice Theory of Social Institutions: Cooperation, Coordination, and Communication". In: *Modern Political Economy: Old Topics, New Directions*. Ed. by Jeffrey S. Banks and Eric Allen Hanushek. Cambridge, UK: Cambridge University Press, pp. 216–268.

Cameron, Charles M. (2002). "Judicial Independence: How Can You Tell It When You See It? And, Who Cares?" In: *Judicial Independence at the Crossroads: An Interdisciplinary Approach*. Ed. by Stephen B. Burbank and Barry Friedman. Thousand Oaks, CA: Sage Publications, pp. 134–147.

Carey, John M. (2000). "Parchment, Equilibria, and Institutions". In: *Comparative Political Studies* 33.6/7, pp. 735–761.

Carey, Sabine C. (2010). "The Use of Repression as a Response to Domestic Dissent". In: *Political Studies* 58.1, pp. 167–186.

Carmines, Edward G. and Richard A. Zeller (1979). *Reliability and Validity Assessment*. Thousand Oaks, CA: Sage Publications.

Carrubba, Clifford J. (2009). "A Model of the Endogenous Development of Judicial Institutions in Federal and International Systems". In: *Journal of Politics* 71.1, pp. 55–69.

Carter, David and Curtis S. Signorino. (2010). "Back to the Future: Modeling Temporal Dependence in Binary Data". In: *Political Analysis* 18.3, pp. 271–292.

CCPR *General Comment No. 26: Continuity of Obligations* (1997). United Nations Human Rights Committee. Technical Representative Document CCPR/C/21/Rev.1/Add.8/Rev.1. Accessed September 20, 2016. URL: http://www.refworld.org/docid/453883fde.html.

Cederman, Lars-Erik, Andreas Wimmer, and Brian Min (2010). "Why Do Ethnic Groups Rebel? New Data and Analysis". In: *World Politics* 62.1, pp. 87–119.

Chapman, Terrence L. and Stephen Chaudoin (2013). "Ratification Patterns of the International Criminal Court". In: *International Studies Quarterly* 57.2, pp. 400–409.

Cheibub, José Antonio (1998). "Political Regimes and the Extractive Capacity of Governments: Taxation in Democracies and Dictatorships". In: *World Politics* 50.3, pp. 349–376.

Cheibub, José Antonio, Jennifer Gandhi, and James Raymond Vreeland (2010). "Democracy and Dictatorship Revisited". In: *Public Choice* 143.1, pp. 67–101.

Chenoweth, Erica and Maria J. Stephan (2011). *Why Civil Resistance Works: The Strategic Logic of Nonviolent Conflict*. New York: Columbia University Press.

Chiozza, Giacomo and H. E. Goemans (2004). "International Conflict and the Tenure of Leaders: Is War Still Ex Post Inefficient?" In: *American Journal of Political Science* 48.3, pp. 604–619.

Chiozza, Giacomo and H. E. Goemans (2011). *Leaders and International Conflict*. Cambridge, MA: Cambridge University Press.

Cingranelli, David L. and Mikhail Filippov (2010). "Electoral Rules and Incentives to Protect Human Rights". In: *Journal of Politics* 72.1, pp. 243–257.

Cingranelli, David L., David L. Richards, and K. Chad Clay (2014). *The Cingranelli-Richards (CIRI) Human Rights Dataset*. Vol. 2014.04.14. http://humanrightsdata.com. University of Georgia.

Clague, Christopher, Philip Keefer, Stephen Knack, and Mancur Olson. (1999). "Contract-Intensive Money: Contract Enforcement, Property Rights, and Economic Performance". In: *Journal of Economic Growth* 4.2, pp. 185–211.

Clark, Ann Marie (2010). *Diplomacy of Conscience: Amnesty International and Changing Human Rights Norms*. Princeton, NJ: Princeton University Press.

Clark, Tom S. (2009). "The Separation of Powers, Court Curbing, and Judicial Legitimacy". In: *American Journal of Political Science* 5.4, pp. 971–89.

CNN (2017). "CIA Torture Report: Fast Facts". In: CNN. URL: https://www.cnn.com/2015/01/29/us/cia-torture-report-fast-facts/index.html.

Cole, Wade M. (2005). "Sovereignty Relinquished? Explaining Commitment to the International Human Rights Covenants". In: *American Sociological Review* 70.3, pp. 472–495.

Cole, Wade M. (2012). "Human Rights as Myth and Ceremony? Reevaluating the Effectiveness of Human Rights Treaties, 1981-2007". In: *American Journal of Sociology* 117.4, pp. 1131–1171.

Cole, Wade M. (2015). "Mind the Gap: State Capacity and the Implementation of Human Rights Treaties". In: *International Organization* 69.2, pp. 405–441.

Concluding Observations on the Combined Third and Fourth Periodic Reports of the Bolivarian Republic of Venezuela (2014). United Nations Committee Against Torture. Technical Representative Document CAT/C/VEN/CO/3-4. Accessed April 13, 2018. URL: https://documents-dds-ny.un.org/doc/UNDOC/GEN/G14/241/72/PDF/G1424172. pdf?OpenElement.

Conrad, Courtenay R. (2011). "Constrained Concessions: Beneficent Dictatorial Responses to the Domestic Political Opposition". In: *International Studies Quarterly* 55.4, pp. 1167–1187.

Conrad, Courtenay R. (2014). "Divergent Incentives for Dictators: Domestic Institutions and (International Promises Not to) Torture". In: *Journal of Conflict Resolution* 58.1, pp. 34–67.

Conrad, Courtenay R. and Jacqueline H. R. DeMeritt (2011). "To Imprison, Torture, Disappear, or Kill? Human Rights Advocacy and State Repression Substitutability". Paper presented at the Annual Meeting of the International Studies Association, Montreal, Quebec, 2011.

Conrad, Courtenay R., Jillienne Haglund, andWill H. Moore (2013). "Disaggregating Torture Allegations: Introducing the Ill-Treatment and Torture (ITT) Country-Year Data". In: *International Studies Perspectives* 14.2, pp. 199–220.

Conrad, Courtenay R., Jillienne Haglund, and Will H. Moore (2014). "Torture Allegations as Events Data: Introducing the Ill-Treatment and Torture (ITT) Specific Allegation Data". In: *Journal of Peace Research* 51.3, pp. 429–438.

Conrad, Courtenay R., Daniel W. Hill Jr., and Will H. Moore (2018). "Torture and the Limits of Democratic Institutions". In: *Journal of Peace Research* 55.1, pp. 3–17.

Conrad, Courtenay R. and Will H. Moore (2010). "What Stops the Torture?" In: *American Journal of Political Science* 54.2, pp. 459–476.

Conrad, Courtenay R. and Emily Hencken Ritter (2013). "Tenure, Treaties, and Torture: The Conflicting Domestic Effects of International Law". In: *Journal of Politics* 75.2, pp. 397–409.

Conrad, Courtenay R. and Emily Hencken Ritter (2017). "A Trump Moratorium on International Treaties Could Roll Back Human RightsâŁ"Here at Home". In: *Washington Post*. URL: https://www.washingtonpost.com/news/monkey-cage/wp/2017/03/ 01/a- trump-moratorium-on-international- treaties-could-roll-back-human-rightshere- at-home/?utm term=.25065e9469ba.

Convention against Torture and Other Cruel, Inhuman or Degrading Treatment or Punishment (1984). United Nations General Assembly Resolution 39/46. URL: http ://www1.umn.edu/humanrts/.

Cook, Sarah (2015). *The Politburo's Predicament: Confronting the Limitations of Chinese Communist Party Repression*. Freedom House. Special report. URL: https://freedomhouse. org/sites/default/files/12222014_FH_ChinaReport2014_FINAL.pdf.

Cross, Frank B. (1999). "The Relevance of Law in Human Rights Protection". In: *International Review of Law and Economics* 19.1, pp. 87–98.

Dai, Xinyuan (2005). "Why Comply? The Domestic Constitutency Mechanism". In: *International Organization* 59.2, pp. 363–398.

Danneman, Nathan and Emily Hencken Ritter (2014). "Contagious Rebellion and Preemptive Repression". In: *Journal of Conflict Resolution* 58.2, pp. 254–279.

Davenport, Christian (1995). "Multi-Dimensional Threat Perception and State Repression: An Inquiry into Why States Apply Negative Sanctions". In: *American Journal of Political Science* 39.3, pp. 683–713.

Davenport, Christian (1996). "The Weight of the Past: Exploring Lagged Determinants of Political Repression". In: *Political Research Quarterly* 49.2, pp. 377–403.

Davenport, Christian (1997). "From Ballots to Bullets: An Empirical Assessment of How National Elections Influence State Uses of Political Repression". In: *Electoral Studies* 16.4, pp. 517–540.

Davenport, Christian (1998). "Liberalizing Event or Lethal Episode?: An Empirical Assessment of How National Elections Affect the Suppression of Political and Civil Liberties". In: *Social Science Quarterly* 79.2, pp. 321–340.

Davenport, Christian (2000). *Paths to State Repression: Human Rights Violations and Contentious Politics*. Lanham, MD: Rowman and Littlefield.

Davenport, Christian (2007a). "State Repression and Political Order". In: *Annual Review of Political Science* 10.1, pp. 1–23.

Davenport, Christian (2007b). *State Repression and the Domestic Democratic Peace*. Cambridge: Cambridge University Press.

Davenport, Christian (2015). *How Social Movements Die: Repression and Demobilization of the Republic of New Africa*. Cambridge, MA: Cambridge University Press.

Davenport, Christian and David Armstrong (2004). "Democracy and the Violation of Human Rights: A Statistical Analysis from 1976 to 1996". In: *American Journal of Political Science* 48.3, pp. 538–554.

Davenport, Christian, Sarah A. Soule, and David Armstrong (2011). "Protesting While Black? The Differential Policing of American Activism, 1960 to 1990". In: *American Sociological Review* 76.1, pp. 152–178.

Davis, David R., Brett Ashley Leeds, and Will H. Moore (1998). *Measuring Dissident and State Behavior: The Intranational Political Interactions (IPI) Project*. Presented at the Workshop on Cross-National Data Collection, Texas A&M University, November 21, 1998.

Davis, David R., Amanda Murdie, and Coty Garnett Steinmetz (2012). "'Makers and Shapers': Human Rights INGOs and Public Opinion". In: *Human Rights Quarterly* 34.1, pp. 199–224.

Davis, David R. and M.Ward (1990). "They Dance Alone: Deaths and the Disappeared in Contemporary Chile". In: *Journal of Conflict Resolution* 34.3, pp. 449–475.

Debs, Alexandre and H. E. Goemans (2010). "Regime Type, the Fate of Leaders, and War". In: *American Political Science Review* 104.3, pp. 430–445.

DeMeritt, Jacqueline H. R. (2012). "International Organizations and Government Killing: Does Naming and Shaming Save Lives?" In: *International Interactions* 38.5, pp. 597–621.

DeMeritt, Jacqueline H. R. (2015). "Delegating Death: Military Intervention and Government Killing". In: *Journal of Conflict Resolution* 59.3, pp. 428–454.

DeMeritt, Jacqueline H. R. and Joseph K. Young (2013). "A Political Economy of Human Rights: Oil, Natural Gas, and State Incentives to Repress". In: *Conflict Management and Peace Science* 30.2, pp. 99–120.

Diermeyer, Daniel and Keith Krehbiel (2003). "Institutionalism as a Methodology". In: *Journal of Theoretical Politics* 15.2, pp. 123–144.

Dodson, Kyle (2015). "Globalization and Protest Expansion". In: *Social Problems* 62.1, pp. 15–39.

Downs, George W. and Michael A. Jones (2002). "Reputation, Compliance, and International Law". In: *Journal of Legal Studies* 31.1, pp. S98–S114.

Downs, George W., David M. Rocke, and Peter N. Barsoom (1996). "Is the Good News about Compliance Good News about Cooperation?" In: *International Organization* 20.3, pp. 379–406.

Dragu, Tiberiu and Yonatan Lupu (2017). "Collective Action and Constraints on Repression at the Endgame". In: *Comparative Political Studies*. 51.8, pp. 1042–1073.

Duncan, Jane (2016). "Why Student Protests in South Africa Have Turned Violent". In: *The Conversation*. URL: https://theconversation.com/why-student-protests-in-southafrica-have-turned-violent-66288.

Dunning, Thad (2008). "Model Specification in Instrumental-Variables Regression". In: *Political Analysis* 16.3, pp. 290–302.

Earl, Jennifer (2003). "Tanks, Tear Gas, and Taxes: Toward a Theory of Movement Repression". In: *Sociological Theory* 21.1, pp. 44–68.

Earl, Jennifer, Sarah A. Soule, and John D. McCarthy (2003). "Policing under Fire? Explaining the Policing of Protest". In: *American Sociological Review* 68.4, pp. 581–606.

Edwards, Alice (2010). *Violence against Women under International Human Rights Law*. Cambridge University Press.

18 U.S.C. 2340A–"Torture (2011). Supplement 5, Part I, chapter 113C, 2340A. URL: https://www.law.cornell.edu/uscode/text/18/2340A.

Elkins, Zachary, Tom Ginsburg, and James Melton (2009). *The Endurance of National Constitutions*. New York: Cambridge University Press.

Ellickson, Robert C. (1991). *Order without Law: How Neighbors Settle Disputes*. Cambridge, MA: Harvard University Press.

Epp, Charles R. (1998). *The Rights Revolution: Lawyers, Activists, and Supreme Courts in Comparative Perspective*. Chicago: University of Chicago Press.

Escribá-Folch, Abel (2012). "Authoritarian Responses to Foreign Pressure Spending, Repression, and Sanctions". In: *Comparative Political Studies* 45.6, pp. 683–713.

Eyewitness News (2014). "Bronkhorstspruit Cop Station Torched". In: *EWN*. URL: http://ewn.co.za/2014/01/31/Bronkhorstspruit-Protesters-set-police-station-alight.

Fariss, Christopher J. (2014). "Respect for Human Rights Has Improved over Time: Modeling the Changing Standard of Accountability". In: *American Political Science Review* 108.2, pp. 297–318.

Feld, Lars P. and Stefan Voigt (2003). "Economic Growth and Judicial Independence: Cross-Country Evidence Using a New Set of Indicators". In: *European Journal of Political Economy* 19.3, pp. 497–527.

Finnemore, Martha and Kathryn Sikkink (1998). "International Norms Dynamics and Political Change". In: *International Organization* 52.4, pp. 887–917.

Francisco, Ronald A. (1996). "Coercion and Protest: An Empirical Test in Two Democratic States". In: *American Journal of Political Science* 40.4, pp. 1179–1204.

Francisco, Ronald A. (2004). "After the Massacre: Mobilization in the Wake of Harsh Repression". In: *Mobilization: An International Quarterly* 9.2, pp. 107–126.

Franklin, James C. (2008). "Shame on You: The Impact of Human Rights Criticism on Political Repression in Latin America". In: *International Studies Quarterly* 52.1, pp. 187–211.

Frogh, Wazhma (2010). *CEDAW Ratification Would Be a Triumph for Afghan Women.* Blog post. Accessed March 24, 2018. URL: http://thehill.com/blogs/ civilrights/ 129753-cedaw-ratification-would-be-a-triumph-for-afghan-women.

Galtung, Johan (1969). "Violence, Peace, and Peace Research". In: *Journal of Peace Research* 6.3, pp. 167–191.

Gandhi, Jennifer (2008). *Political Institutions under Dictatorship.* Cambridge: Cambridge University Press.

Gartner, Scott Sigmund and Patrick Regan (1996). "Threat and Repression: The Non-Linear Relationship between Government and Opposition Violence". In: *Journal of Peace Research* 33.3, pp. 273–287.

Gates, Scott (2002). "Recruitment and Allegiance: The Microfoundations of Rebellion". *In: Journal of Conflict Resolution* 46.1, pp. 111–130.

"Genocide Convention" (1971). In: *CQ Almanac (Congressional Quarterly).* 04-1015-04-1017. Accessed July 26, 2016. URL: http://library.cqpress.com/cqalmanac/cqal70-1292295.

Gerber, Alan S. and Donald P. Green (2012). *Field Experiments.* New York: W. W. Norton and Company.

Gibney, Mark et al. (2016). *The Political Terror Scale, 1976–2015.* Dataset. URL: %5Curl% 7Bhttp://www.politicalterrorscale.org%7D.

Gibson, James L., Gregory A. Caldeira, and Vanessa A. Baird (1998). "On the Legitimacy of National High Courts". In: *American Political Science Review* 92.2, pp. 343–358.

Gilligan, Michael J. (2006). "Is Enforcement Necessary for Effectiveness? A Model of the International Criminal Regime". In: *International Organization* 60.4, pp. 935–967.

Goemans, H. E., Kristian Skrede Gleditsch, and Giacomo Chiozza (2009). "Introducing Archigos: A Data Set of Political Leaders". In: *Journal of Peace Research* 46.2, pp. 269–283.

Goldsmith, Jack (2003). "The Self-Defeating International Criminal Court". In: *University of Chicago Law Review* 70.1, pp. 89–104.

Goldsmith, Jack and Stephen D. Krasner (2003). "The Limits of Idealism". In: *Daedalus* 132.1, pp. 47–63.

Goldstein, Robert J. (1978). *Political Repression in Modern America from 1870 to the present.* Cambridge: Schenkman Publishing Company.

Goodliffe, Jay and Darren G. Hawkins (2006). "Explaining Commitment: States and the Convention Against Torture". In: *Journal of Politics* 68.2, pp. 358–371.

Goodliffe, Jay, Darren G. Hawkins, et al. (2012). "Dependence Networks and the International Criminal Court". In: *International Studies Quarterly* 56.1, pp. 131–147.

Goodman, Nelson (1947). "The Problem of Counterfactual Conditionals". In: *Journal of Philosophy* 44.5, pp. 113–128.

Grief, Avner and David D. Laitin (2004). "A Theory of Endogenous Institutional Change". In: *American Political Science Review* 98.4, pp. 14–48.

Grossman, Hershel I. (1991). "A General Equilibrium Model of Insurrections". In: *American Economic Review* 81.4, pp. 912–921.

Gurr, Ted Robert (1970). *Why Men Rebel*. Princeton, NJ: Princeton University Press.

Gwartney, James and Robert Lawson (2006). *Economic Freedom of the World*. Annual Report. Fraser Institute. Downloaded August 27, 2007. URL: https://www. fraserinstitute. org/research/economic-freedom-of-the-world-2006-annual-report.

Gwartney, James and Robert Lawson (2007). *Economic Freedom of the World*. Annual Report. Fraser Institute. Downloaded August 27, 2007. URL: http://www. freetheworld.com/2007/EFW2007BOOK2.pdf.

Hafner-Burton, Emilie M. (2005). "Trading Human Rights: How Preferential Trade Agreements Influence Government Repression". In: *International Organization* 59.3, pp. 593–629.

Hafner-Burton, Emilie M. (2008). "Sticks and Stones: The Efficacy of Human Rights Naming and Shaming". In: *International Organization* 62.4, pp. 689–716.

Hafner-Burton, Emilie M. (2009). *Forced to Be Good: Why Trade Agreements Boost Human Rights*. Ithaca, NY: Cornell University Press.

Hafner-Burton, Emilie M. (2013). *Making Human Rights a Reality*. Princeton, NJ: Princeton University Press.

Hafner-Burton, Emilie M., Susan D. Hyde, and Ryan S. Jablonski (2014). "When Do Governments Resort to Election Violence?" In: *British Journal of Political Science* 44.1, pp. 149–179.

Hafner-Burton, Emilie M., Brad L. LeVeck, and David G. Victor (2016). "How Activists Perceive the Utility of International Law". In: *Journal of Politics* 78.1, pp. 167–180.

Hafner-Burton, Emilie M. and Kiyoteru Tsutsui (2005). "Human Rights in a Globalizing World: The Paradox of Empty Promises". In: *American Journal of Sociology* 110.5, pp. 1373–1411.

Hafner-Burton, Emilie M. and Kiyoteru Tsutsui (2007). "Justice Lost! The Failure of International Human Rights Law to Matter Where Needed the Most". In: *Journal of Peace Research* 44.4, pp. 207–425.

Hardin, Russell (1989). "Why a Constitution?" In: *The Federalist Papers and the New Institutionalism*. Ed. by Bernard Grofman and DonaldWittman. New York: Agathon Press.

Haschke, Peter (n.d.). *PTS Shiny App*. Application. Accessed April 13, 2018. URL: https: //haschke.shinyapps.io/PTS-App/.

Hathaway, Oona A. (2002). "Do Human Rights Treaties Make a Difference?" In: *Yale Law Journal* 111.8, pp. 1935–2042.

Hathaway, Oona A. (2003). "The Cost of Commitment". In: *Stanford Law Review* 55, pp. 1821–1862.

Hathaway, Oona A. (2004). "The Promise and Limits of the International Law of Torture". In: *Torture*. Ed. by Sanford Levinson. New York: Oxford University Press, pp. 199–212.

Hathaway, Oona A. (2005). "Between Power and Principle: An Integrated Theory of International Law". In: *University of Chicago Law Review* 72.2, pp. 469–536.

Hathaway, Oona A. (2007). "Why Do Countries Commit to Human Rights Treaties?" In: *Journal of Conflict Resolution* 51.4, pp. 588–621.

Hawkins, Darren G. (2004). "Explaining Costly International Institutions: Persuasion and Enforceable Human Rights Norms". In: *International Studies Quarterly* 48.4, pp. 779–804.

Heckman, James J. (1979). "Sample Selection Bias as a Specification Error". In: *Econometrica* 47.1, pp. 153–161.

Helfer, Laurence R. (2002). "Overlegalizing Human Rights: International Relations Theory and the Commonwealth Caribbean Backlash against Human Rights Regimes". In: *Columbia Law Review* 102, pp. 1832–1911.

Helmke, Gretchen (2002). "The Logic of Strategic Defection: Court-Executive Relations in Argentina under Dictatorship and Democracy". In: *American Political Science Review* 96.2, pp. 291–303.

Helmke, Gretchen (2005). *Courts Under Constraints*. Cambridge: Cambridge University Press.

Hendrix, Cullen S. and Wendy H. Wong (2013). "When Is the Pen Truly Mighty? Regime Type and the Efficacy of Naming and Shaming in Curbing Human Rights Abuses". In: *British Journal of Political Science* 43.03, pp. 651–672.

Hendrix, Cullen S. andWendy H.Wong (2014). "Knowing Your Audience: How the Structure of International Relations and Organizational Choices Affect Amnesty International's Advocacy". In: *The Review of International Organizations* 9.1, pp. 29–58.

Hilbink, Lisa (2007). *Judges beyond Politics in Democracy and Dictatorship: Lessons from Chile*. New York: Cambridge University Press.

Hill Jr., Daniel W. (2010). "Estimating the Effects of Human Rights Treaties on State Behavior". In: *Journal of Politics* 72.4, pp. 1161–1174.

Hill Jr., Daniel W. (2012). *The Right to Personal Integrity in International and Domestic Law*. Dissertation. Tallahassee: Florida State University.

Hill Jr., DanielW. (2015). "Avoiding Obligation: Reservations to Human Rights Treaties". In: *Journal of Conflict Resolution* 60.6, pp. 1129–1158.

Hill Jr., Daniel W. (2016). "Democracy and the Concept of Personal Integrity Rights". In: *Journal of Politics* 78.3, pp. 822–835.

Hill Jr., Daniel W. and Zach Jones (2014). "An Empirical Evaluation of Explanations for State Repression". In: *American Political Science Review* 108.3, pp. 661–687.

Holland, Paul W. (1986). "Statistics and Causal Inference". In: *Journal of the American Statistical Association* 81.396, pp. 945–960.

Hollyer, James R. and B. Peter Rosendorff (2011). "Why Do Authoritarian Regimes Sign the Convention Against Torture? Signaling, Domestic Politics, and Non-Compliance". In: *Quarterly Journal of Political Science* 6.3–4, pp. 275–327.

Hope, Christopher (2017). "Britain to Be Bound by European Human Rights Laws for at Least Another Five Years Even if Tories Win Election". In: *The Telegraph*. Accessed April 1, 2018. URL: http://www.telegraph.co.uk/news/2017/05/18/britain-boundeuropean- human-rights-laws-least-another-five/.

Howard, Robert M. and Henry F. Carey (2004). "Is an Independent Judiciary Necessary for Democracy?" In: *Judicature* 87.6, pp. 284–290.

Huff, Connor and Dustin Tingley (2015). "'Who Are These People?': Evaluating the Demographic Characteristics and Political Preferences of MTurk Survey Respondents". In: *Research and Politics* 2.3, pp. 1–12.

Human RightsWatch (2014). *Brazil: Protect Detainees in Police Custody, A Letter to Congress*. URL: https://www.hrw.org/news/2014/07/25/brazil- protect-detainees- policecustody.

Human Rights Watch (2016). "Democratic Republic of Congo at a Precipice: Ending Repression and Promoting Democratic Rule". In: *Human Rights Watch*. URL: https:// www.hrw.org/news/2016/09/18/democratic- republic-congo-precipice-endingrepression- and-promoting-democratic-rule.

Imai, Kosuke, Gary King, and Elizabeth A. Stuart (2008). "Misunderstandings between Experimentalists and Observationalists about Causal Inference". In: *Journal of the Royal Statistical Society* 171.2, pp. 481–502.

Imbens, Guido W. and Joshua D. Angrist (1994). "Identification and Estimation of Local Average Treatment Effects". In: *Econometrica* 62.2, pp. 467–475.

International Covenant on Civil and Political Rights (1966). United Nations. Technical Representative. URL: http://www1.umn.edu/humanrts/.

International Rehabilitation Council for Torture Victims (2014). *Venezuela Appears before the Committee against Torture. Statement*. Accessed April 13, 2018. URL: https://irct. org/index.php/media-and-resources/latest-news/article/789.

Jackson, Griffin Paul (2017). "US Prepares to Deport Hundreds of Iraqi Christians". In: *Christianity Today*. Accessed March 25, 2018. URL: http://www.christiani tytoday.com/news/2017/june/us-prepares-deport-iraq-chaldean-christians-ice-shaou.html.

Johnson, David (2015). "Parlak's 90-Day Reprieve from Deportation Celebrated at Candlelight Vigil". In: *Harbor Country News*. Accessed March 25, 2018. URL: http://www.harborcountry-news.com/news/parlak-s–day-reprieve-from-deportation-celebratedat- candlelight/article 9aa50a5c-66ad-50fb-83ae-5c 2588cc40fd.html.

Johnston, Alastair Ian (2001). "Treating International Institutions as Social Environments". In: *International Studies Quarterly* 45.4, pp. 487–515.

Joseph, Peniel E. (2006). *Waiting 'til the Midnight Hour: A Narrative History of Black Power in America*. New York: Holt & Company.

Kalyvas, Stathis N. (1999). "Wanton and Senseless? The Logic of Massacres in Algeria". In: *Rationality and Society* 11.3, pp. 243–285.

Kavanagh, Michael and Dan McCarey (2017). *All the President's Wealth: The Kabila Family Business*. The Pulitzer Center. Technical Representative. URL: https:// pulitzercenter.org/sites/default/files/all-the-president's-wealth-eng.pdf.

Keck, Margaret E. and Kathryn Sikkink (1998). *Activists Beyond Borders: Advocacy Networks in International Politics*. Ithaca, NY: Cornell University Press.

Keele, Luke and Jason Morgan (2016). "âŁœHow Strong is Strong Enough? Strengthening Instruments Through Matching and Weak Instrument Tests". In: *Annals of Applied Statistics* 10.2, pp. 1086–1106.

Keith, Linda Camp (1999). "The United Nations International Covenant on Civil and Political Rights: Does It Make a Difference in Human Rights Behavior?" In: *Journal of Peace Research* 36.1, pp.95–118.

Keith, Linda Camp (2002a). "Constitutional Provisions for Individual Human Rights (1977–1996): Are They More Than Mere âŁ̃Window Dressing?'" In: *Political Research Quarterly* 55.1, pp. 111–143.

Keith, Linda Camp (2002b). "Judicial Independence and Human Rights Protection around the World". In: *Judicature* 85.4, pp. 195–201.

Keith, Linda Camp (2012). *Political Repression: Courts and the Law*. Philadelphia: University of Pennsylvania Press.

Keith, Linda Camp, C. Neal Tate, and Steven C. Poe (2009). "Is the Law a Mere Parchment Barrier to Human Rights Abuse?" In: *Journal of Politics* 71.2, pp. 644–660.

Kiai, Maina (2017). *Report of the Special Rapporteur on the Rights to Freedom of Peaceful Assembly and of Association on His Follow-Up Mission to the United States of America*. United Nations Human Rights Council. Report to the UN General Assembly A/HRC/35/28/Add.2.

Kim, Wonik and Jennifer Gandhi (2010). "Coopting Workers under Dictatorship". In: *Journal of Politics* 72.3, pp. 646–658.

King, Gary (1989). *Unifying Political Methodology: The Likelihood Theory of Statistical Inference*. Cambridge: Cambridge University Press.

King, Gary, Robert O. Keohane, and Sidney Verba (1994). *Designing Social Inquiry: Scientific Inference in Qualitative Research*. Princeton, NJ: Princeton University Press.

King, Gary and Will Lowe (2003). "An Automated Information Extraction Tool for International Conflict Data with Performance as Good as Human Coders: A Rare Events Evaluation Design". In: *International Organization* 57.3, pp. 617–642.

King, John C. (1998). "Repression, Domestic Threat, and Interactions in Argentina and Chile". In: *Journal of Political and Military Sociology* 26.2, pp. 191–211.

Kirisci, Kemal (2016). "The Geopolitics of Turkey's Failed Coup". In: *Brookings*.

Klandermans, Bert (1984). "Mobilization and Participation: Social-Psychological Expansions of Resource Mobilization Theory". In: *American Sociological Review* 49.5, pp. 583–600.

Klandermans, Bert and Dirk Oegema (1987). "Potentials, Networks, Motivations, and Barriers: Steps towards Participation in Social Movement". In: *American Sociological Review* 52.4, pp. 519–531.

Knight, Jack (1992). *Institutions and Social Conflict*. New York: Cambridge University Press.

König, Thomas and Lars Mäder (2014). "The Strategic Nature of Compliance: An Empirical Evaluation of Law Implementtion in the Central Monitoring System of the European Union". In: *American Journal of Political Science* 58.1, pp. 246–263.

Koremenos, Barbara and Mi Hwa Hong (2010). "The Rational Design of Human Rights Agreements". In: *APSA 2010 Annual Meeting Paper*.

Koremenos, Barbara, Charles Lipson, and Duncan Snidal (2001). "The Rational Design of International Institutions". In: *International Organization* 55.4, pp. 761–799.

Krain, Matthew (2012). "J'accuse! Does Naming and Shaming Perpetrators Reduce the Severity of Genocides or Politicides?". In: *International Studies Quarterly* 56.3, pp. 574–589.

Krupnikov, Yanna and Adam Seth Levine (2014). "Cross-Sample Comparisons and External Validity". In: *Journal of Experimental Political Science* 1.1, pp. 59–80.

Kuran, Timur (1991). "Now out of Never: The Element of Surprise in the East European Revolution of 1989". In: *World Politics* 44.1, pp. 7–48.

Landman, Todd (2005). *Protecting Human Rights: A Comparative Study*. Washington, DC: Georgetown University Press.

Lebovic, James H. and Erik Voeten (2006). "The Politics of Shame: The Condemnation of Country Human Rights Practices in the UNCHR". In: *International Studies Quarterly* 50.4, pp. 861–888.

Lebovic, James H. and Erik Voeten (2009). "The Cost of Shame: International Organizations and Foreign Aid in the Punishing of Human Rights Violators". In: *Journal of Peace Research* 46.1, pp. 79–97.

Leeds, Brett Ashley (2003). "Alliance Reliability in Times of War: Explaining State Decisions to Violate Treaties". In: *International Organization* 57.4, pp. 801–827.

Lichbach, Mark Irving (1987). "Deterrence or Escalation? The Puzzle of Aggregate Studies of Repression and Dissent". In: *Journal of Conflict Resolution* 31.2, pp. 266–297.

Lichbach, Mark Irving (1995). *The Rebel's Dilemma*. Ann Arbor: University of Michigan Press.

Licht, Amanda A. (2010). "Coming into Money: The Impact of Foreign Aid on Leader Survival". In: *Journal of Conflict Resolution* 54.1, pp. 58–87.

Licht, Amanda A. (2015). "Hazards or Hassles: Modeling the Effect of Economic Sanctions on Leader Survival with Improved Data". In: *Political Science Research and Methods* 5.1, pp. 143–161.

Linzer, Drew A. and Jeffrey K. Staton (2015). "A Global Measure of Judicial Independence, 1948–2012". In: *Journal of Law and Courts* 3.2, pp. 233–256.

Lohmann, Suzanne (1993). "A Signaling Model of Informative and Manipulative Political Action". In: *American Political Science Review* 87.2, pp. 319–333.

Lohmann, Suzanne (1994). "The Dynamics of Informational Cascades: The Monday Demonstrations in Leipzig, East Germany, 1989–1991". In: *World Politics* 47.1, pp. 42–101.

Lorentzen, Peter (2013). "Regularizing Rioting: Permitting Public Protest in an Authoritarian Regime". In: *Quarterly Journal of Political Science* 8.2, pp. 127–158.

Lorentzen, Peter (2014). "China's Strategic Censorship". In: *American Journal of Political Science* 58.2, pp. 402–414.

Loveluck, Louisa and Karen DeYoung (2017). "Chemical Attack Kills Dozens in Syria as Victims Foam at the Mouth, Activists Say". In: *Washington Post*. URL: https://www.washingtonpost.com/world/activists-say-gas-attack-kills-civilians-in-syria-as-eu-leaders-discuss-reconstruction/2017/04/04/16093d24-190a-11e7-8003-f55b4c1cfae2_story.html.

Lupu, Yonatan (2013a). "Best Evidence: The Role of Information in Domestic Judicial Enforcement of International Human Rights Agreements". In: *International Organization* 67.3, pp. 469–503.

Lupu, Yonatan (2013b). "The Informative Power of Treaty Commitment: Using the Spatial Model to Address Selection Effects". In: *American Journal of Political Science* 57.4, pp. 912–925.

Lupu, Yonatan (2015). "Legislative Veto Players and the Effects of International Human Rights Agreements". In: *American Journal of Political Science* 59.3, pp. 578–594.

Lutz, Ellen L. and Kathryn Sikkink (2000). "International Human Rights Law and Practice in Latin America". In: *International Organization* 54.3, pp. 633–659.

Mansfield, Edward D. and Jon C. Pevehouse (2006). "Democratization and International Organizations". In: *International Organization* 60.1, pp. 137–167.

Marshall, Monty G. and Keith Jaggers (2009). *Polity IV Project: Political Regime Characteristics and Transitions,* 1800–2007. Dataset. Polity IV dataset version 2007. Accessed July 30, 2009. URL: www.systemicpeace.org/polity4.
  . Polity II: Political structures and regime change, 1800-1986. Ann Arbor, Mich.: Inter-University Consortium for Political and Social Research, 1990.

Martín, Karina (2016). "Despite Government Obstacles, over a Million Venezuelans March on Caracas". In: *PanAm Post.* Accessed April 13, 2018. URL: https:// panampost.com/karina- martin/2016/09/01/despite-government- obstacles- over- a- millionvenezuelans- march-on-caracas/.

Mattes, Michaela, Brett Ashley Leeds, and Naoka Matsumura (2016). "Measuring Change in Source of Leader Support: The CHISOLS Dataset". In: *Journal of Peace Research* 53.2, pp. 259–267.

McAdam, Doug (1999). *Political Process and the Development of Black Insurgency.* 2nd. ed. Chicago: University of Chicago Press.

McAdam, Doug, John D. McCarthy, and Mayer N. Zald (1996). *Comparative Perspectives on Social Movements: Political Opportunities, Mobilizing Structures, and Cultural Framings.* New York: Cambridge University Press.

McAdam, Doug, Sidney Tarrow, and Charles Tilly (2004). *Dynamics of Contention.* New York: Cambridge University Press.

McCarthy, John D. and Mayer N. Zald (1977). "Resource Mobilization and Social Movements". In: *American Journal of Sociology* 82.6, pp. 1212–1241.

Merry, Sally Engle (2006). *Human Rights and Gender Violence: Translating International Law into Local Justice.* Chicago: University of Chicago Press.

Mitchell, Neil J. (2009). *Agents of Atrocity: Leaders, Followers, and the Violation of Human Rights in Civil War.* New York: Palgrave Macmillan.

Mitchell, Neil J., Sabine C. Carey, and Christopher K. Butler (2014). "The Impact of Pro- Government Militias on Human Rights Violations". In: *International Interactions* 40.5, pp. 812–836.

Mitchell, Sara McLaughlin, Jonathan J. Ring, and Mary K. Spellman (2013). "Domestic Legal Traditions and States' Human Rights Practices". In: *Journal of Peace Research* 50.2, pp. 189–202.

Moore, Will H. (1995). "Action-Reaction or Rational Expectations? Reciprocity and the Domestic-International Conflict Nexus during the Rhodesia Problem". In: *Journal of Conflict Resolution* 39.1, pp. 129–167.

Moore, Will H. (1998). "Repression and Dissent: Substitution, Context, and Timing". In: *American Journal of Political Science* 42.3, pp. 851–873.

Moore, Will H. (2000). "The Repression of Dissent: A Substitution Model of Government Coercion". In: *Journal of Conflict Resolution* 44.1, pp. 107–127.

Moravcsik, Andrew (2000). "The Origins of Human Rights Regimes: Democratic Delegation in Postwar Europe". In: *International Organization* 54.2, pp. 217–252.

Morgan, Michael Cotey (2018). *The Final Act: The Helsinki Accords and the Transformation of the Cold War (America in the World).* Princeton, NJ: Princeton University Press.

Morrow, James D. (2014). *Order within Anarchy: The Laws of War as an International Institution.* New York: Cambridge University Press.

Moustafa, Tamir (2003). "Law versus the State: The Judicialization of Politics in Egypt". In: *Law & Social Inquiry* 28.4, pp. 883–930.

Moustafa, Tamir (2007). *The Struggle for Constitutional Power: Law, Politics, and Economic Development in Egypt.* New York: Cambridge University Press.

Mulesky, Suzie and Wayne Sandholtz (2018). *Human Rights Treaty Obligations and State Commitment*. Paper presented at the Annual Meeting of the International Studies Association, San Francisco, CA, 2018.

Muller, Edward (1985). "Income Inequality, Regime Repressiveness, and Political Violence". In: *American Sociological Review* 50.1, pp. 47–61.

Murdie, Amanda (2009). "The Impact of Human Rights INGOs on Human Rights Practices". In: *International NGO Journal* 4.10, pp. 421–440.

Murdie, Amanda and Tavishi Bhasin (2011). "Aiding and Abetting: Human Rights INGOs and Domestic Protest". In: *Journal of Conflict Resolution* 55.2, pp. 163–191.

Murdie, Amanda and David R. Davis (2012). "Shaming and Blaming: Using Events Data to Assess the Impact of Human Rights INGOs1". In: *International Studies Quarterly* 56.1, pp. 1–16.

Murdie, Amanda and Dursun Peksen (2014). "The Impact of Human Rights INGO Shaming on Humanitarian Interventions". In: *Journal of Politics* 76.1, pp. 215–228.

Murdie, Amanda and Dursun Peksen (2015). "Women and Contentious Politics: A Global Event-Data Approach to Understanding Women's Protest". In: *Political Research Quarterly* 68.1, pp. 180–192.

Neumayer, Eric (2005). "Do International Treaties Improve Respect for Human Rights?" In: *Journal of Conflict Resolution* 49.6, pp. 925–953.

Neumayer, Eric (2007). "Qualified Ratification: Explaining Reservations to International Human Rights Treaties". In: *Journal of Legal Studies* 36.2, pp. 397–429.

Nielsen, Richard A. and Beth A. Simmons (2015). "Rewards for Ratification: Payoffs for Participating in the International Human Rights Regime?" In: *International Studies Quarterly* 59.2, pp. 197–208.

Nordås, Ragnhild and Christian Davenport (2013). "Fight the Youth: Youth Bulges and State Repression". In: *American Journal of Political Science* 57.4, pp. 925–940.

North, Douglass C. (1990). *Institutions, Institutional Change, and Economic Performance*. New York: Cambridge University Press.

Nossiter, Adam (2013). "Senegal Detains Ex-President of Chad, Accused in the Deaths of Opponents". In: *New York Times*. Accessed March 12, 2017. URL: https://www.nytimes.com/2013/07/01/world/africa/senegal-detains-ex-president-of-chad.html.

Oberdorster, Uta (2008). "Why Ratify: Lessons from Treaty Ratification Campaigns". In: *Vanderbilt Law Review* 61, p. 681.

Olson, Mancur (1965). *The Logic of Collective Action: Public Goods and the Theory of Groups*. Cambridge, MA: Harvard University Press.

Ostrom, Elinor (1990). *Governing the Commons: The Evolution of Institutions for Collective Action*. New York: Cambridge University Press.

Page, Scott (2006). "Path Dependence". In: *Quarterly Journal of Political Science* 1.1, pp. 87–115.

Paolacci, Gabriele and Jesse Chandler (2014). "Inside the Turk: Understanding Mechanical Turk as a Participant Pool". In: *Current Directions in Psychological Science* 23.3, pp. 184–188.

Payne, Caroline L. and M. Rodwan Abouharb (2015). "The International Covenant on Civil and Political Rights and the Strategic Shift to Forced Disappearance". In: *Journal of Human Rights* 15.2, pp. 163-188.

Pelc, Krzysztof (2009). "Seeking Escape: The Use of Escape Clauses in International Trade Agreements". In: *International Studies Quarterly* 53.2, pp. 349–368.

Pelc, Krzysztof (2014). "The Politics of Precedent in International Law: A Social Network Application". In: *American Political Science Review* 108.3, pp. 547–564.

Perper, Rosie (2018). "After Mass Protests, Iran Bans English in Schools to Fight Western 'Cultural Invasion'". In: *Business Insider*. Accessed April 13, 2008. URL: http://www.businessinsider.com/iran-bans-english-in-primary-schools-2018-1.

Pierskalla, Jan Henryk (2010). "Protest, Deterrence, and Escalation: The Strategic Calculus of Government Repression". In: *Journal of Conflict Resolution* 54.1, pp. 117–145.

Pittsburgh for CEDAW (2018). *Pittsburgh for CEDAW*. Website. Accessed March 26, 2018. URL: http://pgh4cedaw.org/.

Poe, Steven C. and C. Neal Tate (1994). "Repression of Human Rights to Personal Integrity in the 1980s: A Global Analysis". In: *American Political Science Review* 88.4, pp. 853–872.

Poe, Steven C., C. Neal Tate, and Linda Camp Keith (1999). "Repression of the Human Right to Personal Integrity Revisited: A Global Cross-National Study Covering the Years 1976–1993". In: *International Studies Quarterly* 43.2, pp. 291–313.

Poe, Steven C., C. Neal Tate, Linda Camp Keith, and Drew Lanier (2000). "Domestic Threats: The Abuse of Personal Integrity". In: *Paths to State Repression: Human Rights Violations and Contentious Politics*. Lanham, MD: Rowman and Littlefield.

Posner, Eric A. (2008). "Human Welfare, Not Human Rights". In: *Columbia Law Review* 108, pp. 1758–1801.

Posner, Eric A. (2014). *The Twilight of Human Rights Law*. Oxford University Press.

Posner, Eric A. and Kenneth Roth (2014). "Have Human Rights Treaties Failed?" In: *New York Times*. URL: https://www.nytimes.com/roomfordebate/2014/12/28/havehuman- rights-treaties-failed.

Powell, Emilia Justyna and Jeffrey K. Staton (2009). "Domestic Judicial Institutions and Human Rights Treaty Violations". In: *International Studies Quarterly* 53.1, pp. 149–174.

Przeworski, Adam, Michael Alvarez, and José Antonio Cheibub (2000). *Democracy and Development: Political Institutions and Well-Being in the World, 1950–1990*. New York: Cambridge University Press.

Ramcharan, B. G. (1989). *The Concept and Present Status of the International Protection of Human Rights: Forty Years after the Universal Declaration*. Martinus Nijhoff Publishers.

Rasler, Karen (1996). "Concession, Repression, and Political Protest in the Iranian Revolution". In: *American Sociological Review* 61.1, pp. 132–152.

Ratification of International Human Rights Treaties–China (2018). Accessed January 24, 2018. URL: http://hrlibrary.umn. edu/research/ratification-china.html.

Ratification of International Human Rights Treaties–Venezuela (2018). Accessed January 24, 2018. URL: http://hrlibrary. umn.edu/research/ratification-venezuela.html.

Redgwell, Catherine J. (1997). "Reservations to Treaties and Human Rights Committee General Comment No. 24 (52)". In: *International and Comparative Law Quarterly* 46.2, pp. 390–412.

Regan, Patrick and Errol Henderson (2002). "Democracy, Threats and Political Repression in Developing Countries: Are Democracies Internally Less Violent?" In: *Third World Quarterly* 23.1, pp. 119–136.

Rejali, Darius (2007). *Torture and Democracy*. Princeton, NJ: Princeton University Press.

Reuters News Service (2011). "Bush Cancels Visit to Switzerland due to Threat of Torture Prosecution, Rights Groups Say". Accessed September 1, 2016. URL:

http://www. huffingtonpost.com/2011/02/05/bush-switzerland-torture n 819175.html.

Reuters News Service (2018a). "Iran Frees 440 People Arrested during Protests". Accessed April 13, 2018. URL: https://www.reuters.com/article/us-iran-frees-440-people-arrested-during-protests-idUSKBN1F41MP.

Reuters News Service (2018b). "Iran Protests Could Hurt Clerics but Rouhani Has Most to Lose, Say Insiders". Accessed April 13, 2018. URL: https://www.reuters.com/article/us-iran-rallies-leadership-analysis/iran-protests-could-hurt-clerics-butrouhani-has-most-to-lose-say-insiders-idUSKBN1ER1RL.

Richards, David L. (1999). "Perlious Proxy: Human Rights and the Presence of National Elections". In: *Social Science Quarterly* 80.4, pp. 648–668.

Richards, David L. and Ronald D. Gelleny (2007). "Good Things to Those Who Wait? National Elections and Government Respect for Human Rights". In: *Journal of Peace Research* 44.4, pp. 505–523.

Ríos-Figueroa, Julio and Jeffrey K. Staton (2014). "An Evaluation of Cross-National Measures of Judicial Independence". In: *Journal of Law, Economics, and Organization* 30.1, pp. 104–137.

Risse, Thomas, Stephen C. Ropp, and Kathryn Sikkink (1999). *The Power of Human Rights: International Norms and Domestic Change*. Cambridge: Cambridge University Press.

Ritter, Emily Hencken (2014). "Policy Disputes, Political Survival, and the Onset and Severity of State Repression". In: *Journal of Conflict Resolution* 58.1, pp. 143–168.

Ritter, Emily Hencken and Courtenay R. Conrad (2016a). "Human Rights Treaties and Mobilized Dissent Against the State". In: *Review of International Organizations* 11.4, pp. 449–475.

Ritter, Emily Hencken and Courtenay R. Conrad (2016b). "Preventing and Responding to Dissent: The Observational Challenges of Explaining Strategic Repression". In: *American Political Science Review* 110.1, pp. 85–99.

Ritter, Emily Hencken and Scott Wolford (2012). "Bargaining and the Effectiveness of International Criminal Regimes". In: *Journal of Theoretical Politics* 24.2, pp. 149–171.

Ron, James, Howard Ramos, and Kathleen Rodgers (2005). "Transnational Information Politics: NGO Human Rights Reporting, 1986–2000". In: *International Studies Quarterly* 49.3, pp. 557–588.

Rosenberg, Gerald N. (1991). *The Hollow Hope: Can Courts Bring about Social Change?* Chicago: University of Chicago Press.

Salehyan, Idean, Cullen S. Hendrix, Jesse Hamner, Christina Case, Christopher Linebarger, Emily Stull, and Jennifer Williams (2012). "Social Conflict in Africa: A New Database". In: *International Interactions* 38.4, pp. 503–511.

Salehyan, Idean, David Siroky, and Reed M. Wood (2014). "External Rebel Sponsorship and Civilian Abuse: A Principal-Agent Analysis of Wartime Atrocities". In: *International Organization* 68.3, pp. 633–661.

Sariyuce, Isil and Angela Dewan (2016). "Turkey Declares Three-Month State of Emergency". In: *CNN*. URL: http://www.cnn.com/2016/07/20/europe/turkey-failedcoup-attempt.

Sartori, Anne E. (2003). "An Estimator for Some Binary-Outcome Selection Models without Exclusion Restrictions". In: *Political Analysis* 11.2, pp. 111–138.

Schock, Kurt (2005). *Unarmed Insurrections: People Power Movements in Nondemocracies*. Minneapolis: University of Minnesota Press.

Schussman, Alan and Sarah A. Soule (2005). "Process and Protest: Accounting for Individual Protest Participation". In: *Social Forces* 84.2, pp. 1083–1108.

Shadish ,William R., Thomas D. Cook, and Donald Thomas Campbell (2002). *Experimental and Quasi-Experimental Designs for Generalized Causal Inference*. Wadsworth Cengage Learning.

Shadmehr, Mehdi (2014). "Mobilization, Repression, and Revolution: Grievances and Opportunities in Contentious Politics". In: *Journal of Politics* 76.3, pp. 621–635.

Shadmehr, Mehdi and Dan Bernhardt (2011). "Collective Action with Uncertain Payoffs: Coordination, Public Signals, and Punishment Dilemmas". In: *American Political Science Review* 105.4, pp. 829–851.

Shellman, Stephen M. (2004a). "Measuring the Intensity of Intranational Political Events Data: Two Interval-Like Scales". In: *International Interactions* 30.2, pp. 109–141.

Shellman, Stephen M. (2004b). "Time Series Intervals and Statistical Inference: The Effects of Temporal Aggregation on Event Data Analysis". In: *Political Analysis* 12.1, pp. 97–104.

Shellman, Stephen M. (2006). "Leaders' Motivations and Actions: Explaining Government- Dissident Conflict-Cooperation Processes". In: *Conflict Management and Peace Science* 23.1, pp. 73–90.

Signorino, Curtis S. and Kuzey Yilmaz (2003). "Strategic Misspecification in Repression Models". In: *American Journal of Political Science* 47.3, pp. 551–566.

Sikkink, Kathryn and Carrie Booth Walling (2007). "The Impact of Human Rights Trials in Latin America". In: *Journal of Peace Research* 44.4, pp. 427–445.

Simmons, Beth A. (1998). "Compliance with International Agreements". In: *Annual Review of Political Science* 1, pp. 75–93.

Simmons, Beth A. (2009). *Mobilizing for Human Rights: International Law in Domestic Politics*. Cambridge, MA: Cambridge University Press.

Simmons, Beth A. and Allison Danner (2010). "Credible Commitments and the International Criminal Court". In: *International Organization* 64.2, pp. 225–256.

Simmons, Beth A. and Daniel J. Hopkins (2005). "The Constraining Power of International Treaties: Theory and Methods". In: *American Political Science Review* 99.4, pp. 623–631.

Simons, Marlise (2012). "Senegal Told to Prosecute Ex-President of Chad". In: *New York Times*. Accessed March 12, 2017. URL: https ://www. nytimes .com/2012/07/21/world/africa/senegal-to-prosecute-former-president-of-chad-hissene-habre.html.

Sloss, David, ed. (2009). *The Role of Domestic Courts in Treaty Enforcement*. Cambridge, MA: Cambridge University Press.

Smith, Jackie, Ron Pagnucco, and George A. Lopez (1998). "Globalizing Human Rights: TheWork of Transnational Human Rights NGOs in the 1990s". In: *Human Rights Quarterly* 20.2, pp. 379–412.

Smith-Cannoy, Heather (2012). *Insincere Commitments: Human Rights Treaties, Abusive States, and Citizen Activism*. Washington, DC: Georgetown University Press.

Snow, David A., E. Burke Rochford, Jr., Steven K. WOrden, and Robert D. Benford (1986). "Frame Alignment Processes, Micromobilization, and Movement Participation". In: *American Sociological Review* 51.4, pp. 464–481.

Sovey, Allison J. and Donald P. Green (2011). "Instrumental Variables Estimation in Political Science: A Readers' Guide". In: *American Journal of Political Science* 55.1, pp. 188–200.

Staton, Jeffrey K. (2006). "Constitutional Review and the Selective Promotion of Case Results". In: *American Journal of Political Science* 50.1, pp. 98–112.

Staton, Jeffrey K. (2010). *Judicial Power and Strategic Communication in Mexico*. New York: Cambridge University Press.

Staton, Jeffrey K. and Will H. Moore (2011). "Judicial Power in Domestic and International Politics". In: *International Organization* 65.3, pp. 553–588.

Stone, Randall W. (2011). *Controlling Institutions: International Organizations and the Global Economy*. New York: Cambridge University Press.

Stroup, Sarah S. and Wendy H. Wong (2017). *The Authority Trap: Strategic Choices of International NGOs*. Ithaca, NY: Cornell University Press.

Sub-Commission on the Promotion and Protection of Human Rights (1999). *Sub-Commission Resolution 1999/5*. Technical Representative Document E/CN.4/SUB.2/RES/1999/5. Accessed 20 September 2016. United Nations Human Rights Committee. URL: http: //ap.ohchr.org/documents/E/SUBCOM/ resolutions/E-CN 4-SUB 2-RES-1999- 5.doc.

Sullivan, Christopher M. (2016a). "Political Repression and the Destruction of Dissident Organizations: Evidence from the Archives of the Guatemalan National Police". In: *World Politics* 68.4, pp. 645–676.

Sullivan, Christopher Michael (2016b). "Undermining Resistance: Mobilization, Repression, and the Enforcement of Political Order". In: *Journal of Conflict Resolution* 60.7, pp. 1163–1190.

Tarrow, Sidney (1991). *Struggle, Politics, and Reform: Collective Action, Social Movements, and Cycles of Protest*. Ithaca, NY: Cornell University Press.

Tarrow, Sidney (1994). *Power in Movement: Social Movements, Collective Action and Politics*. Cambridge: Cambridge University Press.

Tate, C. Neal and Linda Camp Keith (2007). *Conceptualizing and Operationalizing Judicial Independence Globally*. Paper presented at the Annual Meeting of the American Political Science Association, Chicago, IL, 2007.

Taylor, Adam (2017). "Which World Leaders Are Richer Than Donald Trump?" In: *The Washington Post*. URL: https://www.washingtonpost.com/news/worldviews/ wp/ 2017/03/14/which-world-leaders-are-richer-than-donald-trump/? utm term= .0f1d229603f6.

Taylor, Charles Lewis et al. (1999). "Conflict-Cooperation for Interstate and Intrastate Interactions: An Expansion of the Goldstein Scale". Paper presented at the Annual Meeting of the International Studies Association, Washington, DC, 1999.

The Guardian (2015). "Protests in Poland as Proposed Laws Curtail Women's Rights". In: *The Guardian*. Accessed September 17, 2016. URL: http://www.theguardian. com/world/2015/dec/23/protests-in-poland-as-proposesd-laws-curtail-women s-rights.

PRS Group (2009). "International Country Risk Guide". In: *International Country Risk Guide*. URL: https://epub.prsgroup.com/products/international-country-risk-guide-icrg.

Supreme Court of the United States (1954). "Brown v. Board of Education of Topeka". In: *US Reports* 347 U.S. 483 (1954).

Tilly, Charles (1978). *From Mobilization to Revolution*. Reading, MA: Addison-Wesley.

Torture Victim Protection Act of 1991 (1992). Pub.L. No. 102–256, 106 Stat. 73. URL: https: //www.law.cornell.edu/uscode/text/28/1350.

Tsebelis, George (1989). "The Abuse of Probability in Political Analysis: The Robinson Crusoe Fallacy". In: *American Political Science Review* 83.1, pp. 77–91.

Tsebelis, George (2002). *Veto Players: How Political Institutions Work*. New York: Russell Sage Foundation.

Ulfelder, Jay (2011). *Country Memberships in Selected Intergovernmental Organizations and Accession to Selected Regional and Global Treaty Regimes: Global, Country-Year Format*, 1955–2010. Vol. ICPSR30541-v1. Ann Arbor, MI: Inter-university Consortium for Political and Social Research [distributor].

United Nations (1948). *Universal Declaration of Human Rights*. General Assembly Resolution 217A. URL: http://www1.umn.edu/humanrts.

United Nations (1969). *Signatories and Ratifications of the American Convention on Human Rights*. Multilateral treaty 17955. Inter-American Specialized Conference on Human Rights, San Jose, CA: Organization of American States. URL: https://www.oas.org/dil/treaties_B-32_American_Convention_on_-Human_Rights_sign.htm.

United Nations (1979). *Convention on the Elimination of All Forms of Discrimination Against Women*. URL: http://www1.umn.edu/humanrts/.

Valentino, Benjamin, Paul Huth, and Dylan Balch-Lindsey (2004). "'Draining the Sea': Mass Killing and GuerrillaWarfare". In: *International Organization* 58.2, pp. 375–407.

Vanberg, Georg (2005). *The Politics of Constitutional Review in Germany*. Cambridge: Cambridge University Press.

Vanderschraaf, Peter (1998). "Knowledge, Equilibrium, and Convention". In: *Erkenntnis* 49.3, pp. 337–369.

Vanderschraaf, Peter (2000). "Game Theory, Evolution, and Justice". In: *Philosophy and Public Affairs* 28.4, pp. 325–358.

Vienna Convention on the Law of Treaties (with Annex) (1969). United Nations. Technical Representative 18232. URL: https://treaties.un.org/doc/publication/unts/volume% 201155/volume-1155-i-18232-english.pdf.

VOA News (2015). *Human Rights Day Demonstrators Detained in Cuba*. Accessed March 26, 2018. URL: https://www.voanews.com/a/human-rights-day-demonstrat orsdetained- cuba/3098429.html.

von Stein, Jana (2005). "Do Treaties Constrain or Screen? Selection Bias and Treaty Compliance". In: *American Political Science Review* 99.4, pp. 611–622.

von Stein, Jana (2016). "Making Promises, Keeping Promises: Democracy, Ratification, and Compliance in International Human Rights Law". In: *British Journal of Political Science* 46.3, pp. 655–679.

Vreeland, James Raymond (2008a). "Political Institutions and Human Rights: Why Dictatorships Enter into the United Nations Convention Against Torture". In: *International Organization* 62.1, pp. 65–101.

Vreeland, James Raymond (2008b). "The Effect of Political Regime on Civil War: Unpacking Anocracy". In: *Journal of Conflict Resolution* 52.3, pp. 401–425.

Wallace, Jeremy (2018). "Is Xi Jinping Now 'a Leader for Life,' like Mao? Here's Why This Is Dangerous". In: *Washington Post*. Monkey Cage Blog. URL: https://www. washingtonpost.com/news/monkey-cage/wp/2018/02/27/is-xi-jinping-now-aleader- for-life-like-mao-heres-why-this-is-dangerous/?utm term=.ebc 42727fa5e.

Weede, Erich (1987). "Some New Evidence on the Correlates of Political Violence: Income Inequality, Regime Repressiveness, and Economic Development". In: *European Sociological Review* 3.2, pp. 97–108.

Weingast, Barry R. (1997). "The Political Foundations of Democracy and the Rule of Law". In: *American Political Science Review* 91.2, pp. 245–263.

Weinstein, Jeremy (2007). *Inside Rebellion: The Politics of Insurgent Violence*. New York: Cambridge University Press.

Whitten-Woodring, Jenifer (2009). "Watchdog or Lapdog? Media Freedom, Regime Type, and Government Respect for Human Rights". In: *International Studies Quarterly* 53.3, pp. 595–625.

Whitten-Woodring, Jenifer and Patrick James (2012). "Fourth Estate or Mouthpiece? A Formal Model of Media, Protest, and Government Repression". In: *Political Communication* 29.2, pp. 113–136.

Wolf, Richard (2018). "Supreme Court to Issue Final Verdict on Trump Travel Ban". In: *USA Today*. URL: https://www.usatoday.com/story/news/politics/2018/01/19/ supreme-court-issue-final-verdict-trump-travel-ban/1038126001/.

Wolford, Scott (2007). "The Turnover Trap: New Leaders, Reputation, and International Conflict". In: *American Journal of Political Science* 51.4, pp. 772–788.

Wong, Wendy H. (2012). *Internal Affairs: How the Structure of NGOs Transforms Human Rights*. Ithaca, NY: Cornell University Press.

Wood, Elizabeth Jean (2003). *Insurgent Collective Action and Civil War in El Salvador*. New York: Cambridge University Press.

Wooldridge, Jeffrey M. (2002). *Econometric Analysis of Cross Section and Panel Data*. Cambridge, MA: MIT Press.

Wotipka, Christine Min and Francisco O. Ramirez (2008). "World Society and Human Rights: An Event History Analysis of the Convention on the Elimination of All Forms of Discrimination against Women". In: *The Global Diffusion of Markets and Democracy*. Ed. by Beth A. Simmons, Frank Dobbin, and Geoffrey Garrett. Cambridge, UK: Cambridge University Press, pp. 303–43.

Xiaobo, Li (2009). "China's Charter 08". Translated by Perry Link. In: *New York Review of Books*. URL: http://www.nybooks.com/articles/2009/01/15/ chinas-charter-08/.

Xinhua News Agency (2018). "China's National Legislature Adopts Constitutional Amendment". URL: http://www.xinhuanet.com/english/2018-03/11/c 137031606.htm.

Young, Joseph K. (2008). *Repression, Dissent, and the Onset of Civil War*. Dissertation. Tallahassee: Florida State University.

Young, Joseph K. (2009). "State Capacity, Democracy, and the Violation of Personal Integrity Rights". In: *Journal of Human Rights* 8.4, pp. 283–300.

Young, Oran R. (1979). *Compliance and Public Authority*. Baltimore: Johns Hopkins University Press.

INDEX